Full Circle

Full Circle

✦

From Addiction to Affection

Bruce Codrington

iUniverse, Inc.
New York Lincoln Shanghai

Full Circle
From Addiction to Affection

iUniverse, Inc.

For information address:
iUniverse, Inc.
2021 Pine Lake Road, Suite 100
Lincoln, NE 68512
www.iuniverse.com

ISBN: 0-595-32916-0 (pbk)
ISBN: 0-595-66705-8 (cloth)

Printed in the United States of America

Contents

ACKNOWLEDGEMENTS

First and above all I must give thanks to God for his mercy in allowing me the opportunity for a second chance at life.

To the loves of my life—Janice, my patient, loving, understanding and forgiving wife of thirty-two years, my two sons Kaleem and Kynon, who always encouraged "Pops" to go for it while writing this book.

I cannot list all those in my life that made me the person that I am today, but special thanks to my mom who never gave up praying. Uncle Felix and Uncle Bobby, my strong mentors whom taught me how to always give back. To Renea' and Tracie for taking the time to read my rough draft and gave it a thumbs up, I say thank you.

I dedicate this book to Dad who allowed a second chance at our relationship that I will cherish forever. I miss him dearly.

INTRODUCTION

I felt the need to share my testimony as a recovering drug addict so that I may help to shine a beacon light of hope on someone. That beacon may be for someone that may be struggling with addictive behaviors, marriage issues, or lack of faith. I do not possess any formal educational degrees or certificates on the subjects discussed in this book, however the experiences that I have learned the past thirty-three years of my life are priceless. What benefit would I gain if I could not share my miraculous turn of events that allowed me to live and love once again?

I began writing this book in 1993, as a therapeutic method to cleanse my spirit and soul from much of the pain that I had been harboring for many years. My pain resulted from an amazing series of life altering experiences that I never thought would ever happen to me. I found it very difficult to understand why my life took the route that it did. I also found it very difficult to forgive myself.

The fact that many of us at some point and time sit back and ponder life's mysteries that affect our emotional, spiritual, physical and financial status is a blessing.

The good characteristics of Bruce Codrington had gotten lost for a period of five years. I felt like I had been living inside a person that I did not even know. In fact those five years were during a time when I should have been enjoying the prime of my youth.

I believed that I had considered those tender, precious years stolen from me, and I always felt that I could never make up for the lost time. Once I learned the truth that I gave away those years and that they were not stolen, did I began to experience the pain and anger within myself and wanted to know why.

Having spent five years being addicted to heroin, cocaine, and other illicit mind altering drugs, made me question the man that I am today. I began to search my inner being for the answers to what made me regain control of my life at a particular time and place when all previous attempts at recovery had failed miserably.

My relationships with certain people and family members, even while I was consumed in my negative behavioral patterns, gave me hope for a shot at a positive lifestyle. Although during times when my family had to do the tough love thing with me, I always knew their intentions were honorable and for my own good.

The greatest joy of my life was when I met my wife Janice. I understood when we met the true meaning of unconditional love. This form of love goes too deep and surpasses my understanding. I did not think that I would ever be able to trust, love, understand, sacrifice, be monogamous, be a good father, own a home, and the list goes on and on.

Was I alone in how I felt?

The answer was no.

The more individuals that I had confided in once I became drug free, the more I felt accepted by society's standards. The only problem that I found difficult to accept was why and how could I have wasted five years of my life being a low down trifling dope fiend. I could not see any redeeming value for the time that I had spent living a life of crime, deceit, hatred, uneducated, risk taking, etc.

There are so many people who will never get a second chance in life to make something positive out of their tarnished past. Death, weakness, lack of faith, lack of a strong-willed soul mate and love of family prevent those situations at redemption from taking place. I count that as a sin and a shame.

Once I began to understand through faith and encouragement from people that cared about me, I was able to slowly let go and let God take some of the pain away. I am not yet all the way there, and perhaps never will be, but progress is so much better than perfection because it is ongoing.

By not having a college education, I used to feel so inferior in the presence of those that were fortunate enough to have achieved one. By never having a well paying job, I would feel inferior when in the company of those that did. By not having a 401k plan for my retirement I would worry myself sick over what would happen to me in my latter years. I would worry and become down on myself so often, that I overlooked completely that God had performed a miracle in me thirty-three years ago. I blamed all that I did not have on my past, yet did not credit my past for my successes no matter how small they were.

Now that I have two grown sons, a wife of thirty-two years, and God in my life, I now understand the answer to many of the whys that I had been searching for. I understand that it was *not my business* to intervene in what God had in store for me then, and it is *not my business* to intervene in what God has in store for my future.

It helps to know that there is a divine plan, however, but once I learned to keep my two cents out of certain things, my life became so much more rewarding even without the material things. With the love of God, my wife, children, family, close friends and fellow man, I am rich in so many ways and know that I am truly blessed and kept forever.

GOD RATTLED MY BONES

"Oh Shit! Run! Get back upstairs!" Ronnie yelled as he literally pushed his way past the three of us on that narrow, filthy, piss smelling tenement staircase. The type you would only have to go as far as 116th street in Harlem during the sixties in order to find.

As I ran with the others, I had no idea what the hell was going down. Up until that point all seemed right with the world. Hell, we had just finished getting high off cocaine and heroin, cleaned up our dirty needles for the next time, and still had some drugs and money left over for the next time. We even took advice from "fast Ed," and went to this spot since he claimed he knew the brother that lived there, and now this shit!

What we had forgotten was the fact that dope fiends are the most trifling, and unpredictable kinds of people you will ever find. There we were just forty-five minutes earlier, all of us sitting around getting high in this brother's apartment, and now here we were back in the same spot where we started, wondering what the hell was going on! We felt safe and secure hiding out there thinking the two men, one armed with a sawed off shotgun, would not know where we had escaped to.

Escaped to?

The joke was on us.

To our surprise the brother, who had one of his homies there with us earlier, had made up his mind to rip us off. Why? Because we let our guards down after the dope kicked in and turned our brains to the "off" position. Ronnie, Fast Ed, Ralph and I felt so comfortable around them that we started running off at the mouth about how much money and dope we had left. Well, of course that was all that they needed to hear. The homeboy finished, and then left before we did, which was not unusual, plus whom the fuck even noticed?

The next time we saw him in the apartment, he was telling us to stand, place our hands on our heads, and not to move. One dude held the shotgun, while the other helped himself to what they came back for. It is funny now, but not at the time, remembering Ronnie asking in a manner of the utmost sincerity, if the robbers could at least leave him with a bag of dope for later on.

There we were standing like mad cows on our way to be slaughtered, and he's asking for a favor. Talk about balls! His were so big that he probably had to put Band-Aids on the bottom of them so when they dragged along the ground, they wouldn't get bruised!

I had to just close my eyes since I could not bear to witness him being shot right there where he stood for insulting their intelligence. After all, they had feelings too. To show that the guy did have an ounce of compassion, he politely, I might add, told him he couldn't do it. Meanwhile, Ralph and Fast Ed were made to stand with their pants around their ankles to make sure that they were not holding out.

As for myself, I was just asked to empty my pockets, which I did, and that was sufficient enough for them. Once they were sure that not a stone was left unturned they walked backwards ever so slowly through the two glass doors that separated the room we were in from the room with the exit door. We are talking about no more than fifteen feet in distance.

I was just about through with my second prayer when we were instructed not to move or try anything stupid. Wow what an excellent suggestion. There would be no argument from me. However, I did not know how my fellow dope fiends felt about humbling themselves at a time like this, so I threw in a quick prayer for them also not to do anything stupid, especially Ronnie. He was on full disability from the Navy so you know he was not cooking with all his burners. Add drug addiction to the mix and there was no telling what this fool might do.

When they finally closed the glass doors to the room and left, I knew my third intercessory prayer was answered. My partners had the same thing in mind as I did. We all hit the floor and scurried for shelter behind any chair or piece of raggedy ass furniture we could find, in the dilapidated sparsely furnished apartment, as fast as possible. My feeling was that all of us prayed in our own way that these fools wouldn't start spraying the room with gunfire and leave us all for dead. You know, just like they do in the movies.

Just as I finished pleading with God to spare my sorry ass, a revelation hit me. Duh, you idiot, why would they need to not leave any witnesses? We certainly were not going to find them once they left, and we definitely weren't going to call the police and report that two men with guns just robbed us of our drugs. Naw, I think it is safe to come out from behind our safety nets and chalk this up to a bad day. We reserved cussing out Fast Ed, for bringing us to his "connection," until we got the hell out of there and got back out on the street.

Poor Earl. He had been circling the block all that time as he had been instructed to do each time he gave us a ride to Harlem to score. This was so the police could not tell from the New York license tag, that the car was from Long Island. Supposedly there was some type of numbering and letter system that indicated that a car was not registered in the city. This would be a red flag to the police that you were probably in their fair city looking to buy some drugs.

Earl was not an addict. He wanted to be but was afraid to I guess, so the best he could do was just hang out with us. We used him because he had his own car and it was free transportation to the city. He knew better than to have left us even though we took a much longer time to take care of business than usual.

Where his loyalty came from I have no idea. He was a frustrated Golden Glove competitor who always got his ass kicked before the first round ended. His luck was so bad that once while in the Price's basement throwing darts I accidentally hit him in the temple. Seeing the look on his face as the dart was sticking out of his head, although dangerous, still constituted a laugh from us.

He took more than his fair share of ridicule during high school. He was considered a square by our standards, so one could only imagine what his self esteem must have been like if he had any at all. How sad for a person to have to go so low just to be accepted, that he would jeopardize his freedom and driving privileges to be with a bunch of low life people like us.

He finally picked us up on the corner. Once we got in the car he started mouthing off as to what we should have done and what he would have done. Everyone told him to just shut the fuck up. We felt bad enough as it was, without having to listen to his lethargic rhetoric and bullshit. He was told to just get us across the Triborough Bridge as fast as humanly possible. That was his job.

That almighty Triborough Bridge that connected Harlem to Queens began and/or ended at 125th Street and First Avenue. The adrenaline started to flow as we inched closer and closer to the entrance to the bridge. Sometimes we would take an alternate route down 124th Street, just in case we were being followed. My late mother-in-law years later used to always say I should have been a politician since I hardly ever took the same route twice. This time though it was straight to the bridge, our comfort zone, since we had nothing on us to get busted for anyway.

As we passed through the tollbooth I reflected on the events of the past several hours. I said to myself for the hundredth time that I was going to kick my habit. I can honestly say up until that time only once previously had I ever come so close to getting killed. What made this situation so scary was that your ass could have been dumped in an alley or left on a roof somewhere, and nobody would have known you were there. You'd be just another dead dope fiend and one less for society to worry about.

Of course that line of rational thinking came and went very quickly. In fact, before we were on the Long Island Expressway heading back to "New Castle," I was thinking about how and where I was going to get more money to get high.

A CEREMONY TAKES PLACE

"Well then," said Pastor Rogers, "We will proceed to the second part of the ceremony" Bruce, turn to Janice and repeat after me, "to have and to hold, to love and to cherish 'til death do you part."

Phew! Thank God I got past those words in a hurry.

Of course when Pastor Rogers asked, "Will you love her, honor her, and keep her through sickness and in health as long as you both shall live?" I would have been kicked in the ass if any word other than yes had been the answer.

The exchanging of our marriage vows and the ceremony were a lot of fun. The occasion was not solemn, but was laid back and relaxed. There was a mixture here and there of humor, courtesy of Uncle Bobby, yet taken very seriously. Janice and I wanted things that way. After all this was not the first time we had spoken those words-I do.

As I stood inside our home church in Atlanta, Georgia, filled with family, friends, and fellow parishioners, it was the greatest feeling of accomplishment that I had ever felt. I had never thought that in a million years we would be standing shoulder to shoulder renewing our vows twenty-five years later.

This time around Janice and I had everything done first class all the way: church; tuxedos; wedding gown; 120 family and friends; reception; caterer; gifts; limousine; five-day honeymoon in Ocho Rios; Jamaica; and first-class seats on Air Jamaica. Yes, it was the Ultimate Occasion of my life, and well worth sticking around to witness.

Our wedding on October 30, 1972, consisted of a civil ceremony. We did the justice of the peace thing in front of a judge with the two witnesses. I guess that was good enough to earn us a silver anniversary, huh?

Seemed like it was only yesterday. Where had the time gone?

MY ONE AND ONLY TRUE LOVE

Well our journey to holy matrimony began in 1972 with yours truly having the following irrational conversation with himself. The practiced art of talking to myself, something that I had gotten good at after many years of practice, went somewhat like this:

"You can't be serious!" I said. "No wait; this shit can't be for real. Were we actually going for the blood test to get our marriage license? The next step would be going to the justice of the peace." There was still time to back out Bruce, and save face. At 22-years young, deciding to spend the rest of my life with another person might not be such a good idea; at least not now. Nah, this wouldn't be a healthy move for me.

I may not have learned much during the first twenty-two years of my life, but I always remembered the saying, "You only hurt the ones you love." There she was, right before my very eyes, smacking me right upside my head emotionally. I must have been in love big time, and hadn't even known it. If by me backing out I would have hurt Janice, then the love I had for her was quite evident. That much I did understand.

So when Janice called me from her job to give me the dates, times, and conditions for the ceremony to take place, I just said, "All sounds great to me! Just tell me where, and when, and I will be there."

I was so glad that this conversation took place over the telephone. I would not have wanted my future bride to witness the expression on my face that mirrored my true thoughts during the phone conversation. She might not have wanted to follow through with the most important decision of her life—marriage.

What an idiot I was. I had waited for the right female in my life to come along, someone that I could grow in love with, and there I was thinking about copping out. I knew I did not want to risk losing this beautiful young woman. Although Janice was only 16 when we met, and 17 when we married, she was more mature than most adults were. The Lord knew I needed someone like that to guide me, and see me through life if I was going to survive.

After graduating High School most of the females that I was involved with never got the chance to meet any of my family. The truth was I was too ashamed and embarrassed to ever bring them around my folks. I was hooked up with two other women at the time when I met Janice in October of 1971.

Did I love either of them?

No way!

I was just interested in one thing and one thing only: Sex, sex, and then more sex! In the seventies the most you had to worry about with unprotected sex was catching a little venereal disease. In my opinion, it was a small risk to take. Hell my entire life seemed to have been dictated by risk, so what the hell.

Marrying "*someone like me,*" and vowing to love, honor and take care of me 'til death do us apart, was a risk that Janice thought was worth taking. Again, someone from above was looking over me just like so many other times in my life. The good Lord had been with me.

WHO WAS I?

But who was this "*someone like me*" character anyway?

We all should be so fortunate to dig deep inside our inner souls, and reflect back on our past to explore who we are. What people may learn is that they also may fall into that classification of that "*someone like me*" character.

Hum. Who knows if the person they perceive themselves to be, is not actually who they are?

I have been truly blessed to have had the opportunity to come to know myself. From my dark days of despair, hopelessness, drug addiction, crime, incarcerations, loneliness, and lack of any form of pride, I am damn proud of Bruce.

I said truly blessed because those life experiences have shown me the value of loving another person unconditionally. I might not have reached the point of enjoying thirty-two years of marriage with my soul mate, lover, and most of all my best friend, had I not gone through those troubled times.

As the saying goes, "There is *always* a ministry that comes out of your misery."

I had grown up as this naive, chubby, introverted little boy from Jamaica, New York. My world consisted of anything I could do alone. I loved to draw and dreamed of becoming a famous architect and home designer some day. I would build houses and buildings with my building blocks.

I would play alone for hours and be as content as I wanted to be. I vividly remembered those white and clear blocks of plastic that when snapped together created my fantasies of how my home would look someday. The kit even included little doors and windows to accent the authenticity.

I also used to have little plastic and rubber figures of people that lived in my model home. In 1958 there were no figurines of Negroes to speak of, so I used to color them brown with my crayons. Being black was not fashionable during that time.

Boy, was I the creative eight-year-old kid or what?

In order to live out this fantasy of the big house, furnished with in-ground pool and all, I knew I would definitely have to become a professional. I could never afford those luxuries on a civil servant's salary. Uncle Will was a doctor, and I just thought that was the coolest thing in the world.

For two years, Dad, Mom, my older brother Stephen, and I had lived in an upstairs apartment over Uncle Will's office on New York Boulevard. It was located in one of the roughest sections of Queens. We lived there while we were waiting for our new house to be built in New Castle, Long Island.

Talk about learning to adjust? Moving from a house to an upstairs apartment, and having to be driven to school daily was not much fun. We could not even play out of doors as the neighborhood was so bad.

Often on Saturdays, after Uncle Will had gone home at noon, Stephen and I would sneak downstairs, and explore his office. I thought that those white lab coats that doctors wore were the coolest part of being a doctor. However, since pain, suffering, blood, and Bruce did not get along too well, I had to rule out medicine as a career. It would be kind of hard to treat sick people with those kinds of hang-ups.

Uncle Will had a homeboy, Elwood Low, who was a lawyer. How lucky I was as a young Black kid to have a doctor in the family that was tight with a lawyer. I could have received so much encouragement, and first hand knowledge. Law did not interest me either. Not sure what the reasoning was back then, but I guess it had to be good enough at the time.

The truth was that I had wanted to be a civil servant just like my dad. He drove a bus for the New York City Transit Authority. I used to be in awe of those great big buses being handled by strong, able-bodied men. That could not have been a job for the weak, and timid. I always wanted to be in control of a massive machine like a bus, filled with so many daily commuters, that during the rush hours, they'd be standing in the stairwells cramped in like sardines in a can.

Yes, that was what I wanted to become.

That career choice had nothing to do with money, as I recall how on several occasions, Mom used to ask Uncle Will to cash Dad's paycheck out of his chump change, so she could do food shopping or whatever. I think Dad used to be embarrassed, but never said anything.

If Dad only knew just how much I admired him growing up when he would take me on his route with him from time to time. When he would let the last passenger off and had a ten-minute break before driving back, he used to let me sit in his seat, open and close the doors with the handle, change the destination sign by hand and pretend to be driving. The steering wheel was bigger than life to me. But most of all it was the time we spent together that was important.

No one ever discouraged me from what I wanted to be when I was growing up. My folks used to always tell us, "Whatever it is you choose to be, just be the best at it." I could live with that.

I always had a true sense of family. I enjoyed, cared for, and got along quite well with my aunts, uncles, grandparents, cousins and my own immediate family. Everyone, that was, except Stephen. I loved him dearly up 'til the day he died the third month into the millennium.

Stephen was the type of person that could, and would, get on your last nerve. Not all the time, just some of the time! Yet he was so harmless and often he reacted off of impulse. Poor Mom seemed to be up at the school for some disciplinary problems with him from the time he was in second grade. He was the type that could walk through a lion's den while wearing a pork chop jacket, and have no fear.

There were many situations that allowed me to have so much time to myself. I guess in today's modern way of raising children, a parent would be chastised for "little Brucie boy" not interacting with other children. A stereotypical title that is thrown around so loosely today is Attention Deficit Disorder. This is how the "now generation" views this type of behavior.

Back in the '50's and '60's, this type of behavior was not considered that abnormal. Even if it was, no one would dare insinuate that your child is not normal, not even a family member.

Don't misunderstand now. I did not spend *all* my time alone.

Living in a home with a loving blue-collar, working class father, and a stay-at-home mother was the equivalent to living the *Leave It To Beaver* lifestyle. The only difference noted was the fact that we were black!

No argument there.

Looking back during that era I did not know any other way that people were supposed to live. Unfortunately the negative images of black folks in the media did not discount the fact that my father was a man that always worked hard and put food on the table. Mom was at home taking care of the house, but unlike June Cleaver she was not dressed in high heel shoes, a dress and wearing a string of pearls around her neck. That was where reality began and T.V. land ended.

The comparison to living like the Cleavers or *Ozzie and Harriet* were the only positive images of how a wholesome family was supposed to live. I certainly was not going to compare our family life to that of *"Amos and Andy"* or *"Beulah,"* the only black shows I can remember growing up. Those two programs were so negative, that Mom and Dad forbid us to even watch them on our one and only black and white television set.

1969…A DIALOGUE LIKE THIS TOOK PLACE

Good goodness!

Sheryl you must be kidding!

We just can't believe it. Not our Bruce!

"Yes," said Sheryl, "Unfortunately I am not kidding Anita and Ethel. I just came back from Manhattan after dropping your favorite, darling, little nephew off at Glenview House."

"Sheryl, you mean that drug abuse program for drug addicts on 85th street?" asked Aunt Anita.

"Yup, that's where I just come from". Sheryl said.

"Lord have mercy" both aunts chimed in at the same time.

They were in complete shock and dismay.

Heaven's no, they definitely would not tell Uncle Felix or Uncle Harold. Especially Uncle Felix.

Harold was my uncle through marriage to Aunt Ethel, but he and I were not very close. Uncle Felix was married to Aunt Neat. Since neither couple had children of their own, I was like a son to all of them. They kind of gave me that extra dose of being special you might say, especially at Christmas time and on my birthdays.

So I certainly understood that their reactions to the turn of events for the prodigal nephew must have been like a ton of bricks falling on them. Because our relationship was so special, I tried to keep my dark secrets to myself out of respect for all that they had been to me.

Of course what goes on in the dark always come out in the light so sooner or later they would have caught on to what I was into.

WELL, MY STORY GOES LIKE THIS

Why this young child, who was so content on being independent and just kind of happy go lucky, opted to destroy his dreams can be summed up in one word—insecurity.

I had never intended to ever give up drawing and building those beautiful model houses; but I did. I could not have achieved even a civil service job with drugs on my record. I guess at the time even the thought of having a wife and family was not important because I always felt that I would not live past the age of twenty-one anyway.

Although I did not write the script, I just had a part to play. The only difference was, unlike rehearsing until I had gotten it right; I bowed out and made my exit early. I never did get the crime lifestyle right. I did not need the standing ovation!

Good choice of many more choices to come.

Gee, I remembered the excitement and nervousness in 1959, when our family finally moved from Jamaica to New Castle. We felt just like the "Jefferson's" in that we were moving on up. Mom was pregnant with my sister so she got to stay home and play housewife again. To elevate your quality of life by moving to the suburbs back in those days was the ultimate accomplishment. Way to go Mom and Dad!

New Castle was a small, very unique town on Long Island.

It was a black community with a sprinkle here and there of some Italians and several white families that felt that they were still safe living there. Westbury however, was just the opposite. This town was recognized as the power center for what was said and done for us folks in New Castle.

The two towns, although thought of as one, were separated only by Union Ave. If a black family crossed that avenue you were considered a step above the rest. You could have counted the number of black families on one hand that were living in Westbury at the time. Did not take me long to figure out that we were ghetto bound!

Our neighborhood did not seem to change for the worse until 1965. That was when a multitude of black folks from the South, primarily Alabama and Mississippi, migrated to the North. Once these family members settled in, found jobs, and saved a few dollars, then they would send for their other relatives.

Us "decent folks" started to nickname them "cornbreaders" since they were so countrified. We were not used to seeing so many people from the South at one time in such a small concentrated area. There was a feeling of outward resentment amongst the different cultures. There was a time there when fighting between the good, the bad, and the ugly was a common occurrence.

I guess had I been a homeowner during that mass influx of "cornbreaders," then I would have been upset as well. They seemed to change the status of a quiet, decent, bedroom type of community, to that which consisted of illegal, multi-family style housing. Better put, most of those folks were renters and cared little about the community.

Although I was only nine-years-old when we moved in 1959, I did remember how nice New Castle used to be. When Stephen and I were younger, we used to look forward to us driving out to New Castle from Jamaica, to visit Mom's sister Beatrice, Uncle Will and my three cousins. The only reason my folks even heard about this neighborhood was because of them.

Most of the whites had moved out of the area by 1964. Within a year or two after that, those same areas, where they lived, looked like war zones. The white folks that moved but held on to their property, made out like fat rats in a cheese factory. They would rent their homes to whomever could pay the rent and utilities.

As a result of this lack of vested interest on their part, we had single-family dwellings that would house up to as many as twelve people or more at any given time. There was no such thing as an honest County or fire inspector when it came to the black neighborhoods.

After that poor, old, little German lady and her mother got robbed and put in the walk in refrigerator in their grocery store one night in the summer of 1966, they sold to the first buyer. The Arabs that owned just one of the seven food stores on Prospect Avenue eventually left also because they saw the handwriting on the wall. So to who did both of these shop owners sell to?

You guessed it! Our own people.

Brother Noonan had moved his family up from Mississippi and had worked his way up the ranks from a busboy at a Howard Johnson Restaurant to become the manager. He and his two brother-in-laws bought the store from the German lady. Brother Counsel, who took an early retirement from the Post Office, closed his deal with the Arabs.

What the community thought would happen did not turn out to become a reality. The black storeowners were not there to restore pride and value to the area. They were even a lot worse. They saw this opportunity for entrepreneurship as a chance to become rich off the blood, sweat, and ignorance of their own people.

Every ethnic group went to the same elementary school and there wasn't ever any form of racism that I was aware of. We stayed together as classmates during middle school right up to the day of graduation from Westbury High. Since there was only one junior high school and one senior high school, you did not have to guess which school you would attend. Friends that I made in elementary school at nine years old, I am still friends with some of those same people today.

There were no corporate transfers and relocation opportunities during that time. The desire to move up the corporate ladder for many working parents today, more often than not involve relocating. I can say that the roots established within my school years were solid. This helped a lot because if you had a crush on a childhood girl or boy in school, chances are you might stand a chance at romance down the road.

I was a very quiet person that detested violence in any way, shape or fashion. I wasn't a fighter and was still kind of a loner by time I reached junior high. My boxing career lasted a total of two ass whippings. What made it so bad, they were one day after the other!

Wait. There's more.

My opponent was the same guy both times!

This sticks out in my mind so well because it was so funny. The dude's name was David Sills. We used to call him "the Scholar" since he looked like a nerd with a big head full of brains. I took him for granted. In fact I probably picked a fight with him because I figured I would win. Shows how prejudging can backfire on you.

Back in 1965, Muhammad Ali a.k.a. Cassius Clay was "the man!" I used to watch all his fights. He was so graceful and indeed was "good with his hands" as we used to say. How I ever I thought I could back pedal and bob and weave in the lot across the street from the school, constituted a 15-year-old's dumb mentality.

Of course once the word carefully filtered throughout the school to all the brothers and sista girls, everyone could not wait 'til after school. The audience was there; the stage was set, now all you needed were the two fighters.

I started off with my dancing and defending myself pretty well. Remember I did not like violence. When I was involved, I liked it even less! I remembered the saying, "the best offense is a good defense", and thus that was my fight plan.

Things were going pretty good until I backed up and tripped over a tree stump. Well the rest was history. Not his but mine. It was well within the rules that he had every right to get on top of me and beat the shit out of me. It was my fault that I ended up on the ground so I could not cry foul.

I can't even tell you how many times he went upside my head, but all I knew was I was so glad someone yelled, "Here come Mr. Smith!" He was the assistant principal. Everyone started to run. Although we were officially off school property, the administration could still punish you. Boy that was one rule I was glad they enforced. That meant you had to haul ass so as not to get into trouble.

David had to let me up in order to run also, which left me not only with the few ounces of brains I had left from the hits I took, but a chance to get in the wind myself. By the time I caught up with my homies, I wasn't in the mood to hear that I couldn't let the ass kicking go without a rematch. Far be it from me to show any signs of weakness. I knew they were right, but my head was still throbbing an hour later so that was the last thing on my mind.

When I saw David the following morning prior to the bell ringing to start the school day, he knew even before I opened my mouth that we had to go for it again. He was so damn nice about it too. That pissed me off. I had set my mind on one thing and one thing only for the whole day—I would not and could not lose.

There once was a song with lyrics that went something like this; "my bodies here with you, but my mind is on the other side of town!" I think I knew the meaning of those lyrics when school ended that day.

This time we went to the grassy area along side the Northern State Parkway. It was right through the schoolyard fence and only a short walk. I picked the spot because there were no tree stumps to trip over. Just a flat surface. Others had fought their battles there also. By the time word filtered through the school this time around, I felt like the Pied Piper walking to the "arena" for the main event. There had to be at least sixty people there. "Bruce, you can't lose now," I thought.

I started out good just like the day before. I got in a hit or two and my defense was on the money. Just be patient Bruce. Don't over react. Just keep on doing what you're doing and all will be fine. Since fights back then ended when someone quit, blood was shed, or someone broke it up out of having mercy on the obvious loser, I did not want to be any of the above options.

Well since you know I lost already, no surprise there, so here is what happened.

My body was doing well, but my mind started to drift. I got over anxious, cocky and my confidence level was at an all time high. All of a sudden I remember seeing a fist come straight at me. It looked the size of a basketball. Ah shit, to late to get out of the way.

BAM!

The fight ended due to option number two. Blood was shed—Mine!

I can honestly say I did not feel a thing. I knew I got hit over my right eye, but that was all I knew. Not until I saw the expression on the faces of the audience and I heard Cynthia gasp and let out a low but audible scream, I kind of figured I was not a pretty sight. I wiped the blood as I walked home with you guessed it. The same homies that convinced me to fight again. Not one of them gave me the indication that I was cut over my eye right above the eyebrow.

When I got six blocks from my house, I stopped and looked in the side view mirror of a parked car and almost dropped dead standing up! Not only was I cut, but it was open so wide that you could see some white stuff that I guess is inside your skullbox for some medicinal purpose. By this time only two of my boys were left on the last leg of the journey to my block, so I dare not react like a sissy in front of them.

After Mom nearly fainted, since she was in the kitchen with the back door open as I walked up the steps, she rushed me to the medical center. The doctor was so cool though. As he prepared me for the 10 stitches required to close the one-inch cut, when Mom was not listening he whispered, "Did you at least win?" By my laugh he knew the answer.

The next day in school, patch above my right eye and all, David and I shook hands, laughed and were friends throughout the remainder of our school days.

Funny how we used to settle our differences between one another. Mostly fights happened over something stupid or over a girl. When girls fought it was an even bigger spectacular event cause you got to look up their dresses when they rolled around on the ground. And I thought only guys had hair between their legs! Was I naive or what?

When I was 11 years old, I used to hustle on my block by cutting grass and pulling weeds to earn some money. One of the local builders used to pay me to watch the new homes under construction on our street. I think he knew I liked being around the sites due to my love of houses and building. He built our home so he got to know my family pretty well.

The fact that he started to build our home in error on the wrong lot across the street, I suspect that he was just giving me a job to save face with my folks. Boy were they pissed off when they went out to check on their brand new home and discovered the mistake. We ended up having to live above Uncle Will's office for another whole year. That sucked!

My idea of a good time in the summer during school break was to spend time with my relatives. I couldn't wait to move from Jamaica to the "burbs." Then when school would let out, I wanted to go spend my summer there. Another dumb kid mentality.

I was luckier than most kids my age. I had two aunts and two uncles living under the same roof. Top that! They were nicknamed "the folks." My aunts would take me to Brooklyn and Manhattan on the subways every Labor Day to hang out and go shopping with them. I just went for the eating part. I mean we used to eat up some junk foods. I couldn't wait to eat one of those dirty hot dogs from the street vendor with the red onion sauce and mustard.

They'd shop a bit, and then we'd stop and eat some more. French fries, Knishes, glazed donuts, salted cashews or peanuts in the shell. I never had the taste for a cheeseburger though. Just didn't seem right at the time.

Frankie, my cousin via his mom and my mom being best friends, still lived in Jamaica so I would hang with him and play some hoops back at P.S.116 where I first went to school when I was six. He is three years older than me, but he used to let me hang anyway. I had other cousins through marriages within the family that I hung out with also. Mostly though I stayed close to 104th Avenue down the street from Liberty Park and enjoyed just being around the "folks."

The "folks" had a front porch attached to the house with seven windows. In fact, there was only one wall! We usually took turns as to who got to sit in the chair that rocked back and forth. After dinner we'd retire to the porch and people watch. When we talked about somebody, it was low key so that the people could not hear us. The reason for that was most of the people talked about was their neighbors! Isn't that the way it usually is?

My visits in the summer were no more than two weeks at a time. By staying at the house, I also got to see more of my dad. Since the house belonged to his brother Felix, and his sister Ethel, Dad used to practically live there in between his schedule on the bus route. The house gave him a place to nap, shave if he had to, or just enjoy a visit. There were ALWAYS laughter and good times with the "folks."

My demeanor during the mid sixties was still one of being a nerd. I saw other kids doing things they weren't supposed to do, but did not have the urge to be a follower—at least not then.

We would play stickball, shoot marbles, and ride our 10-speed bikes usually with someone riding on the handlebars or just play ring-a-leave-o under the streetlights on the block. Your parents knew that when they yelled for you, your ass better be within the sound of their voice. It was just understood.

My brother and I were very fortunate. Where we lived on Rushmore Street we had the two Gibson brothers, and the two Price brothers, both within our ages. We were never without anything to do. Sure once in awhile there'd be an argument or a fight amongst us every so often, but we were thick as thieves. In fact, three of us even grew up to become thieves.

Mrs. Price worked on the estate of one of the wealthiest families in New York State. The estate was located in Old Westbury. Sometimes we would ride our bikes the eight miles or so up to the estate and she would let us roam the grounds. We had to promise not to touch anything. I remember the wealthy family's reputation, amongst the rich and famous, was how exotic and exquisite their flower gardens were. They used to give tours for a fee, and then donate the money to charity. I had to be careful not to show my adoration for the flowers. I would have been ostracized from the gang if I showed any sissy qualities.

It was during my junior high school days when I began smoking cigarettes. I used to smoke but never bought a pack of cigarettes. I would steal a couple of Mom's L&M's. Boy, were they nasty! They were like smoking a glass of milk. They had to suffice though as Dad smoked Camels without the filter, which were even worse. They had a kick like a Georgia mule, plus you had to keep spitting out the bits of tobacco that you sucked into your mouth.

I used to think that they chose those brands on purpose just so we would not acquire a taste for smoking. Oh if I had only stopped at stealing Mom's cigarettes and Dad's gin, things might not have progressed to the point of much worse things to come.

MY PUBERTY CAME AND
WENT TOO FAST

I should have been more interested in girls but no big thing. I had time. There were a few girls that liked me, but I was still very naive for my age compared to others. I realized afterwards that at the time when Cynthia let out that horrible gasp at the sight of my eye being cut open, it was because she had a crush on me.

Girls used to do the dumbest things if they liked you. Heaven forbid they just came out and were forward with their feelings. That would be too easy. Usually you found out who liked you from one of their girlfriends, and it was never an accident that they spilled the beans to you. That is precisely why their friend told them in the first place.

There was a time back in 1966, when there was another girl who took a strong liking to me. She was only 14 and I was 16. Her name was Linda Conroy. Her 15-year-old sister Cheri was going out with Bobby who was in my class in school. For the girls it was always cool to say you were going out with an upper class man.

As for the guys, you were either laughed at that you could not get a girlfriend your own age or you were envied that you had a younger girlfriend. Having a younger girlfriend usually indicated that the girl would do just about anything for you to keep you. What an advantage!

I kind of liked Linda though. She was a very pretty girl with long straight hair and an olive skin tone with not one blemish on her face. I believe there had to be some traces of Native American Indian somewhere in her family lineage. The only thing about her was she had not yet fully developed. Her breasts were not like Ceilia's or Joan's. Those two had the biggest titty balls for junior high school kids that I had ever seen.

Perhaps had I known how sensitive Linda was about her breasts, I would have lightened up a little from my usual comedienne self in New Castle Park that hot summer day in May. Damn, all I did was make fun of her blouse because it had a zipper down the front. But I think I crossed her threshold of humility when I said her tits looked like birdseed. Yeah now that I had 38 years to think about it again, I am positive that is what caused the next chain of events.

We used to play basketball as often as we could. I never really applied myself in any sport. I never thought I was good enough. The older guys used to let us youngins hang with them and if you were real good like brother Dewey, you had it made. So on this particular day when Linda did not find my sense of humor funny, she decided since I embarrassed her in front of other people she would get even. She went home and told her entire family that consisted of two sisters and four brothers that I had been picking on her.

Two of these brothers looked like mountain men. They were about six feet two inches, and weighed over 265 pounds each. Rachael, the oldest of the two sisters, could have kicked any dudes ass at any given time. The other two brothers, Phillip and Glenn, were kind of wimpy and Cheri, well she was good with her mitts also.

I guess their fighting skills were the results of watching their father physically abuse their mother for years until he just up and left one day. I would have guessed that their mother would detest violence considering all the years she got her ass kicked. But, I guess back then little was known about abused and battered spouses.

"Man Bruce. You better get out of here. Look!" yelled Ralph.

There they were the entire Conroy clan, marching towards the park. They even were lined up from the shortest to the tallest. We all knew what the deal was. My ass was grass if I didn't get in the wind before they got into the park. Now most of the dudes from the basketball court would have taken my back, but there was no way we could have out fought all of them.

Mr. Clent was one of four park attendants that worked for the County assigned to supervise New Castle Park. He was an ex-light heavyweight boxer that kept his body in perfect condition. Even at forty-eight, he could bench press over three hundred pounds. I know. He lived down the street from us and we could hear him going through his workouts in his garage. Boy was it intense and loud!

He used to have some of his fighter friends come over on Sundays. They would spar in his backyard. Since he lived next door to the Price family, we used to sit on the split rail fence and watch the free show. Without our parents' knowledge, he used to give a few others as well as us in the neighborhood weight-lifting lessons.

Once this dude name Neil dropped a weight on his head by accident and Mr. Clent tried to push the knot back into his forehead—WITH HIS HAND! I had to leave the garage as I was doubled over laughing so hard. Yes, it was fair to say he was one of the nicest adults you could have known with a sense of humor. I was so glad we were neighbors.

There would be no way out of this situation.

This was my first brush with thinking I was going to get killed. My life was going to end and I was only 16. Hadn't even had my first climax yet. Damn!

Of the four park attendants, God must have written the schedule for Mr. Clent to be on duty that afternoon. He was cool with us and we all had the utmost respect for him. That's why he usually could stay in the office in the hexagon park house, and either sleep or watch television. That is how confident he was in us that we would not do anything to screw up his workday. So when he heard the banging of a frantic somebody on the office door he did not hesitate to open the door in a hurry.

By the time I explained the situation to him, Ma Conroy and the troops were not more than 50 feet away and still marching. You could hear a pin drop. No more basketballs bouncing or handballs thumping against the 10-foot wall. All eyes were focused on the "showdown at the New Castle Park Corral."

My explanation to Mr. Clent was quick and to the point. The strongest point being was that I did not want to die. He knew he would never allow a seven to one confrontation to take place; not if he had anything to say about it.

Ma Conroy did most of the talking at first. It was kind of hard for me to hear as I was crouched behind Mr. Clent's massive body of steel. He stood in the doorway with his hands on his hips. He reminded me of that character Mr. Gleam, except without the earring. This was his domain and to get to me you had to get past him. Once the two brothers with brut strength started to chime into the conversation, I not only could hear their anger, but also could see in their eyes that they were prepared to die for the cause. It was time to doubt Mr. Clent' ability to protect me, yet NOT really the time.

Jimmy, Diego, Ralph and some other brothers were ready to take at least the other two wimpy male Conroys out and perhaps at least Rachael. But as for the mountain boys, I was sure that they did not want any parts of them. So the only person that I had to save me was Mr. Clent so it was really a no brainer. He and only he could stop the mountain boys. Period!

I made the mistake of sticking my head out from behind Mr. Clent and when I did, Ma Conroy grabbed me by my Westbury basketball warm up jacket. I was trying to pull away from her grasp (and a mighty grasp it was) when the sleeve tore. That set my adrenaline to flowing. Although I got the warm up jacket from

JJ, who stole it in the first place from the team, it was my favorite. Now this old ass bitch destroyed it.

Don't ask me how or why I said loud enough for everyone to hear, "You bitch."

And that was all she wrote!

I got free, but I made matters worse.

The brothers started their move closer to the doorway, my homeboys were chomping at the bit to get busy, and even timid little me figured, hell, at least I could take Moms if I had to. It was time to go to war and there was no backing out now. When the mountain boys got about three feet from the door, I'll never forget Mr. Clent's exact words to them. He told them, "There is no way you are gonna get past me, and if you throw your hands up, I'll knock you BOTH out!" By this time also, the others knew they were outnumbered. I smelled victory in the air.

They started to retreat back out the park, but not until they finished threatening me that I had to show my face outside the park sometime and when I did well, you know the rest.

Now it was time for Mr. Clent to ask me if I was telling the truth as to what I might have done to set them off. Here he was ready to defend me with all he had, and yet did not even know if the story that I had told him in those hasty moments were true. What a guy.

About an hour later, and yes I was afraid to leave the park until Mr. Clent got off duty, I was sitting on the bench nearest to the gate. I was talking to Doug when I looked up and here came the mountain boys, Cheri, and Linda. Shit! What the hell did they want now? Well I damn sure wasn't running anywhere. This shit had to end sometime.

Who would have thought in a million years, that they would return to the park and approached me an offer an apology? They explained that when they went back home and gave Linda the third degree about her story, she admitted that I never slapped her in the face.

Slapped Linda in the face! Slapped Linda in the face!

I had to repeat to myself what they just told me. She actually went home and told her family that I had slapped her in the face. Aint that a bitch? Here I was having everyone believing that all this shit was because I made fun of her. I could not help but look at her as she kind of hung her head down so as not to look me in the eye. What a dangerous thing she did. I was more shocked than angry. I actually felt sorry for her. To go through all that just to get attention and express her "liking me" took a lot of crust!

The funniest part of their apology was when they told me that on behalf of the family, their mom asked that I stop by and she would pay me five dollars for tearing my basketball warm up. I said, "Thanks, but that was not necessary. My mom can sew it. It aint that bad." There was no way I was going near their house until the ether wore off. No way!

So the story went that Linda and me got together about a month later. I could not help but look up to her as a girl with a lot of guts and determination to get what she wanted at any cost. That was MY type of girl!

Other than us hanging in the park a lot, making out in the field at Grand Street Elementary at night, and playing "stink finger" in the movies, that was the extent of our "going together." I knew at the time she was faster than me in growing up, but she was faster than I could handle.

I am sure I could have gotten all the sex I wanted anytime I wanted, if only I knew how! That was my first real exposure to the boyfriend girlfriend thing. Before that I just went to a lot of blue light in the basement parties and danced the "grind 'em up." Where was a guy to go to learn how to screw? Listening to other dudes was counterfeit because most of them were lying about "getting some" anyway.

She must have felt that my lack of experience was only getting worse before it was getting better, so she moved on to bigger and better things. She found a sorry ass older man that had a fancy car. Talk about selling yourself cheap!

LIFE BECAME A LITTLE MORE DARING

Binky had just moved to New Castle in 1965 before the school term began. I was in my last year of junior high school and he was a year younger and a year behind me. This did not stop us from hanging out together. He moved from Brooklyn with his older brother Alvin, and younger brother Freddie. We used to be wild and crazy for our ages.

We never did anything really bad or destructive. We would cut school every now and then and take the bus to Hempstead, our rival town for partying. Our thirty-five cent lunch money was used for the fare to get there. Eating White Tower hamburgers and fries was our reward after we would steal a March of Dime display full of money off a store counter when no one was looking. Yes I know it was trifling, but we felt at the time the kids would not miss one little box of money.

I smoked my first joint sitting on a park bench with Binky. I had stolen a small handful of pot from Stephen's hiding place—the inside pocket of his jacket that hung in our bedroom closet. I took a couple of sheets of Bamboo rolling papers also.

Together Binky and I rolled the biggest, most awkward looking joint, and was so excited to finally enter into the world of reefer madness. Stephen never mentioned anything to me that some of his stash was missing.

My first experience in stealing a car was also with Binky. It was the day before Memorial Day in '65. We knew just about anyone who was anybody would be going out to Jones Beach to party with the girls. Since we did not want to miss out on any of the fun, we knew having our own set of wheels was the only way to get there.

I'll never forget how we walked around this white neighborhood that was across the tracks for what seemed like the entire night, when he spotted this blue '62 Chevy Impala parked on the street. He knew to choose a General Motors car as they could be started without a key or hot-wired.

Out of respect for not wanting to wake up the homeowner, we quietly opened the front door on the driver's side, turned the ignition switch to "ON," put the gear into neutral and pushed it a block away. Then we got in, started it and drove off. The person was even nice enough to have left us a full tank of gas.

I had never gotten behind the wheel of a moving car, except when I was younger and your dad used to let you sit in his lap and steer while he controlled the gas and brake peddles. This caused us to start arguing since I wanted to learn to drive and Binky already knew since he had stolen cars before.

Finally we returned across the tracks, tracks always seemed to run through black neighborhoods, Binky finally gave me my chance behind the wheel. I didn't do too badly. Other than sideswiping a parked car, tearing off the side view mirror and almost throwing Binky through the windshield. All this was accomplished since I never stepped on the brake peddle. I felt I did fine for a novice.

My car stealing days were during the same time that I had begun drinking that cheap awful tasting wine. I first started with Binky when we used to skip school. Drinking was a part of life for a lot of 15-year-olds. I didn't drink only cheap wine though. The malt liquor craze was beginning to emerge and of course the Jolt was the joint for us. Brother Donnie Ray, who moved out to New Castle in the middle of 9th grade, became my steady drinking partner.

The best part of teenage drinking was finding the best hiding places to indulge and not get busted. If we found a spot, we would never share it with anyone. We wanted it all to ourselves. So when we found out we could access the roof of the one story building attached to the Grand Street elementary school, we struck pay dirt.

Three Arab brothers, whom owned one of the local grocery stores on Prospect Avenue, had no conscience when it came to selling beer or malt liquor to minors; Especially since to them we were just a bunch of crazy niggers anyhow. When they sensed that "the man" was on their asses for doing their thing, then they would ask us for identification. This was our clue to go outside or around the block and ask one of our older soul brothers to buy for us. They were glad to oblige for a small fee of course.

One could not have savored the taste of a nice ice cold Jolt without some BBQ potato chips to go with it. It had to be a large bag too. With our goodies in hand we would be off to the rooftop for a brew and some bullshit talk. Bullshit was the best talk there was.

Once we hung out on the roof for what seemed like hours, the time would come for the part that we dreaded the most; getting down. I was very fortunate to have never fallen, but I look back on those wonder years and do just that; wonder how I never hurt myself.

Donnie and I started to share our hiding place with brother Emmons. Soon we were doing this shit two to three times a week. They both smoked pot too, so we added that to our repetoire of daring things to do. It was like, "Hey yall, let's climb up on a roof, get stoned and then try to get down without becoming a paraplegic!"

Part of the drudgery of going to school was that I had to do things that I did not want to do. Given the same set of circumstances in my adult life, I would choose not to do the same things. For example, I hated having to attend what was called an assembly. An assembly was at least once a month. It was the one-day you were required to wear a shirt and tie. Most of the assemblies were musically motivated, so I guess those interested in music would enjoy something along those lines. I was not one of them.

The only times that I did enjoy the band music was when my man Stephan Garr used to jam with his own trio. I mean this brother was awesome for being only 16 years old. The only reason he was still in the 9th grade was the administrators held him back when he moved from Harlem. At that time a New York City education was not considered as good or equal to a "suburbia education."

Stephan not only played the piano, but he also wrote music and played a mean saxophone. Mr. Norris, the music teacher could not teach him anything. In fact, he could have learned a lot from Stephan.

Basketball as I mentioned before, was not a sport that I was good at. I wasn't the gung ho type that just had to make the squad. I did try out though. I got cut the second round of tryouts. The after school intramural program consisted of those who were not good enough to make the team, yet wanted to play organized sports. Me, I just would rather get high, and then sit in the bleachers and bullshit with the young ladies. Deep down I wished I had been a better athlete, so I got high to hide my feelings.

Since the junior high school games were played around 4 o'clock in the afternoon during the week, I had time to go get my wine or malt liquor, smoke a joint, and get back to the school by game time. If I was late it was all the better. It was not considered cool to be anywhere early and cool is what I wanted to be.

The senior high school games were on Friday nights. Since I wanted to hang out with the older guys, I was a regular at the home games. I would go to some away games, but very few.

Stephan did not play any sports at all. His music was his passion. But he did drink. In fact he could drink a lot! His choice of spirits was "Wilson's." I had never drunk any whiskey before. Every so often I would take some gin from Dad's closet, but I did not like the taste of the hard stuff. Plus it costs more.

Stephan's running buddy was a white dude named Danny Duranz. He wasn't Italian or Irish though. I never did know what nationality he was. All I knew was that he was a white boy trying to be one of the brothers. Against my better judgment, I started to drink what they were into. It was nasty as shit, but hey; sometimes you gotta do what a teenager gotta do.

We had a teacher in Junior High School, Mr. Howard, who I always thought was a little light in his shoes. He knew that after lunch when students had to take his typing class, they'd be kind of lethargic from pigging out. So to prevent folks from falling asleep in his boring ass class, he allowed us to bring a snack or drink to indulge while we learned to type using two hands.

I used this as an opportunity to go to my locker with my orange drink that I bought from the lunchroom, and add some of Dad's gin. There were always a lot of kids hustling and bustling in the halls during changing of our classes, so I never got caught in the act of filling up.

My brother, God rest his soul, had a tarnished reputation during his first two years of high school. The usual stuff. Skipping school, smoking cigarettes and a little pot in the boy's room, drinking and stealing. It is suffice to say that his reputation with the faculty left a lot to be desired. Regardless of what he did, I knew that I had to spend one year in high school as a sophomore with him before he graduated. I was excited. I knew most of his homeboys anyway since I hung with many of them, so I knew I wouldn't get fucked up too bad during initiation week.

Mr. Kickman, the principal, on the other hand was not too thrilled to know that another member of our family would be gracing his school for the next three years. In a way I could not blame the guy. My first encounter with him was not one that you'd want to remember.

It was a Friday and just starting to get dark in the winter of '65. It was not too cold out even though it had snowed two days earlier. There was still about 18 inches of the white stuff in certain parts of town. This Friday night was special, more special than any other. It was the night that the varsity basketball team was playing Roosevelt High School and Westbury's star player, Rudy Waterman, was expected to break the school scoring record. The tickets had been sold out for weeks.

I had met Stephan at his house. He only came to my house one time. My dear old dad had a way of making most of our friends feel uncomfortable. The only thing I could figure was that he knew that most of them spelled trouble. It was not hard to draw that conclusion once they opened their mouths and said hello. For Stephan though, his downfall was not taking his hat off in my father's house. That was considered an insult not to mention a rude gesture.

Stephan's father was a lot older than most fathers that had children in junior high school. Maybe I was stereotyping, but when I first met him, I thought he was Stephan's grandfather that lived with his mom and him. His mother was very naive. She thought her little Stevie was a goody two shoe. This made it easy for me to go to his place anytime I wanted, because I came off the same way too.

Our walk in the cold was about 15 minutes on our way to pick up Danny. We usually waited until the three of us were together so we could chip in and buy our "Wilson's" whiskey. We each bought our own half pint this time. This was a far cry from the usual sharing of a pint amongst us. This was the big game and we had tickets and we were the cool dudes from the junior high coming to hang with the big boys.

The rule was we all had to finish before arriving to the high school. Again this was so much different from hiding it in our inside overcoat pocket to drink whenever we wanted to. Stephan made up this dumb rule. Although I was about half lit by time we got to the overpass at Northern State Parkway and Post Avenue, I went along as not to punk out, and so I killed the rest of my half pint.

The remainder of the journey to the high school was only six blocks and I did not think I was going to make it. When we got into the gymnasium, and of course had to climb about 15 rows of bleacher seats, all my drunken ass wanted to do was flop down and be still. I thought by being still my surroundings would stop spinning. Well I was wrong about thinking that sitting would make me feel better.

I did remember the pounding on the bleachers, the chant of "hey gang, hey gang what's the matter with the Westbury team they all right, they all right", and seeing Rudy make a corner jumper that was all net. I knew I would throw up on somebody or fall over if I stayed in the gym much longer. The heat, the noise, the lights and being several rows up from the ground made for a very bad combination for a 15-year-old that just drank a pint of 86 proof whiskey.

When I made it across the lobby to the boy's room, I ran into Jimmy and Sidney. I knew Sidney because he was going with my cousin and Jimmy I knew from when he was going to help fight the Conroy family for me. They took one look at me and said, "Damn homie, what the hell were you drinking?" When I told them, from their own experiences, they knew to take me outside right away and get some air. They even took some snow from the ground and were rubbing my face in it trying to make me stand straight and sober up some. I told them I was feeling a little better and was ready to go back inside after only 10 minutes outside in the cold.

When I got back inside they headed towards the gym while I headed for the bathroom. The next thing I remember was lying on the marble tile floor in the lobby of the school and hearing adult voices, yet not seeing anyone. When I heard, "stand back I got some smelling salt," I thought I was going to die or better still I felt like I had already done died passed away, and gone on to glory.

The conversations that I was listening to were not the type you'd hear if someone were dying or dead. There was no panic or sense of alarm in the voices I heard. There were no words like, rescue squad or ambulance so I figured I was not that bad off. When I was barely able to make out a visual, the faces I saw were all unfamiliar. Like the song, *"Where are all my friends?"* I wondered why they had left me.

I saw my brother and heard him say my name and acknowledge that I was his brother and that was it. He left and went back to watch the game. When he heard they were going to call our folks to come pick me up, I guess he figured Dad or Mom would make him leave too and he'd miss the game. Couldn't blame him there.

Sidney did offer to stay with me until my dad came. He propped me up on a seat inside the phone booth that they had for the student's use. He kept talking to me and was trying to make my appearance look like I wasn't embalmed. Every time my head would start to drop and my drooling got out of hand, he'd prop me up again and clean me up. He was cool until he saw that red '65 Pontiac LeMans pull up right in front of the school lobby. He said his, "See ya later bro, but I am out of here" speech and that was the last I saw of him. Again can't say if the shoe was on the other foot, I would not have done the same thing.

I was not sure if I was glad Mom did not accompany Dad or not, but I am glad she did not see me like I was. I was clear enough to know that I had to make up a quick story from the time he walked through the door to where I was. It was no more than 100 feet, so my brain had to work fast. This is one time being good at lying and thinking fast came in handy. Once I got my story together and Dad was standing over me in the telephone booth, all that I was praying for now was that he would buy it.

When I looked up at Dad, I said with a shit ass-eating grin, "Hey dad. Gee I don't know what happened. Must have been overcome by the lights and heat in the gym." Dad just looked at me minus the grin. He had a habit of when he said nothing, it meant something, and it was never good. To make the situation worse, he sent for Stephen to come home also. Stephen was pissed and he made me sit in the front seat with Dad as if to say, "Take that."

The ride home was without a sound. No radio. No conversation. No nothing. I knew this shit was bad. Worse situation I had gotten caught in up until then. When we got home, he just went to his room. Mom was frantic, as she didn't know what to expect. Dad took the call from the school to come get me, and I am sure they explained the reason why. I am sure he did not tell Mom. His logic was I would have to tell her myself.

As I got undressed and ready for bed, Stephen warned me that I just made the remainder of his school year a living hell. If they were on his ass already, they would be watching him more closely. Oh well, can't win them all, and I went to sleep.

Oh Lord. I forgot that when Dad opened the blinds as he had a habit of doing on Saturday mornings to wake us up, that I had promised Granny that I would go into Jamaica and clean her apartment. I was to get paid, so I did not want to blow my ten bucks. Plus, my grandma meant the world to me and I would never let her down.

Uncle Will used to be our ride to Jamaica on Saturday mornings. He went to work by 9 o'clock in the morning and usually left around noon. He was one that did not mind giving you a lift and dropping you off where you needed to go in Jamaica, but the rule was you had to be standing at the front door ready. He was not one to wait on anyone.

I was ready, but boy did my head feel like it was in a vice. I had never had a real hangover before. As I was cleaning the apartment, I happened to pick up some magazines under the TV stand to dust, and when I turned the Ebony magazine over, there an advertisement for a well-known brand name whiskey.

I did not retain much in school that I thought uninteresting, but I did remember the story of Pavlov's doggie. All I had to do was look at that picture of the bottle of whiskey, and I got sick to my stomach. I ran into the bathroom I had just finished cleaning so as not to puke on the living room floor. Granny asked me what was wrong, so of course Granny or not, I had to lie and say it must have been something that I had for breakfast.

THE NOT SO MERRY MAILMAN

As I stood in front of the Honorable Judge Simone during my arraignment in January of 1970, I did not understand why he was so upset. He just shook his head and asked, "What is this world coming to?" I reckoned his anger was triggered because I was standing there in my mailman uniform looking all pitiful and embarrassed. During that era the United States government ran the postal service, so the uniforms we had to wear had the insignia of what stood for America.

"Bail $500 cash," he announced.

I knew I was going over to the County jail until I could get bailed out. Something told me I should have gone to work that day, but oh no I had to listen to my brother and go hustling with him.

After lock in, I laid on my bunk in my cell on C&D floor in Nassau County Jail. That wing was for new arrivals and required twenty-three hour lock down. I just looked up at the ceiling and cussed quietly to myself not so much for what I did, but for getting caught. I knew that I was smarter than to let a twelve-year-old kid see me walk into a cleaners, reach over the counter, open the register and take what monies was in there. He then followed me several blocks walking on the other side of the street.

Wait though. It gets better.

The boy memorized the license plate number on my car before I drove off to round up Stephen. No need for Stephen to keep looking for a hustle. I scored so we had enough to go into Harlem and cop some dope.

Dope fiends are too cocky, careless and above all arrogant. I just knew we had gotten away with not being seen. Now the smart thing to have done was to get on the Long Island Expressway or Grand Central Parkway and head straight to the city. But no, we had to stop for donuts, and a cup of coffee to go like we were just two honest working stiffs.

When I pulled out of the parking lot of the donut shop, at least a half dozen of Nassau County's finest in blue, surrounded the car. With their guns drawn as they neared the car, we were not that crazy to do anything stupid to make their trigger fingers itchy.

Oh I could have strangled that little bastard for being so smart to call 911 on me, and why the hell wasn't his ass in school anyway?

I had only been arrested once prior to this. It was for disorderly conduct when I was 17 and a group of us went into the local diner where the owners automatically assumed we were going to leave without paying. The ironic thing was we legitimately went in just to eat. That is what you do when you smoke some reefer and get the munchies. No big deal though. The police came. In 1967 the black movement was hot and heavy. The term "pig," which characterized the white police officers, was the word at the time.

Instead of just dispersing as they asked us to from out in front of the diner, we had to play the militant role. The "just because I'm Black," was another phrase used when it was to our convenience. It was about one o'clock in the morning, and the cops, I must admit, were being very nice to us. That is until I had to open my big mouth and use the word pig. The only reason I said it was they were getting a little rough with Frieda and her older sister Julia.

That was my first arrest.

They grabbed me, threw me against a car, handcuffed me behind my back, and then placed me into one of the squad cars. Frieda and Julia also ended up getting arrested, and they just arrested Brooks because they already knew him. I only spent the night in detention and the next morning I was released in Dad's custody. I was sure glad he showed up. He always vowed that if either of us got into trouble he would leave us there. We always believed him.

However, this time around, I was not as lucky. I moved up to the next level.

I stayed up most of the night talking to Shultz. He was the lobby man. That title was a job that you either earned or got because you were tight with the guards. He was in good with the guards. He should have. He had been in the County jail so often it became his first home. I had never met him before, but he knew Stephen from the time when they spent six months there in the summer of 1969. Shultz and I just talked street shit: how often he had been arrested and for what and who we knew in different towns. Stuff like that. Nothing educational. For my first night in jail, I didn't have too much trouble sleeping.

C-2-12, pack up!

When I heard the cell door crank open the next morning around eleven o'clock I just sat there. I did not bother to remember my cell number. When I heard one of the hacks yell down the tier, "Codrington let's move it. We aint got all day," I got myself together, rolled up my horse hair blanket, my sheet and pillow and stepped out of my cell. I was led through the lobby, which reminded you of a circus. It was a big open area surrounded by bars like you were in a cage.

Stephen was on the other side of the tier on C-1. At the same time I was walking to the elevator, he was coming into the lobby. He asked why I was going home and he was just called down for a visit. I had no idea. He knew more about this place than I did. He knew that if I had my shit under my arm to turn back in, that indicated my walking papers. I felt sorry for him, as he looked so pathetic. He felt as though if Mom had to choose between the two of us, I got the call since I at least had a job.

After being escorted to the elevator, I still thought I was going to visit the jailhouse doctor and then move onto another floor. At the first stop Stephen got off to go to the visitation room and we said our good-byes. He understood. I told him I would come back and get him once I got to the bank to take some money out. What else was I supposed to say?

As the elevator stopped on the basement level, I got the impression that by some miracle, I was really going home. Not that I didn't believe Stephen, but I still was wondering how, and by who would have come to get me out? I had not a clue. Mom was at the arraignment. She used to always be there for Stephen in the past, so she knew the bail situation, and I knew her situation. She did not have $1000 for both of us to get bailed out.

I went into the same room I was in the day before, when I had to exchange my clothes for the jailhouse blues. I thought it very appropriate to make you wear a blue shirt and pants. When they were pressed and didn't have skatey-eight million wrinkles, they didn't look too bad. I was told to once again strip down, bend over and spread 'em. Then I was handed my mailman uniform. I got dressed and then I was led up another floor to the lobby and the visitor's reception room. I was going home.

When the door opened I saw my poor mom's face awaiting me. It was a face of a mother that had to just tell her other son that there was no money for him, but also explained that it was not her money that was used for me. Mom had gone to the bank and withdrew the money from my own savings. There was a reason I had her name on the account with mine. I felt so ashamed seeing what we had put her through. I was also disappointed in myself. After all I wasn't supposed to be in jail, and worse, I knew in my heart I'd be coming back one day soon.

"Please mom," I begged. "Just five dollars for a fix. I'm sick and scared to go out to hustle for money." Plus I knew there was no time for that. I'd been out two whole hours. Mom should have understood the position I was in. The promises to get my act together lasted only for the fifteen-minute ride from the joint to Rushmore Street.

Reluctantly, and I am certain with much remorse and hurt, I watched as my very own mother gave her son five dollars out of her pocketbook so I could get high. Mom also said that she was sorry she did not follow her instinct and leave me in jail where she knew I would be safe from drugs. She was right.

I reflect back now and wonder how we both could have ever had a moment like that. Guess when you love a child like a mother does and sees her child hurting, the natural instinct is to help stop the hurt, regardless of the price.

"Come on Brown. Don't do me like this. I just got out the joint," I said with my crumpled up five dollar bill in hand.

I told him my mother had given me her last out of her own wallet. I even bought the bail receipt to prove I just got out less than two hours earlier. All I was asking for was two for one for my five bucks. One bag of heroin would just shake the chills off, but not enough to get high. He saw I was sick and in need. Why else would I be begging his faggot ass?

But somehow these dealers of death seemed to get their own high having that feeling of empowerment over someone. They knew an addict would sell his soul to get high. People like me just fed their egos by being addicted to that tragic magic called heroin.

Ah! I felt a euphoric feeling as I booted the dirty blood in the syringe for the final time back into my scarred veins at Brown's place. What a nice fucking guy. After begging for almost a half hour he finally let me get two for one. Of course at a later date payback was expected. But hey, just like all the other addicts that he provided dope for, all he wanted in return was sexual favors; a small price to pay when you're sick and in need. This association with Brown did not make you queer or anything. It was just accepted as normal in the drug world that you did what you had to do to take care of business.

When I got home, my mom was glad for one thing that I was still alive. How sad if the money she gave me was the cause of my death from an overdose rather then the healing of my ills. I wondered if deep down inside she didn't pray for God to take me once and for all. Her plea would have gone something like this I suppose:

> "Lord please spare everyone the misery and heartache and put an end to this madness. Don't let him keep killing himself a little at a time."

Guess God had other intentions for me.

I went to work the next day as if nothing had happened. My supervisor Mr. Napers, who knew of me by name and reputation in "the Castle" since I had gone to school with his daughter, was not being fooled. He never could catch me doing anything, but knew that sooner or later I'd fuck up and lose my $3.06 an hour good paying job. Mr. Napers was black and in a position to look out for the brothers in the Post Office, especially since he was supervisor of the carriers. I had the utmost respect for him.

Was respect for him enough to get my act together and show not only him, but also my family that I could be a different person? Obviously not. My fellow heroin user at work was a 20-year-old brother from Wyandanch named K.D. Jones. He really needed the job badly since he had a wife and baby boy at home to take care of. He didn't have a car, so he used to take that thirty-minute ride on the Long Island Rail Road to and from work. It must have been a bitch since we had to start work at six in the morning. However, he never missed a day. We started together and we got fired together. We never made it through the 90-day probationary period.

How I learned my ass was grass was via certified mail. Ironically the day it was to be delivered was the day I was to substitute for Mr. Klinger. He was the regular on the route that included Rushmore Street. I had been racking the mail early that Friday morning in January of '70. It was two weeks after I got busted and after my 20th birthday on the 13th.

When I came across one of those green pieces of cardboard with my name on it marked "certified pickup", I had a gut feeling that it was what I was expecting, yet did not want to happen. I stopped what I was doing and walked over to the clerk's desk to sign for it.

When I opened the envelope, there was a well-written letter stating that my black, dope fiend, lying, stealing, sorry ass was asked out! I felt Mr. Napers did what he had to do for health reason. I would have been the death of him.

That was a blessing in disguise. One of many more to come. Sooner or later I would have ended up in a Federal penitentiary for the things I used to do as a government employee while on duty. I was starting to become very sloppy and careless in my dishonest deeds and actions.

During a visit back home to my folks the Christmas of '87, Dad and I went down to Carol's Italian bakery on Maple Ave. It was a stop I just had to make each trip home for some genuine, real honest to goodness Italian pastries, and warm bread. Couldn't seem to get it right in Atlanta where Italian foods were concerned, so I looked forward to visiting, then going to Carol's and getting my "fix."

When we heard the words, "next please," the gentleman ahead of us turned around as he put his change in his pocket to leave. It was Mr. Napers. At first he seemed reluctant to speak or say hello. His expression was one of a person that just saw a ghost. I laughed at his reaction and I spoke first so he would not think he was tripping or something. He displayed that wide grin that I was familiar with. The one with the gap in his top front teeth. At least he still had teeth. Other than the ring of hair around his baldhead being a little grayer, he looked damn good for a man that survived over thirty years in the post office. Hell, if anyone of should have been dead, he would have gotten my wager.

He was very pleased to see me and to hear that I was married fifteen years at that time, with two sons, and living in Atlanta, Georgia, in my own home. I had to pack in as much information as I could. I was damn proud I could boast like that. He didn't say much other than he had been retired for about five years and enjoying his three grandchildren. He just stared at me while we talked.

Of all the people I had known outside of family that knew me when I was addicted, for some reason I felt blessed to have run into Mr. Napers. I always believed deep down in his heart he felt sorry for me and knew I had more to offer than destroying myself. I felt blessed to have been able to share that moment after 17 years.

During those mailman days there were none of them there little fancy jeeps or vans that had the steering wheel on the right side instead of the left. Oh no. Your ass walked every mile of those routes with over 300 houses. Because I had been a substitute with no seniority or a steady route, they didn't even give you one of those pushcarts either. You were made to feel like a red headed stepchild with no inheritance! You carried all that shit on your shoulder in one of those heavy ass bags that looked like a saddlebag from the old western movies. All that was missing was you did not have a horse.

Also, each house had the mailbox either next to the front door on the house or a mail slot through the front door. This was so lazy folks could just open their door and stick their hands inside the mailbox. For those folks who never wanted to come out the house, their mail was pushed through the slot onto their floor. What did this mean for us poor carriers? It meant you had to walk up to each and every house to deliver their mail. Made for a long day on your feet and your shoulder.

The first thing I used to do was make all those heavy magazines, advertisements, and junk mail disappear—if you catch my drift. Heaven helped those people, who subscribed to publications like: Look or Life, on those days when Bruce was on their route. I considered my thinking as though it was a fair trade off. The less I had to carry, the faster folks would get their mail. My real loyalty to the homeowners was next to none. I had to look out for number one.

Perhaps my attitude would have been a little more compassionate if I did not start my career in the dead of winter. The snow and ice in November was terrible enough to deal with much less having to be made to walk in it for over five hours a day. Whoever penned that phrase, "neither rain, nor snow, nor sleet and hail…" and however else the rest of it goes, did not have Bruce in their thought process.

I found out real soon that Postal union rules stated that if you fell on the ice during your appointed rounds you did not have to finish your route. Chalk up another stroke of luck for the kid here. I "verbally" fell at least twice a week when it was hazardous out. Mr. Napers finally suggested not bothering coming in at all on snow days to save him the aggravation of having to find guys to finish my route.

I will never forget on this one particular day after I set out from the facility by eight thirty in the morning to actually try to put in a full, and honest days work. My good intentions used to always seem to give way to the bad ones. I delivered one street of mail before I decided to go home, get high, relax some, and then go back and finish my route. I was only five minutes from home.

Wouldn't you just know it?

Nothing ever went right for me. I fell off to sleep and when I awoke it was three o'clock; just in time before Mom would come home from work so she could go pick up my little sister from parochial school.

I knew that soon the early winter sunset would be arriving, and darkness would begin to fall. So I did what any good carrier would have done to insure good service to the customers: I called Mr. Napers to send some help in order to finish up.

Boy he was so proud of me. You could hear it in the tone of his voice on the phone. A voice that was saying, "Hey, there may be some hope for the boy after all!" I was showing concern for my job and following policy. What more could a man ask for.

Those good feelings were quick to go south on him when he asked me where I left off delivering so that he could determine where to send the helper. When I told him where, I held my ear away from the receiver immediately. "Good Lord!" he yelled, "What the hell have you been doing all day?"

I forgot what answer I had given to him. It really didn't matter since I lied so much if it were the truth, he wouldn't have believed me anyway. He had to send not one, but two employees out to finish. One guy wasn't even a carrier. He worked behind a desk all day. But, Mr. Napers was desperate. We finally finished around 7 p.m.

After that incident, he soon began following me on my routes when I had to deliver in or near New Castle. I couldn't blame him. He had his job to protect plus he had mouths to feed at home.

When I worked delivering parcel packages during the Thanksgiving and Christmas holiday season, I would park the truck on this dead end side street near old man Brown's place. I don't think there was one legitimate thing going on in his house. Drug sales, bootlegging, gambling, and of course sexual activities were commonplace 24/7. It did not take a rocket scientist to put two and two together and come to the conclusion that I was a man with some serious problems. Despite the obvious, I must say he gave me the benefit of the doubt as long as he could.

Another reason he used to play Dick Tracy with me was that his superiors had received some complaints from the "Castle." These complaints came from a few lazy, fat, and tired looking women that would sit on heir asses all day, screw and then have babies while collecting welfare. I was not against the system mind you. I learned that black folks were not the only ones receiving public assistance.

When I delivered to the lower class white neighborhoods, I stuck many of those same brown government envelopes in their mailboxes on the first and fifteenth of every month also. The difference was, you would never know by their homes and surrounding that they were in the same situation. They were not sitting out in front of an apartment building or a rental property in a broken down kitchen chair, fat thighs gapped wide open, combing little Luanda's nappy hair while sipping on a cold one.

When it came to "our folks", if their check was not in their hands on the first or fifteenth, they'd swear on a stack of Bibles that the mailman had taken it, or didn't deliver it on the exact date just to fuck with them. What they didn't know, was that we were just as pissed if for some reason their 'digit' was not in our stack of mail, because we were the ones that had to hear their mouths.

It would not be fair to insinuate that K.D. and me were the only trifling postal employees in Westbury. There were quite a few folks whose integrity left a lot to be desired.

My favorite person was Clyde. He was a carrier just like we were. He was blacker than soot on a foggy day. His bottom lip hung down so low, that he probably could have used it as a cheat sheet in school. His calling should have been a comedienne since he kept everyone in stitches everyday.

I first got to know him when I had to do his route my second week on the job. It was in an all white neighborhood less than a mile from the jail. I wondered why there was an entire street on his racking bin that was blocked out with masking tape. Not only was it taped off but he had the words, "DO NOT DELIVER," written on the tape. This peeked my curiosity so I had to ask someone what the deal was.

It was explained to me that about a year earlier, some white woman's husband on that street threatened to shoot him if he ever saw his black ass near his house again. The man did not even want him on the street. When I asked why, I was told that the man came home unexpectedly one day and there was Clyde in his house. Supposedly he was just sitting in their kitchen with his wife, sipping on a cup of coffee. Maybe if she did not still have on her housecoat when her husband walked in, his suspicions of something a little more than a coffee break was going on would not have been an issue.

THE RISKS JUST KEPT
GETTING BIGGER

What I felt was the last straw before I was fired, was when I ripped off a lady's wallet at a business on one of my stops. It was just two blocks from the post office. I was in and out in a flash as was my trademark, and continued down the street like any mailman just doing his job. My instincts told me to turn around after doing about three more stops, and low and behold, there was this lady and her boss standing in front of their building and they were pointing at me.

I never once set out or wanted to hurt anybody during my drug addictive activities. All I wanted was the money to get high with. So what I would do as part of my civic dope fiend responsibility was to drop the person's wallet with all the credit cards and other important personal belongings into a mailbox. That way the person would at least get these items returned to them. I thought that those individuals would have appreciated that.

Upon returning to the postal facility around three o'clock as most of us had done, I was confronted by Mr. Willard who was the postmaster. He was the big cheese. He asked if I would mind coming with him into his office. This would be my second trip there in less than a month. I saw no reason to say no to his request, plus I knew better.

When he opened his office door, there stood two Nassau county detectives. "Oh shit!" I thought to myself. "If my knowledge was correct, we're talking not only county, and State charges but Federal charges as well since I was on duty when I made the hustle." This was serious. I wasn't ready for this. They were very polite when they explained the nature of their visit to see me. I didn't say a word. Of course they never accused me. They simply asked if it were not an inconvenience, would I mind going with them over to the 3rd precinct in Mineola: a familiar place for me. I told them sure. I had nothing to hide or fear. What else was I supposed to say to them? No!

Since everybody was being so fucking nice and playing the role, I figured why not crack for some consideration too. So I asked if I could go to my locker and get my coat first. When they agreed and did not follow me, I decided to make a run for it. I had the money I stole and my drug paraphernalia in my pocket. The following items that all responsible dope fiends carried with them at all times were:

1. A hypodermic needle and preferably a spare

2. Bottle cap from a wine bottle. These types were deeper than regular ones

3. Small piece of cotton or you could use a piece of filter from a cigarette.

4. Glass eye dropper with a rubber from a baby's pacifier used as handle. A medical syringe was just too bulky to carry.

5. Piece of shoelace to tie your arm or leg.

These items constituted your paraphernalia referred henceforth throughout the book as "works." You can see the concern I had to not have to go to the police station with my "works" on me. That would be a crime in itself.

I eased out the locker room, slid around a corner and out the back door to the loading dock. There I jumped off and ran like a common thief, excuse the pun. Where I found the time or the nerve to stop at the time clock and punch out in between all of this I had no idea. I didn't even take my car.

I didn't stop running until I reached this brother Rico's house nine blocks away. I just knew him casually when I was in high school and other than a "hey what's up," we hardly knew one another. Under these circumstances, however, I did not have time to worry about our social status. I just rang his doorbell. When he answered the door I asked if he could give me a lift up to the Castle as my car had broken down. He said sure and went and got his coat and car keys. Off we went for the 10-minute drive trying to make small talk along the way.

I knew I would eventually have to turn myself in, but not before I got high first. When we turned into Rushmore Street, I could see far down the middle of the block in front of my house there was an unmarked police car. Guess I could not go home. I asked Rico to drop me off by the local hangout at Don's bar. After I got straight, I hung out until I felt it was safe to go home.

Around 8 PM, I was finally able to go home safely. I was still paranoid though. My thoughts at the time consisted of:

Were they hiding somewhere?

Why did they leave?

I just figured after nothing happened that night that the shit was not serious and maybe they were just trying to see if I would admit what I did by scaring me with the precinct thing.

The next morning I decided to play the martyr. I called Mr. Willard to ask if he could call the detectives back and I would come in on my own accord to answer any questions they had. I even went as far as saying I was scared the day before in his office because I had never been in trouble before and that's why I ran off. It sounded good anyway. Whether he believed me or not was another story. He assured me he would arrange things. I took the bus down to the post office since I had left my car there the day before.

As soon as the detectives placed me in the car, before they even turned the ignition on to pull out of the parking lot, they sat for a few seconds without saying a word. Then one of them whose name was detective Raymond turned around in his seat very nonchalantly and looked me dead in the eye. He said, "OK Bruce where's the wallet? Just give it up and the lady promised not to press any charges. We know you stole it!"

They knew that being a "sneak thief" was my thing from my previous arrest. Plus they did not like to waste their time and efforts on some nickel and dime, petty ante dope fiend that just stole to support his habit. They knew they could be out there making a reputation for themselves on matters of much more significance if they ever expected to be promoted.

I didn't play into their hand. I was smarter than that. The truth was if they had any proof from Jump Street, they would never have allowed me to go to my locker by myself. Also they wouldn't have waited until the following day to come back so humble. They would have slept in front of the house that night. Screw them I thought. Let's play this thing out and see what happens.

So off we went to take the lie detector test to put everyone's mind and suspicions at ease. I just sat back and enjoyed the ride and didn't say shit for the 20-minute ride to Mineola. The test took no longer than 30 minutes. If you've never taken a lie detector test you don't know what you're missing. They are trying to catch you lying and you are doing your best to lie to cover up the truth. What a rush!

When they came back in the room and told me that I passed and that they were sorry to have put me through all this, no one was more surprised than me. Hell, when they asked me during the test, "Have you ever stole or lied in your life?" the needle damn near jumped off the page when I answered, "No." They probably just didn't want to hassle with something this petty. Too much paperwork plus their time in court would have been a waste of a day's productivity.

They were obligated to take me back to the location where they had picked me up from since I was doing them a favor in the first place. This time there was more conversation in the car. Mostly I was talking trash as I had just gotten over on the system.

When we arrived back to the post office, this time while the car was not running, I did get a sermon from detective Raymond. He suggested very strongly that I get my act together before I got into some real serious trouble. So far nothing had been earth shattering. He knew it would be just a matter of time before I did something major and my ass would be his.

He also told me that he knew what happened the first time I was ever in Mr. Willard's office. It took me a few seconds before I even remembered what took place. I had threatened him with bodily harm if he tried to fire me. I don't think Mr. Willard even took me serious.

But to show how small the world is, detective Raymond and Mr. Willard were the best of friends. In fact Mr. Willard was godfather to one of Raymond's kids. He warned me that if I ever made any more threats again he's personally have my butt. "Hey no problem," I assured him as I got out the car and thanked them for the ride.

Talk about basking in the victory!

Since I had the rest of the day off, would you believe I had the balls to go back to confront the lady who was my accuser? I walked in and when she looked up and saw me she almost jumped out of her chair. I told her what I had been through, and felt that I was entitled to an apology from her for putting me through such an ordeal. I made her feel guilty about causing me embarrassment and humiliation not to mention losing a day's pay.

I let her know that I had passed the lie detector test and that I would never and have never stolen anything in my life. She was almost in tears as she apologized. She told me she could not imagine who else could have lifted her wallet from her pocketbook under her desk. She was only away from her desk no more than three minutes. When she saw me going next door on my next stop she put two and two together and assumed no one else had been in the office except me.

I accepted not only an apology from her, but her boss also. After all he was with her when I had turned around and saw them pointing a finger at me in front of his business. He was a little skeptical. As a man, I think he kind of knew I was full of shit but there was nothing he could do or say. I left feeling that it was a win win for everyone. I didn't go to jail. I didn't lose my job. I received undeserving apologies. The lady would probably get her wallet back the next day with all her belongings less the money. A lesson was learned too. She will never leave her pocketbook unattended ever again. All's well that ended well.

My late best friend George had always laughed years later about the time he was on the bus going over to Nassau Community College one day after Christmas break. Traffic had come to a halt for a few minutes but no one knew what was going on. When the traffic was allowed to move, the bus got closer to an accident involving a mail truck and a station wagon at a light at a busy intersection. When the bus finally passed the scene, he said he was shocked to see the driver in the uniform was none other than me. He said I should have seen my hands moving as fast as my mouth as I was trying to explain to the police what happened.

He started to pull the cord to get off at the next stop and come back to see if I was all right but kept on going. He knew later that day over a bag of dope or a joint that he'd get the scoop straight from the source. George was one of those educated dope fiends. He did not have to steal for money. He simply used the money from his grants and scholarships to support the habit he did not think he had. He told me later that day that the real reason he did not stop was he would have been laughing so hard the police might have not believed my story.

I truly felt bad as the lady driving the station wagon had five small children in the car. Seat belts were not used much. There were three in the back seat and two in the rear of the wagon looking out the back window. She was guilty of no more than abiding the law and stopping for a red light.

I was not used to taking downers, known on the street as "red devils." I was used to heroin, cocaine, pot, and cough syrup, but pills were generally not my cup of tea. Kenny gave me a couple to check out. We both used to go out in the mornings and empty the mailboxes as part of our duties as subs. It was fun and we used to race to see who could get back to the post office first. I could have been in the lead, but I'll never know.

If I had known that the pills would make me comatose, I would have saved them for a time when I was not behind the wheel. I swear I never saw the light much less the car stopped in front of me. I didn't even remember how fast I was going. Thank God no one was hurt. At eight in the morning, this happened while folks were trying to get to work.

Seemed as though each car that slowed down and passed me I was given a nasty look. The train station was only a quarter of a mile away and many people I'm sure had probably missed their train. Mr. Napers couldn't cut me any slack on this one since the damage to the truck was quite extensive.

This was not like my first accident a few weeks earlier. That one was not my fault. There had been snow on the ground and the roads were kind of icy. Some idiot was backing out of his driveway on Grand Blvd., which was a busy road. He did not see me. When I went to apply the little bit of brakes I had, and swerved to avoid hitting him, I knocked down someone's pretty white picket fence and I ended up a few feet from their front porch.

I couldn't get the truck out of the mud and snow no matter how hard I tried. I was glad the homeowners were not home at the time. I left it there and walked the half a mile back to the post office. I did not even bother to lock it up. I simply went in, turned in my stuff, punched out, and got in my car to go home.

I would not have left the vehicle unattended but I did call for help and it seemed like foreverary for someone to come. Just to show there were no hard feelings though, I did go past the scene on the way home. There was poor old Mr. Napers and another employee trying to dig the truck out of the yard. One was digging while he was inside behind the wheel. He was gunning the engine and trying to rock it back and forth to get the tires out of the mud and snow. I felt so bad I almost stopped to help instead of just driving by, blowing the horn and waving.

I am sure the possibility of the lady suing the U.S. Post Office came to his mind too. He had no choice but to take my government license away from me. I was relieved because that meant I could no longer drive their vehicles. Yet another blessing in disguise at the right time.

Another reason I was glad that I had my driving privileges revoked AFTER the Christmas holiday was I used to make a killing when I worked delivering parcel packages to homes and businesses. It was disgraceful how I sold so much stuff that people were sending to their loved ones. Some items like baskets of fruit and candy, I used to just give away. I became a psychic when it came to knowing just which envelopes had cards with money. And those that I just knew were shaped like small gift money cards were a no brainer.

I used to just drive the truck right up to Don's bar and grill on Prospect and Brooklyn Ave. where most of the trifling people hung out and park on the side street. I was so bold that I would just pull the rear door of the truck up, and went about my business of selling stuff just like those old time traveling merchants.

Not once did I worry about the police rolling up on me and asking what the hell I was doing. It just never entered my mind. Stamps went for 50% off retail. Boy, talk about putting your integrity on the back burner to save a buck. Most of the buyers were so-called honest, family folks, and most of them I had known for years.

Meanwhile back at the post office, poor old Mr. Gardner was going crazy taking irate phone calls from customers wanting to know where their shit was. He was around 60-yrs-old and as nice and mellow as a person that age could be.

He probably should have taken an early retirement before I started working there. As soon as he found out that most of the calls were coming from the routes that I had been working, he would call me into question. My excuse for as long as it would last was that no one was home and I just left the package by the front door or the garage. He said "I can see something small being left. But a suitcase or a bicycle?"

Shortly after the accident, I pulled the boldest and most daring thing in my life.

While delivering mail on this bright sunny day although about 40 degrees, I had no intention on doing anything dishonest. Really. I knew they did not believe any of my excuses during the Christmas fiasco so I was going to cool it for a while. That is until I innocently pushed the mail through the mail slot to one of those Levitt built homes in an all while community.

These homes had a carport and the door was on the side that entered into the kitchen. When the door opened I was shocked. Who in their right mind would leave the door open like that? I wouldn't have even bothered to go inside, as burglary was not my thing. However there sitting right on the kitchen table was a ladies pocketbook. I just had to go inside since I figured whomever left it open went out for a minute, and that is all I needed. I couldn't help it.

When I got inside I just froze in one spot. I never went into some strange person's home to steal anything. I used to know dudes that all they did was burglaries. I always admired their courage. As for me, I would be afraid a German shepherd or Great Dane would be waiting for me. You had no way of knowing who had what and I wasn't going to go into the abyss. I did know in this situation I couldn't just stand there all day so I had to act quickly. I took what currency was in the purse, quietly left and then continued my deliveries.

When I was coming down the opposite side of the street heading back past the house, a lady was just standing out on the front lawn of the house looking bewildered. A look as if to say, "what just happened?" As I passed by I gave a friendly wave and smile like any merry mailman would do and she gave an unenthusiastic wave and a faint smile back at me. Why would she be rude to me? As far as she was concerned I would be the last person in the world that she would suspect of doing something as bold as what she was no doubt thinking.

A couple of days passed and when nothing was ever said about the incident, I realized what I actually got away with. It was not such a joyous victory for me this time. I thought of what I might have done out of fear had she come into the kitchen. Even worse, imagine what she might have done to me!

EXERCISING ALL OF MY OPTIONS

One of the more dishonest but coolest mail carriers that lived in the Castle helped me out of a jam once after I had gotten fired. Neal had a regular route in the Castle so he knew just about everyone and everyone knew him. I had been back out on the streets the first week of February hustling and collecting welfare. Yes that's right! An able bodied 19 year old man collecting two checks a month just like those people I used to despise in my neighborhood for being lazy and living for a hand out.

The lady that I was renting a room in her home from found out I was collecting a "digit" and almost had a glass baby! So, she made up some bullshit excuse for asking me to move. At first I thought it was because she was a respectful person with a husband, four kids and a decent home. I figured she was appalled that there was no reason her tax dollars should be supporting my lazy ass, especially in her home.

Well, I figured wrong. The truth of the matter was she was collecting a "digit" also and was not reporting her income from the rent she was charging me to live there. So before the welfare folks found out that two checks were going to the same address she had to give me up as a tenant.

Heaven forbid that I should give up my $230 a month income from the system. I made arrangements after I moved out to have my checks sent to brother Emmons' house. I was only entitled to two more checks since my benefits ran out anyway, but I could not even imagine not getting something for nothing. He assured me that he would be home to receive the mail as he worked nights across the tracks in the industrial park.

His mom Ruby was a devout church going Christian lady. So on the first when Emmons' lazy ass was still sleeping at twelve o'clock in the afternoon, Ms. Ruby got to the mailbox first. Why I trusted that he would not fuck things up was beyond me. I went over to the house as planned before he was to leave by four o'clock for work and was met at the door by his mom. By then he was awake and she had already given him the third degree as to why my mail from social services came to her house. I no sooner got my finger on the doorbell than she came to the door and gave me a tongue-lashing. As she was reading me the Christian version of the riot act, she was waving that almighty brown envelop with the little window on it in my face.

Hanging my head in the pretending I was ashamed position, I promised her that I would arrange to not have any more of my mail delivered to her home. She wasn't naive. She knew what was inside the envelope and she knew by then I was not the nice little boy she has known since I was 12-years-old. I even went to church with her family and the Price's. But she gave me the envelope based on my word.

Of course I just couldn't keep my word. I was pissed at her son for blowing my thing but I just had to have that final $115 check on the 15th.

I planned to wait at the park about five houses down the street from theirs on the 15th for Neal. I knew about what time he made his rounds on Howard Street and would be there waiting just like all the other lazy welfare recipients. Now I knew how they felt.

But greed and the dope fiend mentality told me that I had time to spare. I scurried across the tracks behind the park to the industrial area. I don't think there had been one business there that me or someone had not stolen from. But it was worth a shot plus it beat standing around waiting. Time is money you know. I should have been more conscience of the time. When I emerged from the valley of the train tracks behind the park and cut through the park, I saw Neal walking two doors away from the house. Damn. I didn't even make a hustle and now this.

Talk about rotten luck! Well nothing from nothing would have left just that—nothing so I mustered up the nerve to walk up to their door and open their mailbox and remove my check. It didn't matter that it was a federal offense. Plus after all the illegal stuff I had done while I had been a mailman what was one more offense? At least the victims knew me and may not have pressed charges.

As I started down the street to the house I didn't even reach a quarter way there, when I saw Ms. Ruby open the front door and reach to get her mail. I am glad she just stuck her head out enough to reach the mailbox and didn't see me. I could kick myself for being so greedy that I missed out on a sure $115. The only thing left for me to do was to go over there later and belly up to the bar and beg forgiveness. But mostly to beg for her to give up the "digit."

Man! This sermon was longer and harsher than the first. When she was finally finished boring me a new asshole, she told me that she had gone to the Haysville post office and dropped it back in the mail. Return to sender as the song goes. Once I heard that, my next move was to bum a ride up to Haysville and try to con a clerk to try and retrieve a piece of mail I accidentally dropped in the box. My fellow dope fiend Marky had given me the ride so he came in with me. He could lie so much better than me. His entire family was dishonest so he had more practice at an early age.

Now no disrespect to those that work in the postal services, but I couldn't believe the response the clerk gave us. I was shocked when he said he didn't have time to go through what had been picked up from the drop boxes within the past two hours, but we were welcome to look ourselves. I aint making this up! He opened the door from the lobby that led to the back room and showed us where we could begin looking. It was a lot of mail, but we went through all of it within 30 minutes time and found zilch.

Here I was thinking the impossible and yet we had carte blanche to dig through the mail and didn't find the envelope. OK Bruce, the time had finally come to let go. You can't win them all. I wasn't even angry with Ms. Ruby for her standing for what she believed was right. I broke my word to her and she did what she had to do.

Ten days later, I heard someone yell my name as I was doing my regular hanging on the corner of Prospect and Urban Ave. routine. I looked up and it was Neal. I went over to his car and he told me he had been trying to catch up to me since the 16th. I asked him why, and he told me that Ms. Ruby never took the welfare check to the post office like she told me, but instead the next day she personally handed it back to him. He had since been riding around with it to give to me. I could have kissed him right on the cheek. What a nice guy to stick his neck out for a former coworker. He was the most honest dishonest person I knew.

I wanted to do something special for him to show my utmost appreciation. I promised him that I would get him a couple of Italian leather and knit sweaters that were in style. They cost an average of $45. Shoplifting also was not high on my list of chosen means to make money, but this was special.

Here it was that I could live up to a promise to a stranger for being just as dishonest as me, yet I couldn't keep a promise to a nice lady and my friend's mother whom I've known most of my life. Sad.

WRONG PLACE, WRONG TIME

As I fumbled to answer the phone in our room at the Howard Johnson motor lodge on that 6th day of March 1970, I had no idea what was about to transpire. My brother and I took a room there for the night, as we had nowhere else to stay. We had been living in different cheap motels along Jericho turnpike in Westbury for the past two weeks. But, since we had a little extra money this time, we treated ourselves to some real comfort and luxury in Haysville at a HoJo's. The room actually had not one but two double beds.

I was pissed when the voice on the other end of the phone asked, "Is this room 209?" I said, "No, this is 207." The voice apologized and hung up. I could not believe that someone actually woke me up from a much needed and peaceful sleep for some dumb shit like that. Aint that a bitch!

A few minutes later a knock was at the door.

"Who is it?" I yelled.

When the knock continued with no answer, I staggered half asleep across the room closer to the door. I was careful not to wake Stephen who was asleep in the bed on the far side of the room by the window. I asked twice as I neared the door who was there and twice there was no response. When I had my hand on the door handle I yelled again and asked who was there. This time I finally got a response. A male voice said, "Housekeeping." I no sooner got the words, "come back later," out of my mouth when all of a sudden I heard, and then felt the steel door being bashed in.

The security chain was broken right off the wall and in rushed 12 detectives, with high-powered rifles. They immediately threw my face and my body hard against the wall, and I nearly missed the full-length mirror. Two detectives jumped over my bed to get to the other bed that Stephen was still laying in. They put the barrel of the rifle to his right temple and instructed him to rise ever so slowly or they'd blow his fucking head off. It did not take me long to figure that those dirty bastards were the one's who made the call to the room to find out if we were in there.

With my face still turned away from all the commotion going on, out of the corner of my right eye I noticed two familiar faces. They were detectives yes, but also one was a friend of the family. Both were black so we figured we had a chance of making it out alive. Oh Lord! What is going on here? What had we done to deserve this Rambo type of treatment?

We were just two lowly addicts who never held a gun or knife to anyone or knocked someone over the head and robbed them. We were what you would classify as polite thieves and harmless. We stole without you even knowing it until it was too late, and by then we were long gone. Kind of like the Lone Ranger and Tonto except folks were not looking around to thank us as we rode off into the sunset. We got high and did not poison other people's children with drugs. So other than the fact that we were junkies and petty thieves, in a sense we were not all that bad compared to others.

The two detectives the we knew were in narcotics so I figured it had to be drug related. But why were they involved in anything we might be involved with? We were not of kilo status or major players in dealing; just a few $5 bags of heroin and some recreational cocaine were our status. So what was their purpose for being there?

Detective Hank, the family friend, leaned over and whispered in my ear, "You'll got any drugs in here?" I told him yes it was in the top drawer in the nightstand between the two beds. Meanwhile the police detectives were tearing down the acoustic ceiling tiles, overturning the mattresses, and other furniture and even ransacking the bathroom and closet. I found a chance to slightly turn my head around just in time to see one of them find our stash. All six bags of heroin and two sets of "works." Detective Hank just kind of looked at me, shrugged, and gestured with his hands and shoulders that indicated to me that he tried.

I knew that his intentions were honorable bless his heart. He had wanted to find our stuff before his colleagues did so they would have never known anything about it. Like the saying, "a day late and a dollar short," well he was on time, just a second short. How bad a luck is that?

Throughout what seemed like an hour I kept asking what we had done and what were they looking for? I was still standing facing the wall handcuffed behind my back in only my boxer shorts. I cringed, my knees buckled, and I almost peed on myself when one of them answered that they were searching for a gun used in an armed robbery the day before.

Armed robbery!

A gun!

Felony charges!

This was indeed all foreign to me, and needless to say quite scary. I actually couldn't wait to get to the third precinct. There I'd get the facts so I could figure out how they could prove such ludicrous charges against us. It was totally out of character to those that knew us and once everything was straightened out I just knew we could go home.

Trying to get dressed with handcuffs that they were nice enough to move to the front was kind of awkward, but I managed. I put on my sharkskin gray pants, baby blue wool turtleneck sweater, and houndstooth overcoat, the kind Sherlock Holms used to wear. I had to move quickly so not to piss off the trigger happy police who still had us covered.

For a brief moment there I thought that perhaps Stephen did something and didn't tell me. I knew it would have been impossible since we were together for the past 24 hours. Maybe it was "two of nothing Lou." We called him that because he never had two of anything in his whole life and he was 26 years old. He was with us last night when we checked in.

He left with an attitude around 10 o'clock last night because we refused to turn him on so he could get high with us. Not that we were of the selfish nature or anything, but he was always expecting a hand out without doing anything to earn his keep. I doubted that he went out after he left or that morning to warrant a scenario like this.

Dressed, they led us down the outside staircase from the second floor to the awaiting cars. I was shocked not only to find that they had the entire area around the motel surrounded, but there was an audience of nosy onlookers from the Howard Johnson restaurant next door. They were staring at us like we were hard to the core criminals.

However, nothing 'til this day can ever erase the feeling that came over me when I saw our father, dressed in his bus driver uniform, standing with the other officers. His expression tore through my rotten soul. He just stared in disbelief. He did not have to say a word. The look on his face was agonizing. I knew we put him through a lot of changes over the years, but I am sure he NEVER thought he would bear witness to what he was seeing with his own two eyes.

Did he call the police on his own sons?

If he did call them, then for what reason?

Why wasn't he at work?

It was only half past noon and he should have been at the Carter's house playing pinochle right about then. That was his favorite pastime on Fridays. It was not like him to miss work unless he was sick or took a personal day.

I could not look him in the face as they placed me in one car and my brother in the other for the 20-minute ride to Mineola. By now I'm really starting to freak. This shit is getting heavy. Of course there are always the sarcastic detectives that enjoy scaring the shit out of you if they saw you were ripe for the pickings. I was their man of the hour. When I rationalized that the most that could happen, once the truth be known, was charges of two misdemeanors for the stuff they found, I relaxed somewhat.

On he ride over they began to unfold the most bizarre set of circumstances surrounding the events leading up to that point.

After listening I knew there was NO way they had the right suspects.

NO way!

Stephen and I could never have robbed a store on March 5th in broad daylight, shoot the manager in his leg, and run back to my car and speed off. It was impossible for a lady to witness seeing us drive off and take down my license plate number. In fact the more they talked about what we did, the more confidence I showed that they had to be dead wrong.

This one detective whose head was turned around in the front seat talking to his fellow "Dick" seated next to me in the back seat, kept staring through me like I was transparent. I guess my no fear expression must have too obvious and pissed him off. I guess he had to show who was in charge and it damn sure wasn't going to be me. He threw another curve my way that sent me back in to the "freak out" mode.

"Well," he said. "If we find we made a mistake about you both, we'll just take the small quantity of drugs we found and add enough to make it a felony." I had no reason to believe that this could not have been possible. Police officers do it all the time. There is not much within their power that they cannot do. Since Mr. Hank never saw what they found in the drawer, he couldn't take our back on this one. Hey, even if he did know the truth, the police have that silent code of honor amongst themselves so either way, we were fucked.

I don't know if sitting handcuffed to the arm of a hard ass wooden chair from approximately one o'clock that afternoon until three o'clock the following morning constituted cruel and unusual punishment or not. I do know that it was not a pleasant experience. Each moment I thought they would realize they made a mistake and we would be soon free to go, they made another attempt to prove our guilt. Of course detective Raymond had to stick his balding head in the interrogation room and say hi. I know he was thinking to himself, "I told you I'd be seeing your black ass again didn't I?"

An hour or so later, Stephen and I both started to get sick since we had not had any heroin in over 12 hours. Remembering that we did not have a chance to get high that morning due to unforeseen circumstances, the chills, and nose running began to show. We knew we'd be detained longer than we expected so we cracked on the arresting officers and asked if we could get straight. It would be no skin off their back since they had our shit in their possession anyway.

To most civilized, normal, folks this request might seem abnormal, but in the dope fiend world it was as logical as asking for a drink of water. The New York City cops were a lot cooler than the Long Island cops. The rules could be bent and no one got hurt. Having an addict throwing up all over the fucking place was a pain in the ass, not to mention having to clean up the mess. So it was not rare for some officers to cut you some slack and let you go on and get off. Also you would make for a more cooperative suspect. They scratched your back you scratched theirs. That was the way it used to be.

Our request was denied with a smirk. Another notch in our bad luck handle.

They did, however, have enough compassion to take some of our own money and send out for cheeseburgers, French fries, and a cola. I didn't have too much of an appetite but ate as much as I could. Didn't know when I would taste a burger and fries again at the rate I was going. I also was skeptical of their generosity. By accepting their graciousness and act of human kindness, it could have indicated on my part a sign of weakness. The next thing they would expect in return might be admitting to something I didn't do.

Oh, the 'ole familiar lie detector test again. The same person that gave one to me back in January was on duty this time also. We were told that if we passed the test they would have no just reason to detain us any longer and could go.

So far the witness they claimed to have could not pick us out of a line up. I had a gas receipt from a filling station on 122nd street and St. Nicholas Ave. to prove my car was not in Westbury at the time of the robbery. We had up until then been very cooperative and not busting their balls. I was sure they would not add more heroin to their discovery to make the charge a felony. Yup, there was no reason I could find for them NOT to cut us loose.

Gee! How naive I was.

We did not fit the profile for this type of courtesy. We did not have the right credentials. We were not:

A. white

B. didn't snitch on anyone for them

C. They were so far into this bust, they had to justify wasting the taxpayers money on such an over dramatized raid.

Bottom line? It is not that they wouldn't let us walk, they couldn't! So I just sat back and relaxed as best I could. It was to be a long year in 1970 or even longer. But first I prayed I'd get through the rest of the evening.

I felt so embarrassed to have one of my high school classmates, Cory, a patrolman, be part of the police line up. This common practice made for a variety of "suspects" with similar characteristics of the accused. Cory even tried to get us to come clean for our own good. I guess he just barely passed his course at the academy in psychology, because his tactics sucked. He tried to help as brother to brother, but he was pitiful. I kept saying to him that we had not a thing to gain by lying, and if ever a time to come clean, rat on a dealer or for that matter my own mother, this was the time.

Just as I thought would happen happened. We were told that Stephen failed the lie detector test. I knew it was horseshit, but that's the way it goes. They never said if the witness picked us out of a lineup. They even took my coat in a room where she was so we could not see her, to see if she could identify it. A coat! This had become an intriguing drama that kept turning up more and more sabotaged facts and I had no idea when or if it would ever end.

Relief was on the way. It was around three o'clock Saturday morning when the time came for them to transport us to the lockup for the morning's arraignment. At least I could finally lie down. Not sleep, just lay down. It's a bitch when you get there late and have to sleep on the Goddamn floor because all the drunks and other lawbreakers got there ahead of you. Most of the men in the lockup are in there on Friday night for being drunk and disorderly, and they would even get the roll of toilet paper first which was used as a pillow. It was only five hours before court convened so it could not be any worse than what I'd already been through.

After the gourmet continental breakfast of a stale roll and coffee that should have been used to melt the snow, we were herded into the vans for the five-minute ride to court. Chained together like circus animals, you were lead into another holding pen to be locked up until your name is called on the calendar. No sense in being in a hurry either. Unless you were going to make bail, you would have to wait for the afternoon run that went to the jail anyway.

In our case there was no need to be in a hurry. In my heart I knew we weren't going anywhere. I was already out on the $500 cash bail from January and had not even gone to court for that yet. If the police were thinking about cutting us some slack, they had every opportunity to before getting to this point. No Bruce, there was no sense dreaming of them doing shit for you now. All I could do now was pray for the strength to endure being locked up like an animal for who knows how long.

Before the day was out, only three people could not make bail or wasn't allowed to go free in their own custody. The first two are obvious. The third person was some black dude from Manhasset who tried to rape a child. I sat next to him in the holding cell and in the prisoner section of the courtroom and he was definitely a candidate for the nut box.

Let's take a look at our judicial system in this case.

There were two Italian brothers who got busted that morning during a raid and five pounds of marijuana was confiscated. I believe they were even growing their own. They both had prior arrests for drug related charges. Because they had a high profile lawyer, bail was set at only $2500 cash for each. They were allowed to make one phone call, and within and hour they were on their way home.

Our bail was set at only $500 for each misdemeanor charge of possession of a controlled substance, and drug paraphernalia. What a joke! For all we were put through only to have them realize we did not commit the robbery, they charged us for some dumb shit.

Dad did show for the arraignment. Mom could not bring herself to come. He listened but when it was all over, he told us there was no way they could come up with $2000. Even if they had the money, they felt we were safer in jail where at least they knew where we were. I had to agree with Pop on that one. If I were a parent, I would have thought the same thing. So no need to get an attitude with them as they were doing what was best for us in their minds.

Once the judge laid down his little hammer and called the next case, we were led out of the courtroom back to the holding cell to await the ride down Old Country Road to Carmen Avenue to the jailhouse. I called the ride the longest journey.

READY OR NOT, HERE I COME

While I waited for the meat wagon to take me to jail, part of me just wanted to get there and settle in and start "kicking." The other part of me was scared to death to go through withdrawal locked in the confines of a 6 x 8 foot cell for 23-hours a day. The guards or hacks as they were called, had no sympathy for drug addicts. Period. After all we were the ones out there probably stealing from someone they knew or for that matter one of their family members. They had to admit one thing: if not for us, they would not have jobs.

The 20-minute ride from the court to the jail was just enough time for me to start planning my strategy for survival. I had no choice by now. Although I spent one night previously, this time I felt more scared since I did not know how long I'd be there. Once there, Stephen and I would be separated again for the first time in months as soon as we arrived on C and D floors for the incubation period.

It dawned on me that since it was Saturday, the jail doctor would not be back until Monday or Tuesday. The policy was no one went into the general population without given clearance by the doctor. What this meant was, for at least three days I would be locked in for 23 hours with just one hour a day out for a shower and a walk up and down the 20-cell tier.

"Please God," I prayed. "Don' leave me alone in this. I know I screwed up but I need your help more than ever before."

At least when the fellas would hang out and talk about jail life, I listened very closely. Since I had not yet really "broken my cherry" I knew it was inevitable that my day would soon come. I wanted to learn how to "jail," as the lesson was called. Good thing I paid attention and learned from the best, as I would call on these lessons and instincts now in order to survive. The first time was not as big a deal as this was going to be.

As I sat in the wagon with Stephen and the weirdo rapist and absorbed the million bumps along the way to the joint, I was totally numb. I had no idea as to when I would ever be touching my feet on the very soil that I took for granted. As we passed Eisenhower Park, I recalled the times I used to go there with my elementary school class for picnics and fun.

When we slowed down to make the left turn to enter the jail property, reality slapped the shit out of me. There was not a fucking thing that I could do but suck it up and hope, not pray, that I would not loose it.

I knew from only two months earlier that once I got inside to be processed what the drill was. The elevator stopped and we were told to turn around and face the back wall. The hacks faced your back for the short ride. They never let you ride in the elevator facing the front for security reasons. If some shit jumped off in the elevator they did not want you to get the advantage of kicking their asses while they were facing you.

As we were led off onto C and D floors, I was prepared for the infamous welcome to the county correctional facility speech given by Sergeant Fitzhugh. He liked to exercise his authority as most of them did. But he had that Napoleon short man syndrome to add to his character so he was a real first class prick.

I did remember the cardinal rule though from my lessons.

When he explained to answer his questions with a "yes sir" or "no sir", he would next ask you if you understood. Without thinking the normal response would have been just a simple yes or no until you got used to the rule. When, and if someone answered without the word "sir" your ass was his right then and there. I was grateful for the course in "jailing" otherwise I know I would have slipped and got my first ass whipping on day one.

The door to my cell slammed shut with that loud clang. I can't begin to describe the feelings so one could understand, that when they turn the key and slam that door, that you have no way out. That loud clanging sounds that culminates the long, slow, grinding noise of the motor turning when the gates open and close, stay with you for the rest of your life.

At least these doors were made of bars so it was not like you were totally isolated. As soon as I was shown to my suite at the hotel provided by Nassau County, I hit the mattress, grabbed my little pillow with hardly any stuffing, curled up in the fetal position and waited for the sleep that never did come that first night.

The lights had to stay on all night. That was so they could keep a closer eye on the new arrivals in case someone tried to get the sheets up to the bar and hang him or herself. Going through the physical and mental pain of withdrawal would have prevented me from sleeping anyway so the lights on did not bother me. I also knew that there was no way my mind was so fucked up that I would want to end it all by hanging from the bars of a jailhouse cell.

I wasn't in as bad of shape as my neighbor though, who had checked in the day before. He was puking his guts out what seemed like all night long. Oh, I forgot to mention that during this most sensitive time in your life, you dared not share the experience with the hacks. In fact you had better not let them know you were kicking if you could help it. They would make your life even worse.

Another valuable lesson that I had paid attention to is keeping your mouth shut around the hacks. Don' ask for shit, especially to go to the hospital or for something to help with the pain and suffering. What they would do just to be inhumane would be to open the windows if you said you were cold. Those that really got their kicks messing with you would act like they were going to take you and help get you some relief. Then once outside your cage, they would strip you down, wet you, beat the shit out of you, and then to add insult to injury place you in "the hole." This was solitary confinement with no window or toilet.

These underpaid overworked correction officers were neither social workers nor shrinks. Their job was not to make you comfortable so you wouldn't mind coming back again. They were the establishment and cared less about you than you cared about them. So the best you could do for yourself was try your best to get some sleep. In a few days the chills, sweats, shakes and vomiting would go away.

The next morning I was awaken by the sounds of banging, clanging, chatter, the oldies station on the radio, and the smell of food permeating the air. I heard a familiar voice, as the smell of French toast got closer to our tier. When I heard that hearty laugh, I knew it just had to be Shultz. I found out later that he was given the name Shultz as a nickname because he had so many alias' that no one really knew his real name. I don't think he even knew!

He was glad yet not surprised to see me back so soon. It was not unusual. He tightened me up with extra French toast and butter. In the evening an extra piece of chicken would be tossed my way. Normally this was a taboo to accept anything extra as a favor from anyone, but I never worried that he would expect anything in return at a later date.

The jail radio station played some real hip music to keep you at least in an up tempo mood. Vivid memories of songs like; *"Love Grows Where my Rosemary Goes," "Didn't I Blow Your Mind This Time,"* and *"Let It Be,"* are still clearly heard in my head. The one song that the station used to run in the ground that I hated the most was, *"Give Me Just A Little More Time."* I used to think that it was played so often on purpose because they knew the jail played their station all the time. Sounds dumb, but nothing is more depressing than sitting in the joint and hearing the lyrics, *"give me just a little more time."*

Finally the visit to see the jailhouse quack was an even bigger joke and travesty of the judicial system. All I had to do was show him my arms with the needle marks and admit on paper that I was an addict in order to get over. The state of New York would then label you a "certified addict," whatever the hell that meant. Why this was so important was that any crime you committed due to your drug addiction would be dismissed off your record. The catch was that you had to enter into a State run program for a period of time set forth by the State commission on narcotic abuse. It sure beat the hell out of going to jail.

A former late governor of New York needed a campaign platform in 1968 so he vowed to clean up the streets from drugs. His bright idea was to form the New York State Narcotic Addiction Control Commission and design a program for rehabilitation. What a joke! OK so he got over on the voting public, but for us addicts we got over also. Just about everyone voluntarily admitted to being a drug addict whether they were or not! Trying to clean up the drug epidemic was like shoveling shit against the tide. It just kept coming back at society.

I survived the 72-hour incubation period in one piece, got my NACC drug certification, and I was ready to go into the jail's general population for my very first time. Of course by the time you got to your assigned floor everyone knew you were coming, and you already knew who was there. Most dudes I knew were from New Castle, Glen Cove, Hempstead, Roosevelt, and Manhasset. Ralph and his brother, Junebug, were already there, but as adults they were on "F" floor with Stephen.

I knew Clinton had been there for damn near a year already. He was disappointed that I got bailed out in January before he got to see me. Ever since his people moved to the Castle from Queens, we had always been tight even though he was two years younger than I was. His older sister Frieda and I had been in the same third grade class at P.S. 116 before I had moved from Queens.

Clinton was a very good-hearted brother if he liked you. It was your ass if he didn't or if you messed with him or anyone in his family. He was a self taught Black Belt in the martial arts, so nobody messed with him. He had kicked brother Orr's two front teeth right out of his head for saying something about his old lady, even though what he said was true.

Poor Clinton. This brother had no bail and no court dates. With nine felonious assault charges filed against him he used to joke that he was just like one of the bars—a permanent fixture!

Yeah. I knew I would be comfortable going up to "G" floor and surviving.

The part of the jail I was moved to was considered the new wing. The colors were much nicer and brighter, than the dingy green walls on C and D, as was the view at night. I remembered watching the construction going on at the Nassau County Medical Center during the daytime. It used to be called Meadowbrook Hospital before it became envogue to call hospitals medical centers.

At night when I couldn't sleep, which at first was almost every night, I would just stare out at the lights. It seemed so peaceful and the thoughts of what wouldn't I give to be out there again in the "world" kept echoing through my mindless mind.

But reality sets in quickly as the guards make their rounds. When you heard the jingling of the keys and you saw the beacon of light coming from their flashlight, you were reminded again very quickly where you were.

I quickly learned how to use the tools of jailing. It came real easy since I had been tutored by the pros. I didn't ask anybody for anything; not even a cigarette. I didn't go into anyone's "house" as your cell was called, without asking. That was considered trespassing or unlawful entry, just like in the real world. Also the owner of that house would have the right to kick your ass if you were on his property or even kill you. I didn't mess with anyone's "woman" on the tier and the senior inmates got my utmost respect.

Funny how you adapted to such a sick way of living so easily and accepted as status quo the rules. On the other hand, you couldn't accept the simple rules of society that got your ass into your situation to begin with.

My court date was two weeks away. Not that I was looking for a miracle to happen, but somehow just going to court for anything was a day's outing. It gave you a chance to be away from the boredom and confinement for at least a few hours. The 30-minute trip over to the Mineola was also an opportunity to look out the window inside the cars along the way and maybe see some thigh!

My dad, who had never set foot inside a jail before, came up to visit his sons two days after we were settled in to our new environment. There was very little said. I thought something seriously happened to Mom when we walked in to the visiting area and reached our booth and looked through the little glass window and saw him instead of her. I knew that when Stephen used to get in to trouble before this, she would be the one always going over to visit him. "Why was she not here now?" I thought to myself. Dad assured us that she was fine and when we asked for some money for commissary, he offered to leave five dollars on the books for BOTH of us. It sure beat a blank.

I felt so sorry for him to have to see his only two sons behind a glass partition talking on a static filled telephone receiver. My heart was filled with such sadness seeing the hurt in his eyes. I felt deep down inside that Stephen and I were literally tearing apart the house he worked so hard to make a home. I was worried more about Mom than Dad because I had not seen her since a week prior to our arrest. That had been the longest time apart for both of us.

Jail definitely was not the place to show any type of emotion. I just kept my feelings buried deep in my own space within my heart and only took them out at night while I laid down in the quietness of my cell.

THE DRAMA BEGINS TO UNFOLD

A strange thing happened on the way back upstairs to G floor from the visitation room that day. I stopped on the stair landing on E floor and peeked through the door to the lobby. It was a way to kill some time. You couldn't stall for much time because the hacks would call ahead to your destination to let someone know you were on your way. If you took longer than the allotted time, expect an ass kicking and loss of the next visit.

To my surprise I saw a very familiar face standing in the E floor lobby waiting to be let out to go downstairs once I passed. It was Barry Gibson. I couldn't believe what I was seeing. "How could that be?" I asked myself. He had only been home less than a month after doing 22 months in Sing Sing for 15-armed robberies. I was just getting high with him two weeks ago. Did he violate his parole?

I read his lips and he made a gesture with his hand like he was shooting a gun. He had pulled over 15-armed robberies before he got caught running from an ice cream store back in the winter of '67. He was dumb enough to use a car with New Jersey plates. Dee, who was as trifling as any guy, was driving her mother's car. The tags were never changed after they had moved from Jersey because the tag fee was cheaper than New York. I remembered when they got busted. It was written up in the Newsday and they were labeled as "Bonnie and Clyde."

For Dee it was her first time getting arrested so she only got three years probation. She violated her terms less than a year later. Her and Marky boy were shooting up in the bathroom in the basement of Garden Street Baptist Church and got busted by the preacher. Of course it was a low thing to do, but we all felt as a man of the cloth, that Pastor Higgins could have cut them some slack and not called the police. But he wasn't worth shit either, considering all the out of wedlock children he kept fathering.

As I walked the rest of the way upstairs to my new home, I wondered if Barry was stupid enough to start pulling stick ups again. Nah; get that thought out of your head Bruce. No one could be that stupid. All I wanted now was to hurry up and have my court date come around so I could find out what my fate was going to be. March 23rd could not have come fast enough.

Now it was not the family's fault that the only lawyer we could afford was an alcoholic family friend by the name of, you guessed it—Elwood Low. I knew there was a reason I felt a little uncomfortable about him when I was young when I had thoughts of becoming a lawyer. He meant well but trust me, you stood a better shot at the system on your own. With Elwood you could not have made matters worse if you represented yourself. With all due respect, he was useless as tits on a bull!

The 23rd of March finally came around and it was showtime.

Once you got dressed after being thoroughly stripped and searched in every orifice of your body you were then lead to the bullpen. Here you were held until it was your turn to be loaded into the meat wagon for the day's outing. As the door to the bullpen was opened to place me inside I was shocked to discover Rick Timsby sitting there. He looked as if he had just lost his best friend. That probably would have been a better option than losing his freedom.

It was hard for me to imagine Rich doing anything to get arrested for. He used to be our paperboy at one time. He was kind of a nerd even throughout high school. I knew he was dipping and dabbing in drugs but he was considered a hope fiend not a dope fiend. I asked, "What and how did you end up in here?" His response very casually was, "You know that armed robbery that you and Stephen got busted for?"

I answered, "Yeah," then thought to myself, how could I not know you asshole.

"Well Barry and me were the one's that did it!" he said.

I had to sit down.

Not only had Barry robbed and shot the store manager as the police said happened, but he wanted to sexually assault him too. Rick told me that Barry pulled at least four armed robberies within the four weeks he had been home from prison. Just like the time when he got busted in '67, he ratted on his partners.

Jaime was involved in one of the four stickups and the detectives came right to his job across the tracks at T&S Brass and arrested him during his 10 A.M. coffee break. They would have been there sooner but they had to stop on Broadway in the Castle and arrest Rich. It was on the way so why waste the taxpayers money on gas?

"The mystery is solved," I was thinking. "They had to cut me loose after this new discovery."

You knucklehead! Wake up and smell the coffee. Have you not figured this shit out by now? Your ass aint going anywhere. New evidence, admission of guilt to the armed robbery, and anything else did not matter. You had to answer for the bullshit charges and that is all there was to it. So relax. It was going to be a long hot summer.

On the van ride to court Rick began to tell me how he had gotten strung out in the 'Nam. Even though he kept a low profile, in my opinion he was not that trifling. Then I remembered the time that he showed up on the corner hang out trying to sell his little sister's school violin. He was sick and needed a fix.

I felt sorry for him because he really was a nice guy. What a shame he learned his drug behavior as a result of Uncle Sam teaching him in six weeks to go over to a strange land and blow someone's brains out. We were different because I did what I did because I wanted to. I couldn't blame the military for my circumstances.

This time both Mom and Dad were in court for us. Rick's Mom was there also. Mom introduced Elwood to Mrs. Timsby as a gesture of one hurt Mom trying to help another. On the other hand I was saying to myself, "Heaven help Rick!" Even though this was his first bust, it was very serious. You just don't go around in Westbury and rob and shoot a white man in the leg and expect any mercy. Dope fiend or not they want your ass and being Black to boot! Well need I say mo?

As I expected we got a postponement and no bail reduction. I already had my shit figured out anyway. I would cop a plea as an addict, have the charges dropped to include the one from before in January and be home before year's end. As long as I didn't fuck up while on the aftercare probation of 24 months I'd be good to go. So for me as far as I was concerned Elwood could have kept his sorry ass home. He could not have done any better.

So I kind of put the story together in my head on the ride back to the joint. It did not even matter if I caught a glimpse of some broad's thighs as they drove home from work; I wanted to get some closure for my peace of mind.

Rick was the same height and build as Stephen with the same medium length Afro style haircut. I was the same height and build as Barry. Since Rick had no priors he had no police photo on file. Stephen's had to be put in with others of the same description so maybe the lady picked him out. The police assumed just like I did, that Barry could not possibly be back out in the street pulling stickups already, so I had my photo picked out. So far all that was making sense to me.

The only thing that bothered me was why the store manager that was robbed was not brought to the precinct to try and identify us. Also how did my car and tag number get factored in to the equation?

At the time when we were arrested, I told the police our whereabouts and nothing could have been closer to the truth. We were on 117th street and Lenox Ave. at Shep's shooting gallery getting high. Of course the police could not verify our alibi. Were they going to believe a bunch of dope fiends or some elderly white lady?

About two weeks later I was called down for a lawyer visit. "Hey," I thought, "Maybe I might be getting my walking papers sooner than later."

I wished at least I could have gotten just ONE theory right for a change. I figured wrong. Elwood was coming up to the jail so that I could endorse my income tax refund check over to him to pay his fee. For your lawyer visits, a special room was provided so you did not have to talk through glass on a telephone filled with static.

If not for the respect I still had for my family, I'd have cussed his ass out and snatched my check right out of his hand. Since that was not an option, I just signed over my $700 refund. By then I had given up on trying to second-guess anything relating to this whole scenario.

I finally got to talk to Barry returning from a visit. At first I just looked at him in amazement. How could he be back in jail after only being home for four weeks with two years on parole with four new armed robberies and one assault to his credit? This brother had some serious problems.

I knew drugs changed people, but from the time we were all younger growing up on Rushmore Street, Barry always seemed a little different. I personally thought when his moms went in for a simple operation, while he was in the ninth grade, and she died as a result of negligence, he never was the same. Losing his mother, who he was so close to, was emotional enough, but when his dad remarried less than a year later it made matters worse. Of course I was not a shrink, but just someone that still had some rational thinking left in me.

I had never set out to be the type of person that I turned out to be during my teenage years, but despite it all I think I came out of it in one piece. Before peer pressure was as popular as it is today, I never realized how it could have such a strong effect on you. I see now that all the situations I got into that were not healthy or smart in the name of "being cool" were just poor choices.

As I lay my head down to sleep in my jailhouse cell, I wished that I had never smoked my first joint at fifteen and mainlined my first shot of heroin two years later. No sense crying over spilt milk. If I truly wanted to atone for my ways I could only look into the future. Unfortunately jail was no place to show a sign of weakness. Any intentions of getting my act together would have to be done on the sly.

I felt bad that I had to miss my cousin Kellie's wedding. Of all the cousins, we were the closest. She was seven months older than me and we had never had a cross word in our lives, which is kind of rare to find amongst relations. June was the month for weddings and she was to have a big blowout.

Not only had I missed the wedding, but also her dad, who was my uncle Bobby, took ill with a sudden heart attack, and Granny was hospitalized also with a heart condition. I felt like shit behind that.

IF NOT FOR BAD LUCK

When I did finally get a visit from Mom, I had mixed emotions. I did not understand how and why she could not have come in the first two weeks yet at the same time understood how scared and hurt she must have been. The shock of her sons possibly committing such a serious offense was inconceivable. When she came to court and realized that we were not guilty of the robbery and just drug possessions, she could breathe a sigh of relief.

I was so glad to see her. It was easier now that the truth was out in the open. We had nothing to hide. She already knew about our drug habits so it was no secret. I had the whole visit to myself as Stephen was on lock down for something or other and could not have any visits for a week. Glad we had the extra time together because Mom unfolded the most incredible story surrounding the magnitude of the chain of events on that fateful 6th of March 1970.

This is what actually went down.

The detectives had arrived to our home at 6:30 A.M. in the very same manner that they came to the motel-with guns drawn. As the pricks were banging on the door, they threatened to kick the door in if Mom did not open it. The sons of bitches awoke our sister, Lisa, up from her sound sleep, and told her to leave her room while they ransacked it. They scared the living shit out of the two of them. What an experience for an 11-year-old. Dad had already left for work.

In the same manner in which I reacted, when I was told that they were looking for a gun, well my poor mother damn near had a coronary. They demanded to know where we were and she told them the truth. She did not know and had not seen or heard from either of us in a week. She asked to call my father's job. Dad's dispatcher sent someone out on his route to get him right at the height of the morning rush hour. There were no two-way phones in the buses back then. He hauled ass back to New Castle as fast as he could.

Meanwhile Aunt Beatrice lived five minutes away and she went over to get her sister and Lisa. At least my sister could be taken to school so she wouldn't have to be around all the insanity. On Friday's Uncle Will did not go in to the office. It was his day off so he could count his money hidden under the mattress and do his banking business. He suggested they should call on Detective Hank. He lived down the street from them on 3rd avenue, and perhaps he could shed some light on what all this was about.

My cousin Marcia, their daughter, knew we had been staying in different motels in the area but not sure as to which one. By this time Dad arrived at their house the same time as Detective Hank and his partner. They didn't mean to scare the family but he had to be honest with his news that he found out off the police wire. He was told that we were supposedly armed and dangerous and that the police were instructed to shoot to kill if we as much as looked like we had a gun or attempted to resist arrest. We were armed robbers and shot someone so they were exercising extreme precautions. You know, the kind that only Black suspects are privileged to experience.

Of course by now the sense of urgency to find us was on. Either the police would find us first or our own posse would. The odds weren't that heavy in our favor for the latter. With Marcia along, Dad and the detectives started going to every motel showing our picture, but to no avail. The meter was running, and time was about to expire when Marcia remembered "two of nothing Lou." He just might be of some help.

He was no stranger to the police either so when two narcs rang his doorbell, you could imagine his surprise and worry as to the nature of their call. As fate would have it, he told them he was with us the night before and knew where we were staying.

BINGO!

The mad dash over to the HoJo motor lodge was under way. But leave it to Lou. He was never one for attention to details. He got them that far, but couldn't remember the room number. They went through the lobby so they did not see my car around the other side of the motel.

He remembered the second floor but not the room. What he thought was the right one resulted in no answer when they knocked. Thinking we had checked out and gone, they left. After dropping Lou and Marcia back home and giving Mom the bad news that we were still at large, Detective Hank checked in only to find out that my car had been spotted where they had just came from. They made the fifteen-minute ride back to Haysville in eight minutes, but by time they got there the rest was history.

He felt bad because he tried so hard to stop the situation from happening, but it was out of his hands. But, to this day, I will forever hold him in my debt. After retiring and moving to Florida with his wife in '81, he has since succumbed to prostate cancer. I sincerely believe in my heart that the detectives were all pysched for bloodshed and if not for Mr. Hank's presence that day, we might not have lived to tell about it.

SURVIVING PHOENIX ON A WING AND A PRAYER

The only other time that I had actually been locked up was in the Maricopa County Hospital's detoxification ward in Phoenix, Arizona. That was a year earlier in March of '69. Marcia, ironically, was involved in that situation also.

I went out to Phoenix to kick cold turkey. I was sick and tired of the street life. I had no job except driving a taxi so I could hang all day then have a place to sleep at night. In fact I got the job because the owner, Mr. Johnnie found me asleep one morning in the back seat of one of his cabs. He saw that I was harmless. I was just a dope fiend with no home so he let me start working for him that same morning.

Mom and Dad were on my case about cleaning up my act or getting the fuck out the house for good. I was seriously tired and wanted so badly to stop getting high. I took some proceeds from one of my bigger hustles out of the bank (yes as a dope fiend I had a savings account) and called Marcia. She was living in Phoenix with her estranged husband, Sidney, who was in the armed forces and their three-year-old son and three month old daughter. I asked Marcia if I could come out for a visit for a while and she said that it would be all right.

Another good reason for me to make a move at that time was that a week prior Leroy Shipman had held a knife to my throat in front of the youth center on Prospect Ave. This took place right in front of about 15 people. Nobody ever hung out inside any of these establishments for some reason. I was planning to give him the two bags of dope sooner or later. Two bags had been the standard fare for a ride into the city, and the rule was you gave up your fare before you got out the car once you got back to the Castle.

Well in his mind it seemed more like later than sooner. However, I took advantage of him since he was messed up and caught a case of amnesia. I admit I was wrong, but in this instance it could have hurt to try and get over.

What else could I do with the blade to my throat but be humble and beg him to let me at least go home to get his due. I would have been a suicidal maniac if I chumped him one more time and did not come back. He was one of those brothers that had a hard life. His entire family had a history of violent behavior. His older brother Brady got into a fight outside the bar soon after being released from serving time in jail for assault, and almost bit the dude's nose off. Their younger sister Belinda died of a heroin overdose before the age of twenty. At one time she had been Clinton's old lady.

He didn't have to tell me not to cross him. I went home to get his stuff and when I came back he asked me if I had my works on me so he could get off. "Sure" I said. We went to his house to get high since no parental figure was ever there anyway. I thought to myself, "This is great. My life is spared and I get a free high on top of it!"

When we got to his house he apologized about pulling a six-inch blade on me, and threatening to cut my throat from ear to ear. He told me he just had to do that to show those watching he was not a punk. When it was my turn to get my taste of the dope he left me, I asked him in all honesty would he have actually cut me. He told me without stuttering, "Absolutely!" Here's a guy I've known since fourth grade, but the laws of the street were gospel.

I called TWA made a reservation and then I called Mom to tell her I was on my way out West. She thought I was crazy to make a decision within 24 hours to just up and go off to Arizona. I was an impulsive person and that is the way I did things. Not much thought ever had to be involved.

I had to get stoned for the last time, then I went into Queens and said goodbye to the folks and Dad. My grandfather gave me a lift to LaGuardia and I couldn't wait to get away for some R&R. I don't remember shit from the time he dropped me off at the TWA terminal. I was in a nod all the way to Chicago where we had a layover. I'm glad we didn't have to change planes, as I don't even remember waking up but once to see where I was.

When I did get to glance out of my half open left eye during our final decent into Phoenix, I caught a glimpse of the sunset over the mountains. I thought I had died and went to heaven. That photogenic moment was the most beautiful glimpse of anything that I had ever seen. I felt such a sense of relief that I was going to get my shit together, and nothing was going to stop me at this point—nothing!

My cousin Morris had left the street gangs in South Jamaica in '61 and while only 16-years-old his mother signed a consent form so he could join the Navy. It was either that or he would have ended up dead or in jail. He was so blessed to have had a chance to turn his life around. When he was discharged six years later he went on to medical school and became a doctor. His field of expertise dealt with adolescent addictions. I got his number and called to tell him I would be out in Phoenix. Since he lived in San Francisco I told him that I like to come out and hang for a while. He knew the deal but he was family so he extended his hospitality and help.

I never told Marcia or Sidney my real reason for coming there.

The next morning she looked at me and wondered why I was acting fidgety and saying I was cold in 100-degree weather. I told her I might have been coming down with a cold since when I left it was 30 degrees and starting to snow. My jones was coming down hard and although I expected this, the mental state of mind has to coincide with the physical in order for it to work. It wasn't working too tough. I took some over the counter sleeping pills, as I wanted so bad to go to sleep and make the hurt go away. Short of overdosing, I took as many as I could but to no avail.

The next day Sidney came over as he often would since he worked nights. He lived off the base and although they were estranged, he took damn good care of his children. He also was always there for Marcia since he was the only family other than the kids that she had there. They were going to go out shopping with the kids. I was invited to go along, but I had other plans for my shopping needs. I told them I would be fine. I had visited out there in September of '68 for three weeks, and knew my way around pretty well. I told them I was just going to do some sightseeing.

No sooner than I waved as they pulled off from in front of the complex, I searched for the phone directory, and frantically began to look for a drug treatment program. Any program would do. I wasn't particular. Remember, this was 1969 and Phoenix was not up with the times. I believe their tallest building during that time was not even 20 stories high on Central Avenue. If they had a drug epidemic no one obviously was aware of it. There was not one program listed. I called around to several hospitals next in the area and found one that offered some type of help. I felt like I had just hit the jackpot.

After calling a cab and leaving my relatives a note stating," I was out and would be back soon", I prayed relief would come soon. Lord knows I did not want or have to resort to going out and try to score. One thing a dope fiend can do is locate drugs. Drop any dope fiend out of an airplane in a parachute over any town in America, and within an hour he'll find what he is looking for.

There was a famous comedienne that once stated, "If an eight-year-old child can go out on he streets of Harlem on any day of the week including Sunday, or any hour and find drugs, then why can't the police or the government?"

The cab driver that showed up must have been the luckiest Mexican alive that evening. He probably made more money off of me alone than he had all day. It turned out that I hired him to be my personal chauffeur. At each stop I had him to wait then take me to the next stop. I didn't care about the money or anything at that point. All I was interested in was to stop hurting so bad.

The hospital I went to first, that said they could help, misunderstood my needs. They were nice though and referred me to another hospital. On my third stop at this private hospital with the statues of Jesus and Mary on the front lawn, and all over the lobby, I thought this was it. There, I was allowed to talk to a priest. The hospital staff was not equipped to handle a real honest to goodness New York style dope addict. It wasn't their fault, but the truth was I needed more than prayer.

I can remember him putting his arm around me as I cried uncontrollably. I didn't want to ever leave the comfort of his loving arms. I hadn't been held that lovingly and close to someone since I was a small child. Unfortunately all he could offer was to direct me to the county hospital. This would be the next and final stop for me. The next move after that would have been to ask the driver if he knew where I could buy some dope.

When we arrived at the emergency entrance I did not even ask him to wait. I knew this was the last roundup. I paid him and gave him more than a generous tip for his troubles. I knew that someone in there was going to help me and stop the hurting or I was going to die.

But, shit! You should have seen the waiting room! I never saw so many Mexicans in one place in my life. Of course I had to remember where I was also.

I figured if I had to wait before my name was called I just as well have gone back to Marcia's and come back the next day. The dope fiend in me came right out. I said to myself, "Bruce, you've got no time to wait. Nobody in here feels worse that you do. You have got to butch your way ahead of everyone somehow some way."

I looked around and there were some scary looking people in there waiting to be seen or heard. Shit, I couldn't worry about them. I figured if one of them cops an attitude because I get waited on first, what better place to be if I got shot or stabbed than in the emergency room of a county hospital?

I boldly just walked up to the desk and rolled up my sleeves and showed the nurses my needle marks. I thought one of the nurses was going to faint. After almost two years of shooting up damn near everyday, I formed thick black ugly looking "tracks" on my veins from all the hits and the misses. I'm sure these folks never saw anything like this before. I told them I needed some help, and that I not only couldn't wait my turn, I wasn't going to. I was willing to sign anything at this point as I begged for help.

My wish was granted.

As I was led across this courtyard in the pitch-blackness of night to where I was going for treatment, I started having second thoughts. "Hum," I thought. "This is a sure enough mental ward of a county hospital they are taking me to." I knew once inside I aint getting out until the two weeks I signed for is up.

Two whole weeks!

See how a dope fiend's mind works? One minute I would cut off my right arm for help; the next minute I'm thinking about making a run for it before they lock me behind those steel doors. The truth was, had they given me something for my ills first instead of making me wait until I got to the ward, I no doubt would have ran off.

What an experience. After I got my medicine, after almost 48 hours from the time I got high, I finally got to go to sleep. Real sleep is so much more peaceful than a drug induced nod.

My roommate was already asleep when I arrived so I didn't meet him or anyone until the following morning. At breakfast I still had no appetite but did request a phone call to let Marcia, and my family know where I was, and that I was sorry. Marcia was so glad to hear from me. When I didn't come home all night, she was worried sick. She said she would call Mom and reiterate to her that I was indeed trying to do the right thing.

I began to get nervous after 24 hours just by talking to my roommate. He had been arrested for public intoxication. To me it seemed like no big deal, but to the state it was. He said he had to go to a hearing held on the premises to determine if he would become a ward of the state for a pre-determined amount of time if the judge decided to.

I was shocked!

"If they send him to a state hospital for just being drunk, they'd probably give me the chair!" I thought to myself. I did not want to over react, but I was not familiar with their laws.

The next day he had to go to court, and I gave him the old, "Don't worry bro, you'll get your walking papers speech." When he came back to our room with the news that he got three years, and would be transferred within 24 hours to a State facility, I knew I had to get the fuck out of there; if not now, then sooner would have been even better.

I started right off trying to convince my assigned shrink that I was well after only two days. I promised I had learned my lesson and would stay clean forever. Name it I said it. I even used the fact that at the end of the week that it was my

Mom's birthday, and that she would just love to have me home for her 40th birthday.

But a scary thing started to happen as I spoke with the doctor. The more I talked, my voice started to become slurred. My mouth felt like I hadn't had any saliva in a year, and was becoming harder to move. "What if they gave me something to make me a zombie to keep me here forever?" was my first thought.

I made up my mind that from then on, I wasn't going to swallow any more pills. The methadone was helpful for my withdrawal, but, since I was not sure if it was that or the other shit they were giving me, so I stopped everything. There was no way in hell that I got this far in life to end up a babbling idiot stuck in some loony bin for God knows how long. No, the kid aint going down like that.

The slurred speech went away within two days. I never did know what happened that caused it.

A one-story building was where we were housed. Everyday I would sit in the lobby by the nurse's station. When they would buzz for the door to open for "civilians," I would plot how I was going to make a run for it. Out of fear, I never did. So I took my chances playing on the doctor's emotions. I was good at that.

It wasn't until one afternoon when this old lady came up to me and asked pathetically, "If you see my socks please ask them to come home," had I realized how sad and unfortunate those people were. Another man would sit all day in a wheelchair at the far end of the hall and not say a thing. Then as soon as the food carts were delivered at mealtime, he would just get right on up as if nothing was wrong. There I was with all my faculties, yet I was treating my body in the worse kind of way by polluting it with heroin.

The shrink finally allowed me to leave after only seven days.

I was not sure if my con game worked or not but I was not about asking any questions. It was time to move on and close this chapter. I was walking in tall cotton the night before I was to leave. Nothing that went on there mattered to me anymore. So when this big, fat, black female patient threw a chair through the television screen, and smashed it to pieces, it was just another day at the funny farm to me. I didn't think that because someone changed the channel while she was watching a commercial would set her off like it did.

It was hard for me to sleep that last night so I just wandered the halls. When I peaked through the glass window to the room where the fat lady was, I got sick to my stomach. There she was strapped to her bed by these big, leather, straps tied to her wrists and ankles. Her hair looked like she had played a electric guitar standing in a pail of water! She was writhing back and forth and moaning, "I didn't do anything, I didn't do anything."

"Please Lord," I said, "don't ever let me experience anything like this again."

I bummed a ride to Marcia's since she did not want to wake the kids to bring them to come pick me up. At first that pissed me off, but then I was in no position to feel as though anyone owed me anything. Of all the people I could have asked for a ride from, leave it to me to pick some crazy ass orderly that was getting off the midnight to eight shift. He drove worse than some of the dope fiends I used to ride with back home. I just prayed that he would get me where I needed to go before he got arrested for driving under the influence of being crazy.

After my explanation to Marcia, I then called TWA so I could haul my natural ass out of this one horse town the next day. I wasn't taking any chances. She told me that before I had arrived from New York, both our fathers had called her to warn her that I might be coming there to make some big drug buy. They meant well, and they both were looking out for her welfare, but it still hurt that they thought I was THAT stupid.

While I was at the mental bed and breakfast lodge, TWA had gone on strike. I was not aware while I was behind the steel door. I immediately arranged to fly back on another airline but had to wait two days to leave. I was so paranoid that I did not leave the house until it was time to go to the airport.

GOOD INTENTIONS DO
NOT ALWAYS PREVAIL

As the plane taxied to the gate at LaGuardia, all thoughts of giving up "the life" of drugs went right out the door soon as it opened, and I smelt the New York City air. The idea was good on the 3-½ hour flight, but the ether wore off as we got closer and closer to home.

The first thing on the agenda was to answer to the folks. Stephen had not yet gotten kicked out the house again, but now that I was back I knew it was just a matter of time for both of us to have to leave. As I laid down in the comfort of my own bed, I could not help but wonder what the fellas were doing. I couldn't wait to see them.

I went back to what I was comfortable, and familiar with. That meant going back to driving taxicabs. I used to steal food out the grocery bags in the trunk before I helped unload the groceries for old ladies. I felt funny accepting a tip for stealing their food. Before long I was back in full swing as a low life trifling dope fiend. I did have the decency to move into a rooming house. It was the kind where you had to write your name on your shit that you left in the refrigerator, and wait your turn to use the one bathroom.

I did luck out and found a job at Kennedy airport within three weeks of returning from Phoenix.

Alas! I finally would have a job other than hacking all day and night. It could not have come at a better time.

Mr. Jonnie and his ugly ass old lady with the one tooth in her head started acting a fool. Their vast empire of three taxis was in jeopardy of going belly up. Things used to get pretty funny for the passengers as I drove them from the train station to their homes. You would hear Mr. Johnnie and his wife, Lula Mae, arguing over the two-way radios. She was the dispatcher and he was usually driving the third car.

What made this comedy so hysterical was that between the two of them they could hardly speak any decent English. When you took into account all the times she'd call him a "Black son of a bitch", and he would call her "ignit" and tell her that she was "ag-awaiting" him all the time, it did make for a Keystone comedy routine.

I would turn up the volume real loud, especially if the cab was full of men. One time this White man didn't want to get out of the cab right away. When I got to his house he asked if he could just wait until he heard how the argument would turn out. I saw the handwriting on the wall so the new job was right on time.

No need to go into details to say that the wonderful new job lasted only a month!

Still determined to find meaningful employment took me to the home of a family friend Bob Hewitt. He was a real cool dude for an older man, and so easy to relate to. He had told my father that one of his fraternity brothers from Wilberforce University by the name of Ernest Brown, had the hook up with Local 3 of the IBEW.

Ernest was asked to help recruit minorities, primarily blacks, for their electrician's apprenticeship program. So off I went again to take another damn aptitude test. From what I was told the results were very favorable, and so I was accepted as the first black in this new program in New York

I was never sure who was happier each time I found a good job—My dad or me!

The folks in Queens agreed that I could stay with them for a while since my first assignment would be in Flushing. The site was not far from Shea stadium, and near La Guardia airport. I invested in a tool belt, some work boots, a hammer there, and a screwdriver there, and I was good to go. I took the Q-17 bus line up to Kissena Blvd. that first morning. I was so excited that I had even made conversation with the bus driver. He knew Dad since they worked out of the same depot

To say all was well with the world and me that day would have been an understatement. That is until the bus driver said that the next stop would be mine. When I rose from my seat to be ready for the bus to stop, I was in awe of the address that the union gave me.

It was a fucking construction site!

You know, the kind with the noise, heavy equipment, materials everywhere, and most of all "height!" I thought I would start out inside a building at first. I recalled my cousin Gregory's war stories of when he worked as a carpenter during the construction of the World Trade Towers. He and his fellow workers would get wasted during their lunch hour drinking alcohol, then go back up one hundred stories and work the afternoon in that condition.

Where the hell are the walls?

Where the hell are the elevators?

Why the hell was I here?

When I reported by eight o'clock to the foreman, he told me to go to the top floor, which at the time was only eight stories high. Reluctantly I climbed the temporary ladders made of wood to the top. Damn! Why did it have to start raining too? I believe this started my streak of bad luck of me starting outdoor jobs in the worse weather conditions.

My assignment was to just kind of help the others and become familiar with my surroundings. "Get familiar with my surroundings?" I thought. "There are NO surroundings to get familiar with!" My ass was frozen stiff to one spot in the middle of the floor. If I could not hand a tool to someone or observe from where I was, screw it! It just wasn't meant to be.

When a Boeing 727 flew overhead for a landing, and I could see people in the plane looking out the window, I swore I had heard them talking too. I thought I heard a passenger say, "Oh look at that poor young black kid standing there scared to death!"

The guys told me that since I was the new apprentice on the block, the rules of the site was that I would be the gopher. All I could imagine was me making trips up and down these rickety ladders all day long carrying stuff on my back and falling over the edge and killing myself dead as a doornail. Their comment was my cue to start scheming on how I was going to get out of this situation.

A miracle happened next.

To the rescue came a blessing from above. I guessed that since I was nearer to God on this site, His response to my prayers got back to me quicker than usual.

It was time for the morning coffee break, and I was the one to have to go to the corner bakery and deli for the Danish and coffee for everyone. While they were all busting my balls and laughing about me having to walk two blocks in the rain and carrying all this shit back for them, I was tallying up. I was figuring that the last laugh would be on them, and if they were waiting for me to return, well more power to them.

I was making my way slowly down the ladder one step at a time moving like Stepin Fetchit's brother. I was scared to death. I knew right then and there I had nothing more to fear. Brother Bruce knew it would be a one-way journey.

For days I actually felt guilty about those poor guys wondering what happened to their breakfast. It was not my intent to steal from them, but I only wanted to survive. I bet they'll never trust another "newbie" to go off with their money again. I'm sure the issue wouldn't have been a black or white one. My theory on the matter was that it would be a long time before they opened up their union to let another one of us in anyway.

So there I was, sitting on the same bus less than three hours from when I got off earlier. The only difference, this time I was all muddy and soaking wet. The driver remembered me from talking his head off and must have wondered what kind of job I had putting in less than three hours a day. I could sense and feel the passengers staring at me for looking so pitiful. At least I was smart enough to have taken my tools when I left. At least I could sell them to someone that really needed them.

I survived the rest of the summer of '69. As soon as the test results came back from the civil service postal exam, I'd become a respectable citizen. A civil service job was considered by my dad's generation and the generation before his to be the ultimate security as far as jobs were concerned. I also had gone for the test for the Transit Authority, but I only earned a 70% passing grade. Dad told me that I would be so far down on the list that I would be old enough to retire by the time they got to my name.

October rolled around and when I got the news that I passed the test and would be starting that November, not only was I happy but Dad and my grandfather were also. The same grandfather that drove me to the airport to go off to Phoenix just eight months earlier was a retired postal worker. He was ecstatic that his grandson would follow in his footsteps. The only negative to the joyful news was that I had been assigned the one post office that would spell disaster—WESTBURY.

Just another of my many obstacles that I had to overcome.

The next leap of faith was Dad signing a loan for me to buy my first car. I was so excited. I had bought a 1965 gray Oldsmobile Starfire from a Franklin Square businessman for a whopping $800. It was loaded. Steering wheel that moved up and down. Rear radio antenna that worked by pushing a button. Seats moved six different ways. I mean this was luxury at it's best. The loan called for payments of $34 a month for 36 months. If I fucked my new found blessings up this time, I'd be a first class jackass.

While in jail, just three months later, I thought back to the day I was so proud when Mom took me over to pick up the car and I handed the man a check for $800. Now there I was sitting up half the night talking to some half-wit loser named Shultz, and wondering what went wrong. Two months after that, I became a victim of mistaken identity.

During my most recent incarceration, Dad sent Mom over to the jail a month later in April to inform me that he was going to sell my precious car. On one hand I knew this meant I was not going home anytime soon, and on the other I could understand where Dad was coming from. Protection of his good credit history was very important to him.

OH WHAT GOOD TIMES I THOUGHT I WAS HAVING

In high school I gained the reputation of dressing my ass off and being a ladies man. Super cool and always with the right answers was my image. Talk about peer pressure! I had what a lot of brothers wanted yet they were smart enough to want that piece of sheepskin even more. Inside I was a very unhappy teenager. I always knew I could have been more academically successful, but my image kept me from being the real me.

Kelvin, whom I've known since we were both in Ms. Bennett's fifth grade class, went on to become a very prominent Radiologist in Mountville, Tennessee. He had told me several years ago that back in high school he had wanted so badly to reach out and encourage me to get my shit together so I could go on to college like him.

I never realized that another classmate even cared about me back then. I was very touched by what he said. For one of my peers to have seen potential in me, although I knew it was there all along made me wish I had been more approachable. Perhaps things might have turned out differently, who knows.

The faculty members in high school were of little help to me. Hell, most of them knew we were using dope and pissing our lives down the drain, yet did nothing to help. The majority of them looked the other way in hopes that we would get out of their school before their good reputation was tarnished.

There were no more than six black faculty members out of a staff of 65. They tried to be positive role models but they actually caused me to feel that there was little hope for the marginal black student. Out of the six teachers, one of them used to ask me to bring him back a pint of booze when we used to sneak out during second period to go to the liquor store. I could not blame him for drinking. It must have been very depressing teaching the "special class", and I was not talking about the gifted and talented either!

Mrs. White, who had been married to a County Police Detective, and had four school age children, worked at the school as an aide. We had little respect for her because she was screwing Mr. Lundy, the special education teacher. He was married also, but his children were grown. Then we had Mr. Rogers who was struggling with his sexual identity. The other three educators kept a low profile.

Don't misunderstand. I don't blame any of them for my drug addiction. However, I will say that now that I am an adult I can understand just how important those tender years are for a 16 or 17-year-old seeking positive role models. Teenagers are always searching, and if they cannot find that strong positive role model within the family or at school where most of their time is spent, then a negative role model is as good as any.

I realized how labeling or stereotyping a child could also be very detrimental. I was expected by the powers to be to end up just like Stephen. It's sad but the school had me on their shit list before I even began attending. I was the "other one" in their eyes, yet they did nothing to help prevent a possible bad situation. In the eyes of the administrators I was a problem student for the next three years and they just accepted that. So the pressure was on for me to live up to their expectations, and damnit, I did my best to prove they were right.

The easiest thing I could have done, after looking back, is to have done well in school and proved them wrong. It is easy to say 36 years later, but what does a 16-year-old know about playing adult games?

How sick and disgusting to know that the only way I could graduate from high school was by having my English teacher change my final grade. In the '60's a 70% was a passing grade. My teacher gave me two points so that I could pass, even though every project she gave me to hand in for a grade I did ZERO. I did everything but tell her to go screw herself. I did not even do the required final Regents term paper. I even threatened her that that with any luck she would have me back in her class if I had to return for another term. I knew I'd be damned if I was going to fuck up my summer going to summer school either.

She did what she had to do, and I did what I had to do.

I threw my diploma in the trash two years after graduation. I did this to express my anger. My anger was directed at a system that would allow people like me to be so intimating that teachers would sacrifice their integrity and standards to pass us through to society so unprepared.

Graduation night was another horror story.

That night, after I had gotten wasted, I had fallen asleep on the front seat of my Mom's '62 Mercury Comet that I had parked in the parking lot. When I woke up, and looked around, I saw that the parking lot had filled up with what seemed like 1000 cars. Next I looked out across the football field several yards away where the ceremony was taking place. I then realized that the commencement ceremony had already begun.

I quickly got myself together and ran as fast as I could, holding on to my cap, while lifting my robe so I would not trip over it, and bust my ass. By the time I made it within a few feet from the seating arrangements for the graduates, I listened to Mr. Kickman calling last names beginning with the letter "H". Just when I thought I had seen or done it all, this had to happen on graduation night in front of everyone including my family members.

There I was, just like when one enters a movie or play late, excusing myself as I climbed over people to get to my seat. How much worse could that have been? I recall Mr. Kickman, and his assistant, Mr. Southern, just looking down at me and shaking their heads as if to say, "Thank God after tonight he's out of here for good!" They called my name near the end, and I went through the bullshit of shaking the hands of the hypocrites while receiving my much-undeserved diploma.

I used to write the weirdest stuff in people's yearbooks or on the back of my senior wallet size pictures. One slogan that comes to mind was:

> *"Now I lay me up the street, I pray to God I hope I sleep.*
> *If I should die, before I see here's something to remember me."*

Now try understanding writing that as an 18-years-old just getting ready for the world and all it had to offer, and feeling you are not a part of anything that was good.

The best times I remembered about my teen years were before I started to snort heroin at 16. The only activities my partners and I wanted to do was smoke reefer, drink a wine named "Bali Hi", get the munchies, laugh, get your rocks off, and chill. Not one of us were thinking about robbing people, and going to jail. Though none of us were Einstein's in school, we did do our work, and never really were much of a threat to anyone.

How fast all of that changed was mind-boggling.

I could not really place my finger on how, and when everything started to change for the worse. What I do know is this: once you aligned yourself to a group of peers, whatever was the "in" thing to do at that time, was so subtle that you hardly had a chance to stop before things got completely out of hand.

No need to worry like today about HIV, and all these bizarre forms of sexually transmitted diseases. Getting a girl pregnant, or catching a dose of the "clap" was about all you had to concern yourself with. For me, I was so naive when it came to sex. I mean I actually thought I was doing girls a favor by NOT trying to do the nasty. I had no idea that the girls were faster in that area than I was. It did very little for my self-esteem and reputation not knowing how to satisfy a girl.

In reality, deep inside of me was the fear of the negative results from such behavior. The risks at that time did outweigh the pleasures derived from it.

There were no pornographic videos or "how to" movies to watch to learn about sex. Sure we had access to the old eight-millimeter, black and white movies where the actors wore a mask, and they kept their socks on, but there was no sound. My friend Jimmy Berber's old man used to keep plenty of dirty magazines, and movies in their house.

Jimmy had a fine ass sister also who was only 14-years-old. The only reason none of us ever liked going over to their crib was because his folks were kind of strange. They liked to go both ways so you never knew which one of his parents would try to hit up on you. Jimmy's mom was fine also, and she liked young boys. I guess compared to families that are dysfunctional today, you might say their family was quite normal.

I was not much of a sexual partner to any of my companions during high school. I had a hell of a rep so I was never without a girlfriend. Since no one likes to feel insecure, I stayed stoned all the time so I wouldn't have to deal with the real issues. Made life so much easier plus I could use the fact that I was too stoned to perform, and thus keep my dignity in tact. My image was all that mattered to me.

I often times wondered what the attraction to me really was. I never went out of my way to put on heirs or do anything special to be well liked. I was so insecure in a lot of ways towards the opposite sex, but it never stopped me from being popular.

The reason that I see this part of growing up as important is there are many youngsters that cannot express the root of their unhappiness or insecurities to anyone. As a result, they bury themselves deeper into the pit of despair and frustration. Then their situation is too far-gone before they realize what happened and more often than not, it is too late.

If given the opportunity to step outside the box for a moment in time, they would see that the baggage carried around is not that critical or significant to ruin one's life over. Unfortunately the understanding of what this all means to someone comes all too late to prevent so many sorrows and pains for yourself, loved ones and the community.

Being socially acceptable was all that mattered to me during those turbulent teenage years. The irony of that statement was that no one wanted to be caught hanging with a dope fiend except other dope fiends. I never saw it at the time, but when we all thought we were the hipsters and all, people of a more serious nature were laughing at us.

Lynn was only 15-years-old and I was 18-year-old. She was from another town so I saw her infrequently. Her cousins lived in New Castle so I met her at one of their parties. She was even faster than Linda was. Where did I keep finding these young girls that were ready to give up their "cookies" as soon as I had meet them?

Once her Mom found out that she was involved with a dope fiend, it didn't take long for Lynn's visits to end. I had no car so I could not go to visit her. Eventually after only three months, and screwing only once, we parted ways. I still have a senior class photo of hers that she signed back in 1970 an mailed to my parent's house.

Her Mom was so worried about the influence I would have had on her, that she let Lynn's next boyfriend from the Castle get past her parental judgment. He had started using drugs after he graduated high school, and wouldn't you know it Lynn began using heroin soon after. Goes to show parents cannot know for sure who is going to turn your child out.

After I was instructed to stop seeing Lynn, in '68, I would forget having any type of relationship with anyone until I was 21-years-old. The time was never there, and who wanted to spend time with a dope fiend except another dope fiend? So I spent my time around dykes, female dope fiends, and to get a free high now and then, good old Brown, the neighborhood fag was always an option.

It would be nothing for me to spend the night, when I needed a place to sleep, on the floor in Brenda's room. I would curl up on the floor at the foot of the bed that was occupied by her and Luanne, her "boyfriend!" I could not help but to have to listen to the two of them go at it all night. No, it was not a turn on. If you saw these two you'd understand. The little bit of sleep I got was better than no sleep at all.

I really missed the relationship of someone other than family members that cared about me. At the rate I was going I would not even have the family. Oh well. So I kept on getting high to forget how lonely, and unhappy I really was. Tomorrow would bring a brand new day.

TIME TO PAY MY DUES

"Damn! Who the fuck is banging on the door so loud?" Brown wanted to know.

No sooner than AC reached for the knob to open the back door to Brown's kitchen, Fuzzy managed to open it by himself. With the last ounce of strength that he had in him he tried to utter something then fell inside on the floor.

Fuzzy was a big strapping brother. But human nature being what it is, when you get stabbed several times, and you are trying to hold your intestines in your tee shirt; your ass is going down. I don't give a shit how big, and bad you are physically, behind something like that your ass is history. We thought the dude was dead when he hit he floor. Brown's first reaction was, "Ah shit, why here?" Now someone would have to call the police and all, and he certainly did not need the hassle.

The same old shit went down. One drug dealer versus another to see how many lives they could destroy for profit usually meant a beef now and then. I left before the cops came as did most of us, but heard later that day that Fuzzy ended up surviving. The son-of-bitch should have died as far as I was concerned. He was in my mind the worse kind of dealer—he preyed on kids.

Fuzzy was by far the lowest form of human scum there was. He used underage youngsters to deal for him. To those of us that still had an emotion or two left in our warped bodies, his actions violated our code of ethics. Those ethics were; go ahead and ruin your life, and body with narcotics, which was fine. But to inflict young kids with this poison was a sin, and those that felt it to be OK should be shown not one ounce of mercy.

Most of those cradle rockers lured their victims with all these false promises of making big money. Several of his dealers had quit high school, and never made it to the 11th grade. It hurt me personally to see that happen. I had known some of these kids by knowing their older brothers or sisters. I vowed that no matter how low I had become, selling dope was never going to be part of my character. Plus the time given out to dealers vs. users was something I knew I could not have handled. Hell, I had a hard enough time dealing with waiting in jail to go upstate to the "bigfoot" country as we used to say.

I pled guilty just so I could qualify for the State's bullshit program, and was sentenced on the 12th of May 1970, just two months after my arrest. Now there was nothing more for me to do but to sit back and wait to find out where I would be going to serve my sentence.

Once sentencing was imposed then I was moved to G-1 tier. This was for inmates waiting to be transported to their destination. I just kept laying low because out of the 20 inmates on the tier, three were sentenced for murder! Mind you, we all were minors. I just played a lot of cards, and I got to read the book, "In Cold Blood", in one day during a lock down for doing something I can't even remember.

I would like to have believed that during my 60 days on that tier, I realized how lucky I was to be going to a program. Everyone else was sentenced to prisons in upstate New York. I will never forget Willis Smith. At the age of 18 he was involved in an armed robbery of a train ticket office located just five minutes from of all places, the Nassau County Courthouses.

During the robbery, one of the other three participants shot the clerk and killed him. I never understood the need to shoot someone, AFTER they have given over the money. Willis got 7 ½ to 15 years in prison. Another inmate named Nixon got only five years for being present when his partner blew the side of a man's head off. Then there was Ramaldo Maldonado, who lucked out also. This crazy ass Puerto Rican only received five years for beating his co-worker to death over the desires of a woman. Gee, wasn't I the lucky one to be around so many nice guys all in the same place at the same time!

July rolled around, and I was starting to become impatient waiting my day to move on; not that I said anything to the authorities. Then the morning of July 11th, while playing basketball in the yard around 9:30, I heard over the speaker, "G-1-10 pack up!" This time around I knew what to do. I said my good-byes, slapped a few high five's, and gave my spot over to Cosmo who had winners anyway. I went back upstairs, packed, and gave away shit to the less fortunate that I couldn't take with me anyway. It was show time!

Mid-Hudson Rehabilitation Center was part of the Matawan State Hospital for the Criminally Insane. It consisted of four unused, all brick buildings, which were turned into a place for dope fiends to get their act together. This was just one of the several facilities that were set aside for the State program.

Twice a week you would be allowed a three-minute telephone call as part of the few privileges that they had to offer. One day in September when I got on the phone, after Dad accepted the charges, and we spoke for a while, I asked to speak to Mom. Dad's response to my question was quite shocking.

Other than Dad's 83-year-old father who died when I was only eight, I had never experienced a death of a family member. I could not fully grasp the emotion when you lose someone you love very much. Well Mom was not dead thank goodness, but she did move out of Rushmore Street and took my little sister Lisa with her. I had felt like I really fucked things up for good. I felt like shit. I felt so guilty. I felt so sad for Dad. I felt sad for everyone involved.

He sounded as though he was handling it well, but oh how I wished I could have been there with him to give comfort at a time like this. If only I had not starting messing my life up, and causing so many arguments between them. If only I had heeded the warning signs that were there, and intervened by cleaning up my act. Fuck it! There wasn't a damn thing I could do now so might as well deal as best I could.

Since I dear not show any emotion in front on the others, or the hacks, I just held my feelings in that same dark place that I had carved out for myself. I handed the phone back to officer Barns, whom I swore, was a member of the KKK, and then I went on to my room.

My guilt feelings could not last too long. I had to start thinking about a place I could come home to by the end of that month. This pathetic excuse of a program was offering, ready for this?

INSTANT AFTERCARE!

Was that not a joke or what? Here was a state run program designed to help you get your life back together, and become a productive citizen, and they are putting you back on the streets in 90 days. The poor aftercare officers were already underpaid, and overworked, and now here comes a new caseload every 90 days for them to monitor.

It was no secret that all of their eight facilities were overflowing with addicts. To alleviate some of the overcrowded situations, they had to come up with a solution and that was the best they could come up with. Now I had to write Dad and ask if I could come back home. If I had no place to go to, guess what? Rehabilitated or not, I would have been detained until I could provide to the powers to be a place to call home.

I was tickled to death that Dad's reply was favorable. I would not let him down ever again.

Stephen arrived in Mid Hudson within the next 48-hours of my arrival. One more time we were reunited by some act of negativity. The only positive thing that came from this was Mom could make one trip up the Hudson River every other Sunday and kill two stones with one bird! One visit she bought Granny, and because her name was not on the list of visitors they weren't going to let her in.

Mom told us afterwards that Granny cried in the car when she was told she would have to wait outside. By God they sure knew how to encourage rehabilitation by doing some cold shit like that to a family that drove two hours to visit. At 68-years-old, maybe they thought Granny might sneak some contraband in or try to help us escape.

Some of the less fortunate addicts preferred to delay their release date. I didn't understand at first the rationale behind doing something so stupid, but then there is ALWAYS a reason. In this case for a junkie, usually the first thing noticeable that deteriorates is their teeth. Some were worse than others, but if the state pulled out your choppers while you were in their care, then they were obligated to replace them. I mean I saw some serious acts of dental work during the little time I was there.

I knew not where they found these state dentists. They could have been apprentices or those who could do no better on the outside in private practice. Regardless of their credentials, the brothers looked at them as a blessing. That is why they would opt to wait until their false teeth were ready, and in place before they went back out into the world. One must protect one's image all the time.

Most of the guys would be walking around like zombies after being given these strong painkillers after they had their mouths butchered up. When the Novocain would wear off, and they couldn't stand the pain, down the hatch went the pills. What a pretty site seeing a bunch of dope fiends walking around high on painkillers while getting rehabilitated.

Group therapy twice a week was a joke for most of us. We had some college educated, blond, blue-eyed social worker, calling herself trying to encourage a bunch of drug addicts to rehabilitate. Her task was like trying to push a car up a hill with a rope. Totally impossible yet she tried. She had her job to do.

Yes it was mandatory that you went. However, most of us used to enjoy going only because she had nice thick thighs, and a great body. Every so often when she crossed her legs, and you got a shot at some thigh, you'd have some fantasies to take to the shower that evening. I personally thought she got her jollies by having a room full of horny men undressing her with their eyes.

"Why are you crying Belle?" I asked. "Is everything O.K.?"

Once she got herself together, she told me her and her boyfriend, who happened to be my roommate Sam, had a very bad fight. Sam had a bad temper. He was the son of a boxer, and so he was good with his hands. He broke a glass jar on the side of her face, and cut her ear. Shit, from the size of the gauze and bandages I was expecting she might become another Vincent Van Gogh!

I tried my best to comfort her. The reason she was so upset was not because of what he did to her, but because the hacks had taken him to solitary for three days as punishment. She felt it was her fault since she did something to tick him off. Belle was the ugliest fag that I had laid my eyes on. She looked like sin on a pickle truck! She didn't have near a tooth in the front of her head. Of course she had a purpose for that.

I learned to play pinochle so the ninety days went by pretty fast. My partner and me named Shorty used to spend eight to ten hours a day playing for cigarettes, which was used to barter for commissary. We were awesome. We might have lost one or two games but for the entire day we kicked some ass.

The usual shit was the order of the day. Blacks hung with blacks, Whites with whites. Hispanic with Hispanic. The only group that was kind of different was the "five percent's." They were part of the Nation of Islam. How a person could be five percent of something was beyond me, but out of respect I didn't question their beliefs. Bottom line was if they were practicing what they believed and preached, their asses wouldn't be in rehab for drug addiction.

They tried to brainwash you in to not eating "the poison animal", which was pork. They also were expected to fast. In an environment that used to serve food that was prepared next door at the insane asylum, if you did not have any money to buy commissary or barter with cigarettes you would not have to be asked to fast. Your ass would starve to death! Once I found pieces of metal objects in what we used to call "a murder burger."

Other than a small disturbance on 4C, my stay was quiet and uneventful.

ADDICTION IS NOT PREJUDICE

Before you are discharged, the State used to provide you with a State suit from a placed called Robert Hall. Even though they took your measurements, the jacket was too small, and the pants too big. They also gave you a pair of black shoes that would have let the world know you were a convict! Who gave a shit? It's only for the ride down state, and then you could set the clothes on fire if you wanted to.

All set with a place to go home to, new shoes, new suit and $40 waiting for me when I got to New York City, I left the 18th of October. The ride in the van was much nicer than the ride coming up that July when it had to be at least 98 degrees outside.

Since we got busted in March, the month known for cold and snow, I had to wear what clothing I went into the jail wearing.

That July, just picture yourself sitting in a station wagon in the seat that faced the back window directly in the sun on a 98-degree sunny day. For the safety of the officers that did the driving, you were shackled at the ankles as well as handcuffed at the wrists. Remember now, my arrested wardrobe consisted of wool turtleneck wool pants and a woolen houndstooth overcoat. The ride from the jail in East Meadow to Beacon, NY where Mid Hudson was had to be a little over two hours the way they drove. I did not know where I was being taken until I got there.

Little did I know that when I arrived in the Big Apple to report to my aftercare officer, all but $10 of the $40 was kept in their care. Well aint that just a bitch! I was counting on that money to get high with as soon as I got to the Castle. Then it dawned on me that the State knew what a dope fiend's intentions would be too.

Mr. Sands was a brother and was very nice. Too nice to have the type of job that he had. I kept getting these black men in my life that was overly nice to me. When I screwed up I felt so guilty for turning around and kicking them in the teeth.

I was allowed to report once a week on Long Island versus going to downtown Manhattan. He would have to drive out to Mineola where the probation offices for Nassau County were located. I felt for him as he lived all the way in Brooklyn, and would have to drive back and forth twice a week to handle his caseload.

I boarded the train for the ride out to New Castle. I could not wait to see my mom and my dad. Getting high was a priority, but not before seeing the folks. At least that's what I thought.

I would have made it to Rushmore Street if had I not run into George. He was so glad to see me that he almost started crying. He used to get all mushy at times, but that was just his nature. We hugged, and he got emotional while telling me how his oldest sister Joan had died from an overdose two weeks earlier. He must have forgotten that he wrote and told me, but I let him release anyway.

He meant well in his heart by offering to get me high. Forget that I had not had any heroin in my system in eight months, and that the shock from even a morsel could kill me right on the spot. Nonetheless like an asshole, I went with him to the bathroom in the gas station on Prospect Avenue to get off.

Of course I didn't die, but I felt so ashamed that I did not even make it home first before relapsing once again. We even used the belt, and the tie from the State issued attire to tie our arms with. I could just imagine if I had died the paper would have read:

> "Dope fiend overdoses several hours after his release from State program, and never even got a chance to change out of his State clothes into his own."

When I finally did make it home, Dad knew from just looking at me, and the way I was talking, that I had gotten high. He didn't over react though. He more than likely wanted our relationship, and my life to work this time around. This act on his part made me feel even more like a shit. After Thanksgiving, I was back in the treatment program with those that failed their urine test. It was just a two-week stay in the city facility. The usual hanging out and watching television, and playing cards keep me occupied. Therapy was not offered; God forbid.

Once I got out, I decided to try one of those programs that were popular in the 70's like Phoenix House. There was one on 85th street near 7th avenue. It would definitely be on a voluntary basis and only for the day care program. I wasn't THAT ready to get my act together. My first visit there Mom was with me to make sure I went. By going it kept both of them off my back; at least for a while.

I used to like to go just to hear the stories shared in-group. I mean there was plenty of personal stuff thrown out there in the circle. I would sit and listen, and then I would tell my little middle class sob story to act like I belonged. At lunchtime, I'd go out with one or two of the other dope fiends and get high. We'd always made it back on time since you only had one hour. The counselor's favorite saying when everyone returned was "O.K., who had junk for lunch?" Most of us would lie, and unless you were so stoned you couldn't sit up straight, they could not prove you weren't high.

The afternoons went by pretty quickly, and then it was time to head to the subway on 81st street to make my way back to New Castle until the next day. That was my daily routine Monday through Friday. It was like having a 9 to 5 job with an hour for lunch, except I wasn't getting paid.

Since the location was on 85th street, we had some pretty sophisticated junkies in our group. Eight-fifth street was definitely not like being in Harlem. This was a pretty affluent part of Manhattan. I met a lot of people using drugs that had a lot of serious hang-ups. It did not matter what status or social circles I traveled in, I learned that a dope fiend is a dope fiend—PERIOD! Drugs were not prejudice.

In the group I had attended there was Dave. He was a white, private, parochial, 5th grade school teacher who was gay, and shooting heroin. He confessed one day how he had been attracted to another guy in the group. He said it started when the two of them would walk to the subway station together. The dude, who was the object of his desires, almost fell off his chair. He had no earthly idea that he was being drooled over by this highly educated queer.

There was a white brother and sister who were screwing each other.

We had a black female who had both of her parents shooting up with her. She was only thirteen years old.

The grossest story I heard was a guy sharing how he would have sex with his own mother.

The counselors were super cool recovering addicts. They had to be to work there. Most of them graduated from the program with no less than two years in treatment. Their stories were even better than ours were, and they were sincere in trying to help the cause. They also cut you NO slack regarding your excuses for getting high.

This young brother who I used to go out and get high with during lunch had a sure enough sob story to tell. He had most of us on the verge of tears as he confessed his story of why he began using drugs.

Seems his mother had left his 11-month-old baby brother alone in his crib one day. She had nobody to watch him, and she needed to go up to the school because this brother was misbehaving. When she returned home about an hour later, she found that the baby had suffocated under a pillow. I remember he even had to stop talking because he broke down, and cried uncontrollably. Several of us got up and went over to console him. My thinking was "Wow the brother made a breakthrough of his old baggage that he had been harboring for years."

The counselors didn't utter a single word during this moment.

To my surprise, after everyone sat down, and he had gotten himself together, the counselors responded to his story with little to no compassion. In fact all three counselors told him he was full of shit! He was told that his excuse was bullshit. They even went further and called his mother a stupid ass person to leave a baby home alone under any circumstances. I mean they talked about the lady like she should have been placed before a firing squad for what she had done.

That was some cold-hearted shit they shot at him in his time of feeling his lowest. I wondered if these counselors had any compassion whatsoever. I got kind of pissed off but kept my mouth shut as usual.

After thinking about what they said on the subway ride home that afternoon, I had to admit that they were right. Instead of him blaming himself all those years for his brother's death it was not his fault, but his mother's. The point they were trying to convey to everyone was; dope fiends can, and will always find a reason for their actions. It mad no difference if they are valid or not, an excuse is an excuse, and that is all there was to it.

After I had gotten out of the drug lifestyle, I was surprised at how many of my fellow classmates from high school ended up strung out. At first I used to say, "fuck 'em," because many of them acted like they were better than me when I was addicted. While their candy-ass, goody two shoe reputations were cool in their eyes, I knew that at anytime or given the right circumstances, their but for the grace of God could go any one of them. So I was not surprised that while I was getting my ass out, they were just getting in. I always remembered a saying; "There is nothing worse than a dope fiend, other than an OLD dope fiend."

THE THRILLS ARE
BEGINNING TO FIZZLE

After working odd jobs around April of 1971, my new residence was a dorm room at Stony Brook University. My late friend, Jimmy, was a student there, but he was shacking up with his old lady in her room. He was paying for a room anyway, so he let me stay in his room for free. Well free at least until I made a hustle, and had some drugs, then I had to turn him on.

During the one month I lived there, I was starting to give less value to my life than any other time since I started using. One night about four of us was in the room and someone had given Keith some hashish. Like fools we tried to cook it down into a liquid form to shoot up. We succeeded in doing so and it looked just like mud. Of course I just had to argue that since I had the "works" I got to shoot up first.

I had smoked hash before, but never tried to shoot it into my veins, and here I was arguing to be the Guinea pig. Of course I got no argument from Keith and Jimmy. Why should they argue? They had more at stake to lose than I did at the time, so if I died they'd know not to be stupid enough to do the same thing.

Now this rational way of thinking was not always valid. Once Stephen went out on me in a motel room, and I could not bring him around. There he was lying across the bed with his eyes closed, mouth hanging open, making these labored breathing noises; and I went ahead and shot my portion anyway. This type of behavior was not unusual. Dudes would go out on ya all the time if the dope was that good.

The rule of thumb for an addict was if the heroin was that good to cause someone to overdose, then it just had to be what we called a "smoker!" I mean addicts would go out of their way to find the same thing if they heard that someone overdosed and died from a particular dealer's stuff. Talk about getting the most bangs for your buck.

If this wasn't the sickest way of thinking, then not trying to call for help for my own brother before I got high first was even worse. He came around on his own. It just took a matter of a few minutes.

In May I got arrested again. It was for one stinking bag of dope that two policemen saw me throw on the ground when they pulled along side me in their car. I was walking along Prospect Avenue around three o'clock in the morning after the bar closed. I waited too damn long to get rid of it since it was all I had for the next morning's fix. I was holding on for dear life.

I argued that it was not mine because it was not in my possession. I didn't recognize one of the officers so I figured he was a rookie, and probably had no seniority. That was probably why he was on the graveyard shift. After they stopped laughing at my Perry Mason defense, off I went to Mineola.

At headquarters they were nice to me. After so many times there, once they got to know you they'd let you take your own fingerprints so they wouldn't have to get their hands dirty. When it was time to go to my sleeping arrangements, the rookie cop approached me and pulled me off to the side.

The police were looking for Georgia Red, one of the many dealers in the Castle. He got word that they had a warrant for his arrest, and took the first thing smoking. It was commonplace for the police to offer some leniency if you gave up a name or two.

It was my turn to laugh now.

I told the officer that he had better get with the program if he was to survive the streets. Since it was just the two of us, I reminded him that the time to offer a deal was BEFORE this point in the arrest process.

The rule was to take a suspect and ride them around for a while away from the neighborhood. Then, after you gave up the information that was asked for, valid at the time, they would drop your ass off so that no one in the Castle would see anything. There would be no way an arresting officer could cut you loose after you have been fingerprinted, and had your name put in "the book." And all that talk about putting in a good word to the judge when you got to court was horseshit. No, I wasn't telling him shit even though I did not know where Georgia Red was anyway.

I could tell when the officer turned two shades of red that he was pissed off. He could not even kick my ass since I had already been photographed, and any bruises would have required an explanation. I was not going anywhere by then so I could care less about his feelings.

As usual, I would always think that getting busted was a sign from above. When the time would come to act positively on these visions was another story. I was really starting to feel myself going further and further down into the valley of being a real low life.

The feelings I once had for this type of lifestyle weren't there for me anymore. I was being pulled in two different directions. I knew I was not cut out to exist day in and day out just being a dope fiend. I was not sure how to turn this shit around before I got into some real serious trouble. Not only did I not know how to change myself, I just about fucked up every opportunity I received from those that tried to help me.

I got sick to my stomach this one evening in particular as I was hanging up at Don's place. Sheldon came into the bar to announce that there was this lady who had passed out in the back seat of someone's car. She was stone cold drunk and was taking turns with different guys.

My sex life wasn't about anything and when your "collar gets tight" you have no respect for yourself. All you want is some tension release. I followed Craig out to the car. Sure as shit, someone was just finishing up when we got there. When he opened the door, I was surprised to discover that it was Helen who lived at old man Brown's place. Even though he liked men especially young ones, every so often when he wanted to exhibit his manhood, she was his main squeeze.

You have to first understand what Helen looked like. She looked like someone beat her in the face with a bag of nickels. She was drunk and smelling like Chinese cheddar and a sight for sore eyes. Damn Bruce are things that bad? I answered my own question and knew there was no way, regardless of how hard up I was, I was going near her stuff. While I was making my decision, by now there had to be ten men that came out to the car for some of Helen's stink loving.

The scenario got more comical when Jody came outside. He was one of four brothers who were in seventh heaven working as garbage collectors in the Castle. They all worked for the same company and you never saw them without a smile on their faces. They lived in this nasty, filthy house one block from the bar on New York Ave.

Their crib was a house that had a lot of stuff going on, but nothing compared to Brown's place. One of the brothers' name Jamie was strung out on drugs. Jody liked to gamble and chase women even though he was married with two kids. Their parents sold drugs. The good sons that they were, they would always bring home all kinds of junk they would find on their routes and leave it right in the front yard. One time they had all the fixtures to have created a bathroom outside.

Anyway, Jody decided instead of screwing her in the car, he would take her to his house in the basement. Surely it would be more comfortable. His folks wouldn't know much less care since they stayed drunk all the time. You should have seen how he just picked her up like one of those big sacks of flour. He damn near hit her head as he placed her in his beat up old car. The poor woman didn't have a stitch of drawers on and she never once woke up.

I rode in the back seat and thought more and more as to how people could be so cruel. Being hard up is one thing, but to screw something as awful as her was pitiful. I bet she was a hurt puppy the next morning. We've all seen her drunk before, but she honestly looked like she was dead. No I never participated but I knew that it was time for me to make some serious changes real quick.

While sitting in the "bullpen" waiting my turn to go across the hall for arraignment everyone was sitting around telling the biggest lies about their crimes. I couldn't help but notice this very petite guy sitting next to me. He seemed in a different world. He never said a word to anyone. He was dressed nice in a sport jacket, shoes, a nice shirt and pants. I figured him at best to be a drunk arrested for D.U.I.

When the cage opened and they called his name a strange thing took place. As soon as the door opened for the court officers to escort him across the hall to court, all I heard them saying were, "Get back! Get back! Let us through!" There were camera flashes going off everywhere in the hallway. "Damn," I thought. "I wonder what the hell he did to cause this much notoriety?" We asked the guards what the deal was. They told us the previous afternoon he shot his estranged wife and mother-in-law to death in the parking lot of the hospital where she worked as a nurse.

The story went: he arrived at the hospital after her shift around 3 PM to try and talk to her about visitation rights for their 3-year-old daughter. One thing led to another and he shot her point blank in the chest. Meanwhile her mother, who had been waiting in he car with the little girl to pick her up, heard the shots and ran up on the scene and he killed her too.

After hearing the gory details I knew why he had been so quiet. He was probably in shock over what he had done. When he was brought back in the bullpen since he had no bail, everyone slowly moved away from him. Since I had been sitting next to him all day I was more curious than afraid of him. I had never been that close to someone who had just killed two people in less than 24 hrs. Like the fool that I still was, I started to check him out to see if I could see some of the blood on his clothes.

We later found out that he was one of New York's finest. Yes, the man had been a cop. He had been on disability leave for six months due to mental problems yet still allowed to carry his service revolver.

My bail was only $100 cash, which I had on me so I went home, and skipped having to go to jail.

I went back to driving cabs again, but this time it was with a more reputable company. They had no provisions to let me sleep in one of their cabs so my new home by the end of May was the Westbury train station. The benches were hard as a rock, but then again they weren't designed for sleeping either. I never once worried about getting mugged or anything. I felt absolutely safe in my new surroundings. So long as I woke up by 6 A.M., before the morning rush hour, it wasn't too bad. The whistle from an express train that did not stop in Westbury used to be my alarm clock.

I recall one morning for some reason I overslept. How you could sleep so soundly as to not hear a train whistle blowing practically right in your ear was a mystery to me.

When I yawned as I woke up, and opened my eyes, I looked around to a standing room only waiting room. The look on some of the commuter's faces told me that they were pissed for having to stand since I was taking up about five seats on the bench.

This was more embarrassing than the graduation thing because I had no idea how long these people had been staring at me. I sat up straight, stretched and played it off like I fell asleep waiting for the train. I was good at acting like something was not what it appeared to be. In my world everyone else was crazy but me. To save face even though I did not know these people, when the train arrived I boarded with everyone else like I was going to work. I hid amongst the crowd so I wouldn't have to pay and got off at the next stop less than 5 minutes away.

One morning I decided to go up to the mall in Haysville to do some shoplifting and I didn't feel like walking the five miles. I had stolen from just about every business along the route to the mall so checking for possible opportunities to steal anything was not an option.

I stuck out my thumb to hitch a ride and low and behold, this nice elderly white lady in a blue Volkswagen stopped. What a nice jester on her part and she was even going all the way to the mall. As I opened the front passenger door, I noticed she had her pocketbook on the floor right behind my seat. This couldn't be for real. Not in my lifetime would an easy situation present itself to me at the right time.

This lady must be some kind of nut to pick up a black male even though it was broad daylight. By not moving her bag over to her side behind her seat was a rip off waiting to happen.

As we drove and made conversation, I eased my right hand between my seat and the door and placed my hand inside her bag. Once inside the pocketbook, I took her wallet out and bought it ever so carefully back up to my side and into my coat pocket. This all took place while I was looking her dead in her face while we talked.

Once we reached the entrance to the mall, I asked to be let out. My excuse was I needed to stop at the Post office across from the mall and she had been more than kind to carry me this far. After she stopped and I got out, I thanked her and told her to make sure her doors were locked. One cannot be too trustworthy you know. We said our good-byes and I waved as she drove off no doubt feeling a sense of pride that she did her good deed for the day.

Of course the reason why I didn't want to go into the mall was that once she discovered her wallet missing, I'd be a sitting duck in a captive pond with no where to run or hide. I took off as fast as I could and headed directly to the Haysville train station six blocks away. The station was elevated and quite big so I thought I'd be safe until the train came. I was so glad it came within 10 minutes since the police station was nearby and if the call went out with my description, I'd be on my way to jail. I boarded the train and headed back out to Stony Brook.

THE CURTAIN IS ABOUT TO COME DOWN SLOWLY

I was over at Marcia's and my other cousin Myrna's house one-day right after the Memorial Day weekend. Both still lived at home and had small children of their own. They were going to take a ride up to my favorite place—the mall. Their folks agreed to watch the two boys who were five and three at the time, but they had to take Sonja, the 2-year-old. I asked if I could take a ride with them and both agreed I could if I gave my word I would not do anything stupid.

When we arrived at the mall, Marcia went to take care of what business she had and left Sonja in the car with Myrna. She would only be gone a few minutes. Again she warned me not to do anything stupid that would get them in trouble. She knew from my Arizona trip that nothing would surprise her about me anymore. I promised I would be on my best behavior and got out the car to go into Gertz department store. She told me that if I was not back when she was ready to leave I could get home the best way I knew.

That only pressured me to do my shoplifting a little quicker than usual. What that equated to was I had no time to be careful. The race was on now to do my thing and beat Marcia back to the car. I always enjoyed a challenge so off I went. I went into the store like I was on Supermarket Sweep! The style at the time was nylon tee shirts and boxer shorts in a variety of colors for men and pantyhose were the thing all women would buy from you.

I came back to the car in less than 10 minutes and asked Myrna to put the goods under her seat. She should have said no but she was always the adventurous type since we were kids, so to her this was exciting. With the meter still running, I went through the shopping plaza like the bandit that I was. I mean I must have zipped in and out of at least 10 stores without spending no more than a minute in each and stealing nothing.

Instead of just going back to the car and calling it a day, I had to go back into Gertz to steal some more pantyhose. I sensed the store detective was following me so I didn't go immediately back to the car. I was surprised my cousins hadn't left yet. When I walked back and forth in the parking lot in between cars for a few minutes, like I was looking for mine, I headed back to the car. As soon as I put my hand on the door handle, I was caught. Little Sonja watched as I was handcuffed and led away back in to the store.

I was dragged through the store to the security office with my arm twisted behind my back. He had his other hand holding the back of my pants so tight it felt like my balls were coming out through my belly button. There was another store detective that had his back so I knew I couldn't even try to make a run for it. Everyone in the store was staring and I felt like I was on display like a zoo animal.

The two of them laughed about how they saw me the first time I came in the store and stole the underwear and was about to arrest me then. But then they saw me go back in to the plaza and they followed me in and out of every store I went in. They said they had never experienced a thief come back to steal from the same store within 10 minutes.

This was no big deal so I figured the best option was to cooperate and I told them that if they went to the car and asked, my cousin would just give them their merchandise. Maybe they would let me go with a warning. My thinking was my cousins would be gone by now or be good citizens and just bring the stuff back on their own.

Still clinging as I usually did to what little faith I had, I prayed for a miracle. I did not want to go back to jail three weeks after my last arrest. My chances of walking that day went completely out the window as I head Myrna's voice screaming, "Get your hands off me you pig! I know my rights and you searched my car without a warrant!" I thought to myself how many motherfuckers she must have called him before they got to the security office. I knew right then and there that any hope of them cutting me some slack was dead in the water.

What began as a simple trip to the mall turned into a disaster. Marcia ended up finally driving home with Sonja to break the news to Uncle Will and Aunt Beatrice. Myrna and I got a free ride to the precinct. This was the Second precinct in Woodbury this time, and not the one in Mineola. Lord knows I did not want to see detective Raymond again.

By the time we arrived, Uncle Will was standing on the steps right in front of the entrance to the precinct. He probably had ten grand in his pocket to bail his darling youngest out of jail. I felt so sorry for him as I saw in his eyes just how scared he was and did not know what was going to happen next.

When we were bought in right past where he was standing, he kept saying to me, "You know what to say Bruce. You have been through this before. Tell them she didn't do anything. It was all your fault."

He was talking a mile-a-minute so I just let it go in one ear and out the other. He was right. However, had she just given up the merchandise instead of doing everything short of talking about the guy's mother, she wouldn't be here in the first place. Of course I kept my thoughts and comments to myself. I had caused enough trouble up until then, so why make matters worse. Some things are better left unsaid.

The store detectives knew that she wasn't involved, but no matter what I said it was a personal thing now. She was definitely going to have to go to court. They gave her an appearance ticket for the next day's arraignment. That meant she could go home and come back in the morning. I asked for one also and the detectives just looked at me and smiled. One thing I could say for myself was that I would exhaust all my resources and was not going down without a fight. Most of the time I would lose but hey, that's life.

So as I watched my relatives leave, I took the ride to Mineola. At least I got there early since it wasn't even 8 PM and I was able to claim a bench and didn't get stuck on the floor again.

I really thought long and hard this time about putting an end to all this madness. No, not the serious end to it all just the part that was killing me. If only I could have mustered up the strength and resolve to say no to drugs I'd be in seventh heaven. I knew deep down inside that I wasn't cut out for this type of lifestyle and I always seemed to get a lucky break. Just the thought of going to prison scared the shit out me, so why was I still out there tempting fate?

The lock up for some reason got so crowded that night; they moved some of us over to the jail until the next morning. I was sick so sleep wasn't part of my program. I couldn't have slept even if I wanted to, so I stayed up all night being fascinated by this elderly con man from Brooklyn. The man spent his entire adult life conning people. That was his job. He told me he never put in an honest day's work after he turned 17. He promised if we both were released in the morning that he'd give me $20 for my pocket. He had a bankroll when he got busted with his partner trying to con an elderly woman at the Green Acres shopping mall in Valley Stream.

The next morning at the arraignment aunt Beatrice was there with Myrna since my uncle was at the office healing folk. My aunt shot me the meanest look I ever received from anybody much less your own family.

I lucked out after I gave the judge some hard luck bullshit story about being a college student trying to make a better life for myself. I was wearing a sweatshirt with the Stony Brook logo so I took a shot at using it to my advantage. Since he had documents to show I had priors and out on bail just a few weeks earlier, it must have been a tough decision to release me on my own recognizance. He must have had a child in college himself or just in a good mood that day. What a lucky break for me. I was happier that I would be getting $20 from the "old man" if he was released also.

Myrna had never been in trouble in her life so she was continued free in her parent's custody until our court date. The "old man" and his partner were released also, so it was my lucky day all around.

While I was getting my belongings from the property room, I asked my aunt for a lift back to New Castle. It was a shame I couldn't even use the term, "a lift home," since in a sense I was considered homeless. At first she said no, then she said she would, but she was leaving as soon as Myrna's paperwork was completed.

I knew it would be a little longer for the brother to sign for his property, so I had the audacity to ask Aunt Beatrice if she would just wait a few minutes so I could take care of something. I could tell she was livid that I had the nerve to ask for anything after she went against her better judgment in the first place. She said if I wasn't downstairs in the parking lot in 10 minutes, she was leaving. Sounded fair enough to me.

Seems as though the property clerk knew my situation and was taking his sweet ass time checking over the "old man's" stuff. He was a man of his word though. He peeled off a twenty spot but not before giving me some sound advice. He advised me to get off the dope and use my brain versus my body. He told me it mattered not what I did for a living, legal or illegal, I'd never be successful as long as I was using dope. He shook my hand wished me well and made me promise I would not use the money for drugs.

I gave my word, only this time for some strange reason I meant it. I felt that I owed him something but did not know why. We went our separate ways, and I never once asked nor did he offer to tell me his name. He and his partner were kind of like the Lone Ranger and Tonto also.

I almost fell down the courthouse stairs taking two at a time, trying not to miss my ride. A second later I'd have blown it. I had no choice but to accept the long lecture from my aunt for the entire 15-minute ride back to Prospect Ave. She was adamant when she asked that I not darken her door again until I got myself together. She didn't even want me to ask for a ride if I saw my cousins on the street.

As hurt as I felt, I agreed to not bother them anymore and held no animosity towards a parent just trying to protect her children. I knew I had crossed the line by doing something so stupid, especially with one of her grandchildren in the car at the time.

As they drove away something told me to heed the "old man's" advice and give this shit up now. Even though the man was dishonest all of his adult life, he didn't live to be 62 years old being anybody's fool or taking drugs. A dope fiend would not have given up $20 or even that kind of advice to someone they knew, much less a total stranger. Somehow this all began to make sense to me. That's when I saw just what kind of people we were and I realized that I did not like it.

You begin to live so deep into your own sick world, that you never see how dirty, nasty, stinking and sickly you look. I began to think back on all the times Stephen or myself would show up to my Mom's workplace and wonder why she started asking us not to come by there anymore. Her coworkers became her dear friends and out of respect for her, they kept what they felt inside to spare her feelings. Poor Mom was always embarrassed of both her sons.

I have often wondered who this man was that touched me in such a way that no one else had. Why was he moved from the lockup to the jail that night along with me? What made me start to talk to him? How could he have known my heart to even imagine that I would take advice from a stranger? I was so conditioned to be skeptical of others that I never even tried to listen to anything positive they had to say. Why did any of these circumstances take place that 7th day of June 1971?

I wish I could say I didn't use the $20 to get high.

THE ROAD TO RECOVERY IS ABOUT TO BEGIN

Things started to change within my circle of friends around the beginning of June of '71. Tommy was my best friend and partner in crime since 1967; however, we began to go our separate ways. He was a very troubled brother who had absolutely no respect for women whatsoever. Having a mother that was a high-class call girl more than likely had a lot to do with his hang-ups.

We used to do everything together and like me, he had a knack for smelling where money was. We would be riding down the street and he'd yell to the driver to pull over. Hell, he would be out of the car before it even came to a halt. More often than not, he'd be dead right. We used to have our share of arguments if he felt I withheld some money from him. If I got a moneybox or a wallet and had to meet up with him several blocks away, he would never believe I was honest about the amount that I got. He'd swear I took something extra for myself.

He and I skipped the morning session of school one day. I was a senior and he was a junior but we were thick as thieves anyway. We only needed time out of school in the morning to get stoned and hang out at Alma's apartment with Carol and Maxine. Pot made your inhabitions go out the window, so after we all got high, he went in a bedroom with Alma and I into another with Carol. Maxine was married while she was in high school so we didn't want to screw a married woman.

My sense of humor was always on the money and with some pot and wine, look out! While Tommy and Alma were in the bedroom getting it on, the door was cracked open just a little. All I saw was his little high yellow ass working hard and she was moaning with pleasure. I called Maxine and Carol over to sneak a peek and while they were looking through the opening, I pushed them and the door opened and they both fell in on the floor. Tommy was pissed as he was just about to make his sperm donation and Alma was so embarrassed. I couldn't stop laughing and Tommy did eventually speak to me after we got back to school that afternoon.

To illustrate how demented we both were, he got mad at me after I "skin popped" heroin first without him. Here I was the 17-year-old who as a child used to be so scared of getting a needle, I once ran out of a doctor's office with my Mom in pursuit. So sticking one under my skin myself was hard for even me to imagine doing. In Tommy's mind it was as if I were a traitor or something. Since we started snorting heroin together, it was expected that we graduate to the next level at the same pace. So to get even with me, he went ahead and "mainlined" five months later with Arnold Blackburn.

Boy, talk about payback being a bitch. I could have killed him and I was truly hurt when he showed me the tiny needle mark where he broke his cherry. Going right into the vein was the ultimate for a drug user. He had finally taken the big plunge and the thought of doing such a thing without his partner was devastating to me.

So what did I do in return? The very next day after he told me his news, I just had to experience flirting with death myself to catch up to him. My first time shooting heroin into my veins was in the winter of '67. It just wouldn't seem right that my best friend should be strung out without me. Arnold was more than happy to let us use his place.

Just around the same time in '71 when I was contemplating getting my life together, Tommy had gone off by himself and robbed a bank at gunpoint. He was such a smooth thief in the night, so the thought of him doing something to that magnitude just blew me away. Had we still been hanging tough like in the old days, I could have been right there with him. My gut feelings had paid off. He was starting to become careless with his shit and I knew he was headed for some big time. Better him than me!

When he got out after 48 months behind the prison wall, he was even more fucked up than before he went in. He got right back in to the same ole thing and after two trips to a mental hospital, he was released only to jump out of an eight-story hotel window in 1976. He was only twenty-five-years-old.

The days of fun and petty crimes were no longer there. Seems as though the time to come to the cross road of my addiction was staring me right in the face. The bottom line was; if I was going to stay out there, I would have to be prepared to do some real heavy time in jail. I knew what I had and needed to do and if not now then sooner would have been even better.

The real deal was; life was playing for keeps and only the fools would find themselves totally fucked up. All the slack and considerations that society was allowing in the name of compassion and rehabilitation had gone out like button shoes. The system was tired of being made to look stupid by us and they would not stand for it too much longer. I sensed the ax waiting to fall. I wasn't sticking around to have my head handed over on a silver platter to the establishment. Naw, they could kiss my ass.

TOUCHED BY ANGELS AND DID NOT EVEN KNOW IT

Although I was still hanging out and doing my thing for the next three days, I could not stop hearing a voice saying, "You need to do something now before it is too late." I mean it was 24/7. Each time I shot up, I felt more and more like I could do without it. Something about my inner being came alive in me and I felt myself gaining the courage, strength and desire to give recovery another try and this time mean it.

On the fourth day of this tug of war with these feelings, Butch was on the corner gathering his regular passengers for the ride to Harlem to make our buys. Since I was one of his regulars to ride in his tired old beat up 1965 red Plymouth Valiant, I knew my seat was confirmed.

Butch's brain was always in a holding pattern. I mean his mind was out there where the buses didn't run! He was just another country ass northern transplant that thought he could make a killing selling drugs. If you saw this car and where he lived, you'd agree that he was not too successful in his chosen profession.

He made the all time list of the dumbest things anyone had done in New Castle. In 1972 he was sentenced to 15 years for selling drugs to undercover agents and then appealed when it turned out that his lawyer had never passed the bar exam! And no, his name was not Elwood Low! His new lawyer that handled his appeal was no better. He ended up getting 10 more years at his new trial.

I had my money together, over $100, and got in the car with the others for the ride to the city. This time, even the ride did not have the same feeling as before. I would usually be part of the bullshit talk and laughter, but this time I just sat quietly and stared out the window. As we crossed the Triborough Bridge, I had my mind already made up and NOTHING was going to change it. I wasn't going to buy any heroin or cocaine.

We arrived on 117th street to our regular connection at a newspaper and candy stand. The dealer would give you your merchandise in a brown paper bag when you bought your candy. When it was my turn, I asked for $40 worth of methadone. My fellow addicts looked at me in astonishment. To not see Bruce buy any drugs was out of character for me and I was asked why I wasn't indulging. I just opened my mouth and said with a calmness that I had never felt before, "I don't want to!" It was that simple.

The $40 worth of this synthetic drug that some egghead came up with to make you a legalized addict would last for five days. Methadone became popular when it was evident that the state programs weren't worth shit other than to employ people. It was just like this Country to go to a plan "B" when plan "A" fails.

Put the finger in the dike was the cry from the citizens that were being victimized by all the crime imposed on them by addicts. So the solution was to make up in a laboratory, only God knows where, a drug that is supposed to take away the cravings for heroin. The rationale was that at least the druggies can work in society as long as they got their daily fix of methadone.

Now what happens when an addict sells their allotment on the black market for money to get drugs? You now have a market for another product that dealers could offer in their line of goods. If people ever wonder why the drug problem in this country will NEVER cease to exist, here is a good example.

I bought a soda from the candy store also and immediately took one tab to take the chills off. I felt a vote of confidence that made me believe that I could do this thing right. Having dope right under my nose yet not giving in to the temptation was a high that I hadn't experienced in a long long time and it felt damn good. This time the ride across the Triborough Bridge to buy drugs was a one-way journey.

When I got back to the Castle, I knew the next step in my self-help process was to get out of the environment before the ether wore off. The only problem was where could I go? I wore out my welcome at my grandparent's. They let me stay there for about three weeks in March while I worked in Kew Gardens delivering party supplies.

I thought the folks in Jamaica were a little paranoid having me around. Nope, couldn't go back to Phoenix since my cousin had moved back to New Castle. My options were few, yet I knew the only way to survive was to leave New Castle on the hurry ups.

During that time in my life I was feeling like I had nowhere to turn. I thought about the saying, "I aint seen times this hard until I saw a rat sitting over in a corner nibbling on a red onion, and crying like a natural baby!'

I hadn't considered the relatives in Wyandanch. I think I had too much respect for them to bother them with my problems. Uncle Bobby had enough on his plate trying to make his community a better place for black folk. That alone is stress enough to last for a lifetime. He also had his heart attack the June prior and he did not need any more stress in his life.

He'd give a stranger the shirt off his back if necessary so it wasn't about thinking he would refuse me. However, this was not the time to be all sentimental and considerate. I was desperate and had to pull out all the stops. This shit was serious. I had to cry out for help. He was a blessing to have in the family and no one needed him now more than me.

I fished out a dime from my dirty pants pocket and called him. After the third time of talking myself out of letting the phone ring more than once, I rang until I got an answer. His secretary Mollie answered the phone and put me on hold as he was on another call. I was glad Mollie was sober that day; otherwise like in times past, she'd disconnect you and never know it. When I heard his voice say, "Hey man! What's up?" I knew I could not back out of what I needed to ask.

He listened and I am sure he could sense the desperation in my voice since I was talking a mile a minute. Without even a hesitation, he said, "sure man. I can introduce you to a lady that works with me that can hook you up in a program." He also said something that I have held dear to my heart and will never forget. He said, "I know everyone in the family right now is down on you, but I'll never turn my back on you. OK?" He made me promise to catch the next train out and to come to his office at the community action center where he worked as the director.

I remember crying after I hung up. I just knew with all these blessings and signs from above were telling me that it was my time to shine. Another first for me was that my mind and my body were in synch to handle rehabilitation. This made for an equation that could only equal positive results.

With brown paper bag with all my belongings in hand, I walked down to the same train station that had been my home earlier that year and caught the train out to Wyandanch. The 45-minute ride seemed an eternity. I was nervous yet confident. I could think of nothing else but success. Yes, this lifestyle has seen the last of me. I'm out of here.

Mrs. Ruth was a very nice lady. Her and Uncle Bobby did not always see eyeball to eyeball on matters of business, but the respect for each other was there. She had a heart of gold. I know she could have been nice to me just because I was her boss' nephew, but I did not get those vibes. My first impression was her intentions were honorable. Her job was to outreach and help those in the community that were in need. With drugs in the all Black community, there was no bigger need than getting those addicted some help.

She took me straight out to a town called Patchogue, which was about a twenty-five-minute drive. There I would be screened at the intake office of a program she was affiliated with called DETER. It stood for Determined Effort To Encourage Rehabilitation. Later after I got there we joked that it stood for Don't Expect To Eat Regularly. Mrs. Ruth knew from experience that while an addict's desire to kick the habit is fresh and sincere, time is important. Her nephew was a recovered addict and worked on the staff there, so I knew I would be accepted.

Their residence facility was in Ellenville, a small sleepy town in upstate New York. The town was about a 2 ½ to 3-hour drive depending on who was driving. Mrs. Ruth talked about how nice it was all the way out there so I couldn't wait to go.

I met Louis, Juan, Kyle Rosenberg, Sean and Bertha. I felt like I was at the United Nations. Just goes to show the that the common denominator regardless of race, religion or nationality is DOPE! I had to be interviewed and Mrs. Ruth waited to make sure everything was OK before she left. Heaven forbid she go back to Uncle Bobby all confident that she took good care of me, only to get a call that I ran off after she left.

I had been through the usual bullshit from other programs so I knew what answers they wanted to hear. I also agreed to what they called a "contract" that required me to shave all my hair off. This was to see how committed you were to your rehab so they would think of something that they thought you valued a lot. I had a big Afro at the time so that is what they went after.

But, there was one problem. A big problem.

Unfortunately I was told that I had to finish with the withdrawals first before they could accept me. Since they could not be responsible for any health problems if I got really bad off while in their care, they could be held libel. They also were not authorized to dispense methadone or even allow it on the property, so I had to complete the doses, be clean, and then I could hang out with them.

I prayed that this would not be an obstacle that I couldn't handle. I did not want anything to stand in my way. I was there ready, willing, able, and most of all had support from my family. What else did I need to prove?

Louis told me that if I could be done with my methadone and was totally clean by Monday, they'd send me upstate that afternoon. He truly was a sincere therapist and knew Uncle Bobby personally also. Since this Friday and I had already been drug free for 24 hours, I knew this would be a piece of cake. The only thing I worried about now was getting through the weekend and not relapsing. For Uncle Bobby, his challenge was to convince Aunt Helen to let me stay with them until Monday. She was kind of the nervous type. Although they had allowed different people to live with them from time to time on different occasions, a drug addict was never one of them. I was her nephew and all, but a drug addict is just what the name implies regardless of who you were.

Uncle Bobby was smart enough to know that if I went back to the neighborhood he might never see me again. He convinced Aunt Helen to let me hang out with them just for the weekend. The issue was not why she agreed, as it was that she did. The good fortunes just kept on coming. It was starting to get more and more exciting and I couldn't wait to see what was in store next.

To keep me busy, and my mind off drugs, he had cousin Howie and me to paint the outside of the house Saturday. Thank God it was just the front! They had that old fashion shake asbestos siding with cazillion groves and it was a bitch to do. It had to be done only by brush so I felt like that dude named Huckleberry Finn. By the time we got finished that day my ass was too tired to do anything but sleep. I wasn't worried about getting any withdrawals since the methadone actually did do the trick.

The next day they had plans to go to Harlem to visit my great aunt. Aunt Helen was cool with me as long as they were around to keep an eye out. There was no way she wanted to leave me in their home while they were gone. Not wanting to push his luck any further Uncle Bobby said I would have to stay at my Mom's apartment. They had to swing by there to pick her up anyway, and she knew what I was trying to accomplish with their help. Mom was OK with the arrangements. She figured if I was to do anything asinine then at least it would be on her and not them. Of course I was in no position to say anything so I just went along with the program. I only had one more day to go so why mess with what seemed to be working.

Sitting around Mom's place on a Sunday afternoon watching television started to get boring. I did not like to read so that option was out. The negativity came through what little once of common sense I had left in my head right away. I picked p the phone and called Myrna. I knew that my aunt and uncle had gone with the other family members to Harlem for the day, so I wasn't worried about them answering the phone. I tried to con her into coming out to where I was so I could hang out for the last time. She did me the biggest favor in her life by saying no to my request. She knew what I would do.

I felt myself getting an attitude until I realized how lucky I was that at least she still cared enough to want to see me make it. So we stayed on the phone for about an hour just talking and shortly thereafter I laid down on the couch fell off to sleep.

I was awaken by the sound of several car doors slamming shut. When I looked at the clock it was about 7 PM. Thank you dear Lord that I made it through another day drug free. I couldn't wait to get back out to Wyandanch so I could get ready for the trip Monday to what I considered my destiny ride.

I WAS SERIOUS AND WANTED THE WORLD TO KNOW IT

Before Aunt Helen left for work that Monday morning, we hugged and she wished me good luck. I promised I would not fail. She said to do it for myself and not for anyone else. Uncle Bobby took me with him to work so I could hook up with Mrs. Ruth for the ride back to Patchogue.

I don't remember what I said to Uncle Bobby before we left, but I am sure words could not have expressed how I felt. I could tell just by looking at him that he was confident that I would do well. That was enough for me to get in the car with a renewed vigor that was beyond my wildest dreams.

The hardest part of the day was waiting around the intake office until the van was ready to leave around 7:30 PM. This was not unusual since they had residents that were down for the day going to court and they also held group therapy until 6 o'clock. Once the food rations were loaded into the van and heads were counted we were on our way. I honestly never once had a change of heart, but I was still anxious to get going since I didn't know how long those feelings would last.

Three hours later when we pulled to a stop in the pitch-black darkness of night, I thought we were stopping again to go tot the bathroom or something. When Mary turned off the engine and headlights and headed towards this building of some sort, I said to myself, "where the fuck are we and this can't be the place I heard so much about!" But it was. Welcome to DETER in Ellenville.

Thinking they had forgotten that my contract was to give up my hair, the next morning I got familiar with my surroundings. The place was a cluster of old buildings that used to be a resort for the Jewish folks. It was kind of beat up and run down but I've stayed in worse.

I got to meet Jose Pizaro the executive director that morning. He was also and ex addict. He had been up there for two days taking care of some business pertaining to a soon to come move to a better location. He was about to leave after breakfast when he overheard Bertha and me discussing why I shouldn't get my head shaved. I was concerned that in 2 days I had to go back to court and did not want to go bald headed. Her response was she could care less how I looked, it was either honor my contract or leave. When he heard what was going on, he very calmly told me that she was right and if I wasn't going to cooperate to leave right then and there.

I knew that after the ride up to this God forsaken disolete location that I did not even have a clue as to how to get back to the main highway. When the dope fiends wanted to "split" the only way back down state was to hitchhike. But first one had to find the road to stick the thumb out on.

My decision was to leave and I could always try and come back after my court appearance. I asked if I could catch a ride back to Long Island and Jose just smiled and said there's the road have a nice journey. With that he and some others just got in the van and pulled off into the horizon.

This brother name Vernon was the resident barber. His top piece was shaved and he tried to convince me that it aint too bad. He said the summer is here and it is more comfortable not worrying about washing your hair and all that. I went ahead and told him to go get the clippers; because of something else he said when he sensed I wasn't buying into that theory. Vernon said to me, "Bruce, who are you going to run into in court that gives a shit about you? Is it your image you are trying to protect or are you looking for an excuse to cop out again?"

Man, will these individuals stop coming into my life just at the right times. I mean how can I figure out a way to resort back to my negative behaviors, when lately I am constantly surrounded by people I hardly know giving me good advice? Either accept or reject Bruce. The ball is in your court. Is it worth leaving after you were all geared up to get it together and come here in the first place over an Afro?

My baldhead actually looked pretty good.

I found out from Vernon also that the reason they bring your ass up in the dark is so you won't know where the hell you were. Made for running off kind of scary for some of us. Good strategy. Leave it to Jose to know all the tricks. He had to be the most intelligent person I had ever met and it was nice to see him using his brains for something positive.

With baldhead and a few articles of decent clothing on my back that someone had loaned me, the next afternoon I was headed back to court. I had to leave Tuesday so I could be in court by 9 AM Wednesday. I was to stay the night at Mrs. Ruth's since she was trustworthy and on the board of directors of the program.

This time the ride was in the daytime. I had never in my life experienced the beauty of upstate New York except for the summer prior when I was going up to Mid Hudson. This time however, the scenery was breathtaking and I could fully appreciate God's wonders without being handcuffed and shackled at the ankles.

Myrna came out to Mrs. Ruth's in Deer Park to pick me up. She cleared it with her Mom since I was trying to help myself. The assistant director of DETER name Tony Rosario went also to represent the program. Mom took the day off to go with Myrna and me. Aunt Beatrice and Uncle Will felt that their daughter was in good hands to go alone since Elwood would not let anything happen.

The judge was nice. He sentenced me to the care and custody of DETER with the stipulation that I complete the program. Not only did I have to complete it, but also I had to be on my best behavior while in their care, otherwise I could be sent by them back to court and then to jail. I was so glad that the judge was kind enough to do that for me. Can you believe that my cousin got probation for two years? Chalk up another victory for Elwood!

When our court duties were completed, Mom took everyone out to lunch and especially thanked Tony for his help. He promised her if he had to kick my ass to stay in line he would. He was a 250-pound Italian with 15 years on the streets as a junkie, so I knew he meant business. I promised Mom that her worrying days for me were over. This one was for her. My promise to Mom was sealed with a kiss and hug, and I knew in my heart that this was one promise I would keep. Somehow I just knew it.

My advice to youngsters or anyone that is struggling with recovery is to pick someone if necessary to do it for. I know the old philosophy says that one must do things for themselves and not anyone else. Who cares about traditional philosophy when it comes to saving a life was how I felt. To me, if you love someone THAT much and do not want to see them in pain and heartache over your behavior, then I believe it can be a strong enough force to keep you drug free.

Myrna dropped Tony and me back out to Patchogue. I kissed her, told her how sorry I was for all the trouble I caused and asked to convey those sentiments to her folks. She hugged me and cried. We were so close since we were the same age. We were even in the same class together in 4th grade. When I moved out to New Castle in 3rd grade, she used to protect me and once found me outside the school crying because I was scared to go inside. So for her seeing me successful meant a lot to her also.

The ride back upstate was ready to roll by 6 PM this time. I could not wait. Not once did I ever entertain the thought of getting in the wind like I did in

Phoenix at the mental hospital. I realized that I had a reason now that I never had before and I was not sure where it came from. I always had a mother. I always want to not hurt her. I always wanted to do right. I don't know why these feelings of courage and determination manifested at this time, but they did.

TALK ABOUT A PROGRAM THAT SUCKED!

My stay lasted until October of that year. The program was 18 months, but there was no way in hell I was going to hang for that long. I left on my own accord or in other words, "I SPLIT!" I must have had a thing for the month of October since a year earlier I came home from Mid Hudson during that month to. Two other milestone events in my life took place in October also.

My mind told me that never again in my lifetime did I want to subject myself to anymore drug rehabilitation programs. I am not against therapy or self help groups, etc. but only if those in charge are sincere: truly sincere! This program sucked big time. It did not take me very long to figure out what was really going on in the name of rehab. Once I saw the handwriting on the wall, my motivation to be confident enough to make it on the outside became stronger and stronger. This time my gut instincts that had always gotten me through tough situations was right on.

What I learned in a hurry that it was a self supported program. They would ask the parents or guardians of the residents to make monthly donations similar to tithing. They would solicit goods and services from just about anybody you could think of. I did not see anything wrong with that, but what I did see that was not too cool was the small fortune Jose was making off the program. It was being run like an enterprise.

Three weeks after I was there Mom thought since the program seemed to be helping me, she borrowed $1000 from Granny to bail Stephen out of jail. He got caught with enough heroin to be charged with possession with intent to distribute. I did not mind her trying to get him some help, but I told her not to give up any donations. Let the other suckers make Jose wealthy. He already had the daughter of a very prominent well to do family in his program so I knew their checks were substantial.

It didn't take Stephen long to act like the program was just like being in jail. He was hustling from day one and trying to change the system to be more beneficial to his needs. The needs were to do as little as possible yet stay long enough to keep out of jail.

There was a wood shop set up to make items such as: bookends with those little globes on them, business card holders and six varieties of ashtrays. The shop operated at night so you could get your therapy during the day. There was a sales team that was considered an honor if you were selected. This got you out of the shop and the smell of shellac, sawdust and turpentine. I got sick to my stomach at first until I got used to it, but I knew this wasn't for me. I had not done any manual labor in two years.

In order to get on the sales team, you either knew someone that would recommend you or you were hand picked based on how trifling you were in the streets. To Jose, the more of a con artist you were as a dope fiend, the better you'd be at going out to the marketplace and soliciting "donations" in exchange for his products. You would in a sense be doing the same thing only for a different purpose.

I would have been a bigger fool to also believe that late night trips down to the city once or twice a week was to pick up some home made ethnic foods from Carlos's mother. When the program moved to the more modern location about 45 minutes further upstate, Jose had a cabin that was transformed into a castle fit for a king. He had an old lady who was a so-called graduate of the program living there with him.

Donations from a well-known bakery chain would donate day old products three times a week and they would be bought up for us to eat. I couldn't believe the first morsel of coffee cake I was presented with at breakfast. You needed a jeweler's eyeglass to find it on the napkin.

After Jose got his rations, then the rest was for us. While we ate oatmeal and cold cereal damn near everyday, he was up in his ivory tower eating waffles, pancakes and other normal breakfast foods. Dinner was the same. We got a meat or chicken maybe 4 out of 7 days.

I knew I just had to be a part of the selling crew since they ate three squares a day while they were out in mainstream society. Joe Goddard was a cool white dude from Queens that was the best salesperson they had. He put in a good word for me plus one of their other members got busted for sneaking off for an hour so the timing was perfect.

My decision to split was based on fact not theory. After being fed up with not learning anything more about myself that I did not already know, I just grew sick and tired of the bullshit. I wondered just how great the program could have been if all the negative energy to deceive and use people were put to positive use.

Sound familiar? There were hundreds of people just like me that were crying out for help and sadly some ex addicts never lose their negative ways and take advantage rather than help. In less than a year's time from when I left the program went down for the count.

After 2 ½ months of all the traveling in the vans selling all day and sleeping on the long rides back, I got burnt out. The only thing that I looked forward to near the end was the meals we got to eat. I saw damn near every town in New Jersey during that time. There was very little planning involved on a daily basis. We just used the old dope fiend method of just going on instinct to go where the money was. It worked every time.

I even got to see Niagara Falls. We were up in Buffalo one time and our leader Carlos thought it would be nice to visit the wonder of the falls. All my life I had heard about all the romantic vibes you got from the view and how breath taking it was. My aunt Ethel and uncle Harold spent their own honeymoon there in 1958. I had always envisioned that the day I did visit Niagara Falls it would be with that special someone. Instead there I stood sharing the moment with a bunch of dope fiends. At first I wasn't even going to get out of the van but figured what the hell. It was exactly as I had heard it was, minus the warm fuzzy romantic feelings.

GOT TO SPLIT FOR MY
OWN SAFETY

The selling part wasn't the deciding factor for me wanting to leave. What I was concerned about was my own safety and losing my life during the rides in the van. Since you don't lose your bad habits overnight, the way some of the them drove left much to be desired. I felt I stood a better chance out on the street surviving than to risk my life in an accident.

Once as we were coming back from Long Island in this old donated car, the hood came loose and almost went through the windshield. Another time I opened my eyes just in time to catch brother Al nodding behind the wheel doing 70 mph and yelled at him just as he was changing lanes without knowing it.

We lucked out again crossing he Tapan Zee Bridge. While Ken was turning his head while he was busy running his mouth, he didn't notice the traffic ahead had come to a complete stop. Of course when he went to slam on the brakes and discovered there were none, the natural reaction was to swerve to avoid a rear end collision. Finally the car stopped right at the barrier where a few more feet would have taken us over the rail into the Hudson River.

I never believed that God could actually be a copilot; I just thought it was a cliché. That was until the last accident I was involved in before I left. This one was far worse than the first two since we almost went off the New York State Thruway down the side of a mountain. Those passenger vans were very light and the weight of eight people plus the merchandise did not make for a good combination while driving in the pouring rain; especially while going down hill.

Several of us asked Marty to slow down, but since he suffered from the "Napoleon syndrome" he was always trying to be macho. I personally never liked him. He was Jewish and I never had any compassion or sympathy when one of them got strung out. To me they had the world at their feet and if they wanted to blow it, fuck 'em.

I felt sorry for Blacks and Hispanics because unless we had a family member that owned a business, if we messed up it was twice as hard to live down the stigma. Being Black was hard enough. Being Black with drugs and an arrest record was harder to be accepted by society.

As we were heading down this hill there was a curve ahead that this fool was about to take at 50 mph. His ass should have been a Kamikaze pilot. It was like he had a death wish or something. Instead of slowing down he went for it and all of a sudden the van went in to a tailspin. All I could remember was closing my eyes and hugging the guy next to me as the van fishtailed like one of those carnival rides.

As I took what I thought to be my last look at my surroundings, I knew what people meant when they say, "I saw my life flash before my very eyes." All of us let out screams in unison and braced for the end to come. I was in the last row on the left side, so I figured I'd be the first one to go since we were heading towards the edge from the left rear side first. Just my luck!

"Heavenly Father at least you can put down in the books that I did try to turn my life around and if this is the price for rehab then I've paid," I prayed to myself. I had no time to include anybody else. Fuck them. To me, if ever a time to be selfish this was it! To say I was ready would have been a lie. I still had a lot of living left in me.

Suddenly and with extreme caution I opened my eyes only to discover that we had come to a stop. The front doors had flung open somehow and the rain was pouring inside. "Could this be true?" speaking again to only me. "Had God once again spared my life by these death defying wake up calls?" If so He no doubt had my undivided attention this time.

Ah, but it was for real. His hands not only spared me but all of us from death. It was a miracle that the steel cables that are placed along the roads to serve as a guardrail actually stopped us from going over the edge.

My reaction once I finished giving God his due was to jump over the other two rows of seats and try my best to kill Marty for putting our lives in danger. I felt his egotistical attitude prevented him from listening when he was told to slow down due to the weather and road conditions. The others pulled me off him as I had my hands around his little Jewish neck. He was screaming for me to stop but I was determined to kill his ass.

I was angry that I was being subjected to all of this bullshit, and felt that I had very little control over my destiny. I hated feeling like that and was determined to never feel like that again, one way or another.

A twist of irony took place right before my eyes again while I stood outside the van catching my breath. Another vehicle was rounding that same curve that almost cost us our lives, when all of a sudden it went into a tailspin. I watched in horror as I relived the moment when I thought I was going to die. The vehicle stopped short of the guardrail, and when the door opened on the driver's side, to my surprise out came a priest all dressed in his attire. He was shaken, but I could tell that he knew the Creator protected him.

To show how little they cared about us, they sent the other van to pick us up. Right out there in the inclement weather on the side of the thruway there we were emptying our van and loading up the other to continue our journey. This time we didn't let Marty drive.

Once I made up my mind to leave, the next step was hustling up enough money to get back to Long Island. Fate would deal me yet another hand and two days after the near fatal mishap, Carlos decided to drive to Long Island and sell there and drive back the same evening. This made for an exhausting day, but remember, it was not about us just about Jose. For me it was perfect since I could split right from my home area and not have to worry about hitching a ride.

That weekend I finally got to have sex after who knows how long going without it. A new resident name, Barbara, who had only been there a week, became my savior. She was from Uniondale, Long Island, and was there because she was using and her folks put her out of doors until she got herself together. The fact that she was white mattered not. There were no color barriers for female addicts. When they got the horns it was anybody that was available. I just happened to be the lucky one as usual. We just found an abandoned cottage late one evening, and took care of much needed business for both of us.

On Tuesday after I returned from busting my ass all day, I was asked to go to the therapist's cottage. I knew some shit was going to hit the fan but knew not why they called for this special group at 10 PM. Turned out that when I made a phone call to my Mom from the mall we were hustling in, this "brown nose" ratted on me. We were not allowed to make any contact with our family members without their permission or supervision.

After sitting through the typical bullshit about how bad a person I was, they placed me on a no talking contract for three days. Now how the hell was I supposed to go out and sell anything without talking? They had an answer for that which did not surprise me. The head therapist in charge came up with the brainstorm to only have it in effect while riding in the van, and when I came back to the property. It was also mentioned that it was rumored I was planning on splitting so they was going to keep a close eye on me. Yeah right!

Soliciting donations from the working class people was like taking candy from a baby. Most of society was so gullible that little to no effort was needed to get them to go in pocket. Jose even had special boxes made up to place the products in, and he printed receipts for tax deduction purposes.

Joe and I were the best they had. They knew it and we knew it. We would always be the first to clean out our allotment, and then go back and ask for more so we could get on the road early. If we waited for some of the others to finish their inventory, we would have gotten back at midnight everyday. Some were jealous while others could care less.

Aside from getting money for our goods, we would also hustle our food, gas, and cigarettes. Joe and I used to always con a retail store manger/owner to donate an article of clothing. We used to say that the 11 and 13-year-old kids had nothing at all to wear. I once told a female storeowner that the program was starting to look like a nature camp. The need would always fit the size that we wore but they never questioned a thing. So on top of being the best at selling and hustling, we also were the best dressed.

The funniest thing that I experienced while going from town to town hustling was getting some r-e-l-i-e-f, from this young black sista girl in a lawyer's office. Either girlfriend was just plain stupid, hard up or kinky to allow me to convince her that my rehab would be helped immensely if only I could have sex. She said her boss was in court for the afternoon so we had time to get it on in the waiting room on the sofa. I thought she was just teasing, and joking until she actually locked the door, hung the "out to lunch" sign on the doorknob, and led me to the leather sofa.

Well I was so wound up that before she could even get her pantyhose off I was done. She looked disappointed but so what? I would never see her again in life so what did I care.

I had selected that Tuesday to split. I had nothing to gain from staying another day.

What I had learned in those four months was what changed my thinking about drugs for the rest of my life. I came to the realization that programs or jail are not the necessities of life. I no longer felt dependent on them to change who I was. The only way to stop being a part of it all is to change my understanding of the drug life.

I began to feel used, abused, and embarrassed by being a part of the culture. There was not anything I had control over. I knew that in order to stand by those new beliefs I had to replace my lifestyle with something more conducive to living. I had told myself, "This shit aint living. It's was a mental incarceration." I once heard the saying, "A mental death was far worse than a physical death because you had to live with it." I no longer wished to be part of the living dead.

The day to leave finally came. I had told my best friend Boonky Boy that when I left that morning I wasn't coming back. He understood and wished me luck and that he wasn't too far behind me. The brother had more at stake than I did since he was in the program for an armed robbery.

Boonky Boy kept me in stitches everyday. He once told me how he and his partner stole his parent's console color television and stereo. His family had gone out for the day, and left him home alone. He then sold the T.V. to a man in his neighborhood. After learning the man was going to the racetrack that afternoon, they knew he would not be back for at least several hours. In that period of time they went back to the man's house, stole the T.V. and had it back before his family returned that evening. I told him I'd see him again since he lived in Wyandanch, and I would be living in Deer Park, which was the next town over.

TALK TO THE HAND THAT
WAVES FAREWELL

We were planning to go all the way down to Long Island that Tuesday. I knew Stephen, and this other dude name Bubba, were splitting that day, and the white chick Barbara was going along with them. I could not have my own brother hitching back to Long Island so I threw him a couple of dollars that I had not turned in from a cash donation. We slapped high five's, and knew we'd see each other back in the Castle.

Oh, I almost forgot, brother Stan. He was also splitting that morning so he could be with Barbara. He had gotten to her "cookie" like I had, but the only difference was he thought his ass was in love.

As we approached New Jersey, the van had started to act up. I wasn't worried though. With all of the near death experiences in so many unsafe vehicles, I knew that a little indicator light would not stop us from our mission. Well they fooled the hell out of me. Of all the times to start thinking about our safety, that Tuesday was not the time to begin.

Our fearless leader Carlos, the most trifling staff member of them all, made the decision to go as far as Fort Lee, NJ. Since I was still on a no talking ban I could not put in my two cents so the decision was final. At that stage of the game, if they had talked about turning back, and returning to Ellenville I swore I would have opened a door and leaped out first.

That day was the usual. We ate breakfast of our choice in a diner. There were no fast food places offering breakfast at the time, otherwise that's where we wouldn't went. The teams were split up, our times to return to the van for lunch were established and we were off to sell, sell, and sell. We never left a town until ALL the items were sold. It was not unusual to collect close to $2000 a day in cash or checks.

Now I told you their plans, now I'll tell you what mine were.

Bruce's plans of action for that day was eating my last breakfast as a resident of DETER. Next I would have tried as hard as I could to solicit a cash donation or sell an item for cash as soon as possible. The last step was to haul ass the first chance I had as soon as I got enough money in my pocket. It was that simple.

As fate would have it, and as good as I was with my mouth, the first several customers gave me checks. I could not get a cash sale to save my life. After I received a nice sweater from a clothing store, and I finally got about $20 in cash, it was lunchtime. "What the hell." I thought. "Might as well hang for my last free lunch from the golden arches, and maybe afterwards I could hustle up a little more cash." I knew it was a long way to Long Island from where we were. Either way I would have been on my way across the George Washington Bridge no later than two o'clock that afternoon. I wanted to avoid the Friday rush hour.

Just sitting around eating my favorite filet 'o fish sandwich, fries, and orange drink, I got to thinking that I had better not take any chances by being greedy. I knew I had it in me to get home without having to swim across the Hudson River. After I finished my gourmet meal I gestured with my hands if it would be O.K. for me to go back to the van for a smoke. I was given permission although I was still on a no talking, no smoking contract.

As I went back to the van to grab a whole pack of cigarettes to take with me, this poor, hopeless soul name, Tom, followed me. He reminded me of the character from that movie, "*Of Mice and Men.*" He stood about 6'1" and weighed about 220 lbs. He once told me that the only reason he is still in the program after 18 months was because he was scared to go back out on the street. He also used to let the staff treat him like he was less than human. He once allowed them to give him a Mohawk haircut as a punishment.

As I was lighting up a cigarette, and just about to close the door to the van, and do my adios amigo, he just stood in front of me, and begged me not to go. I asked him how he knew what I was fixing to do, and he said, "I have seen so many go that I can sense it." That is why I followed you out to the van in the first place."

I told him I would be just fine and that I was ready to stay drug free. I'm sure he must have heard those famous words a hundred times. I did not expect him to believe me, but what I did suggest to him was he needed to start believing in himself. He could hardly stay in the program for the rest of his life to feel safe and secure. I gave him a hug, and with tears in his eyes he wished me well. I turned the corner, and was off to start my new life as a human being.

The first gas station I came to I rested, and gathered my thoughts once I felt safe that I was far enough away from the others. I was about three blocks from the entrance to the George Washington Bridge. No sooner had I lit another cigarette while staring at the New York City skyline, my ride appeared out of nowhere. All of a sudden I saw this beautiful white woman around twenty-five-years-old with long blond hair. She was driving a green Fiat convertible and she was pulling in to get gas. When she got out, and took off her sunglasses as she headed inside the station I could not believe how tall, and sexy she looked.

She came back out after the attendant finished pumping her gas, and she noticed me just standing there admiring her car. I just knew she was sent there by God to part the Hudson River, get me away from my enemies, and lead me into the Promised Land. From the friendly expression on her face I took it upon myself to boldly just come out and ask was she heading across the bridge. She replied, "Sure get in. I just have to wait for my change first."

How nice it was back then to have felt safe around strangers. Picking up hitchhikers was a common thing to do without fearing for your life. I felt good about myself already as I never once thought about doing anything dishonest.

We cruised across the bridge, as her blond hair blew in the wind

Sure felt good riding in a decent car for a change. As she turned her head my way to talk, I saw the reflection of the sun shining brightly off her sunglasses. I wanted to yell out a scream of joy from the bottom of my lungs that I was about to start my life anew. She told me she was a college student from New Hampshire. She was beginning her fall break from school, and was down in New York to visit a girlfriend who lived on 79th and 5th Ave.

I did not get into my life story so I just told her that I was also a student on break trying to get to the city, and left it at that. In a way I would not have been lying. My education came from the "University of Hard Knocks" and I was close to graduating.

When we arrived in the Big Apple, I felt a sense of relief. Since she was going downtown she drove me as far as 59th street. I was only twenty-five blocks from Penn station, and the walk would do me good. I felt compelled to give her a hug and kiss on the cheek but opted not to. I am quite sure she would not have been offended, but I wanted to start anew, and I thought it best to just shake her hand and say thanks.

Had she known just how much her act of kindness meant to me I think she would have started crying. What she showed me on that day was that she trusted me. When she saw me she did not see that filthy, stinking, trifling, and pathetic looking Bruce. That meant so much to me.

FREE AT LAST, OR WAS I?

The walk down 7th Ave. to 34th street was so invigorating. I just looked straight ahead like I was in my own little world, and kept stepping, and did not stop until I had reached the train station. It felt strange buying a ticket to Westbury to go home without having any drugs on me. There were times when I could not get a ride to the city, so I had to take the LIRR, and then the subway uptown to 116th and Lenox Ave.

As I boarded the train, I found myself, out of habit, walking through several cars to make sure I was not being followed. When I finally chose which car was most comfortable for me, I looked ahead, and towards the back of the car I saw Stan and Barbara. They looked no worse for the weary. I asked them how they made it to the city from Ellenville, and the first words out of Stan's mouth was, "Man, your brother's a dirty, rotten, mother-fucker!"

That was all I had needed to hear to know that Stephen and Bubba had ripped him off. As the train slowly pulled out of the station Stan proceeded to unfold the series of events from that morning when I last saw them until they got to Penn station.

Stan was kind of a square even though he was a dope fiend. He was from the Castle like us but was not in the same league that we were. Anyway, what happened was the four of them decided to split together. Stephen and Bubba knew Stan had some cash on him from twice filling in for someone on the selling crew. They also knew that Barbara was hot to trot. Once they made their way about three miles from the facility they came upon an abandoned resort with cabins that were not secured or boarded up. A good place to rest Stephen decided before they reached Route 17 that lead to the New York State Thruway.

I listened as Stan said how they took turns screwing Barbara. When it was his turn, which was of course AFTER Stephen and Bubba got their rocks off; he let his guard down. While Stan had his butt to the sky, and dead in the saddle, Stephen and Bubba rifled through his pants pockets, and stole what money he had. He talked about it like Barbara was not even sitting next to us on the train; that's how stupid he was. Believe me, I tried my best to keep a straight face as I looked at the two of them so I would not burst out laughing.

When I though he was finished with his tale of whoa, he kept going until he came to the funniest part of the story. When he came out of the private room in the cottage and put his pants back on, he had discovered that his money missing. They had no choice then but to put the ole thumb out, and hitch to the thruway, and then stand out there and try and hitch a ride down state before nightfall.

Meanwhile Stephen knew there was a bus station in nearby Woodbourne from the time he spent six months there in a rehab center there in '68. He and Bubba hitched there so they could ride back to the Big Apple in a nice, comfortable, air-conditioned, coach. As they were cruising down the thruway sitting in the back of the bus chilling out, they saw Stan and Barbara out on the side of the highway with their thumbs out. While the two continued their saga I thought what pissed Stan off the most was as they passed by they waved at them, and he could see them laughing. I did get through the ending without laughing. I dare not have asked them how they got the money to get on the train. He probably felt bad enough as it was.

By the time we got to our stop, we had convinced ourselves that we deserved to get high one more time before calling it quits. I had a few dollars left but I'd be damned if I was sharing anything. My gut said not to, but my mind said what the hell. Stan did have a few articles of clothing he had stolen before he left so I decided it was my turn to get over on him.

I sensed that after Barbara got stuck spending an entire day with someone so dumb, she would go along with my idea just to get away from him. We planned on getting rid of his tired ass, get some dope and go to a motel for the night and party. I suggested that Stan give me the clothes he had and I would go up to the corner hang out and sell them. I would then buy some drugs and the three of us would go shack up for the night and get high. He wanted to come with us, but I told him to let Barbara go alone. I had known because she was white, the brothers would probably have given up a few more dollars than they would have if it was just two brothers.

He bought the irrational idea without an argument, and he waited like he was told to do. I told him to stand on a corner about 10 blocks away. It had not even dawned on him that he was about to get beaten twice in the same day. I told him that once we had everything we needed we would meet up with him in front of the liquor store on Union Ave. He was so excited, and again I was trying not to laugh at how stupid he was.

I don't know where he went or what he did while waiting, but I knew what we did.

We got about $40 for the merchandise but we never did buy any drugs. It was not because of lack of desire but I was more concerned about not "gettin it up" when we got to the motel. Heroin, unlike cocaine, dulls your sex drive. I had been there before and did not want to go there again so I suggested we buy a bottle of wine instead. This was a more rational decision as far as I was concerned.

We bought a bottle of good wine, not the $2.50 kind, and checked into one of the motels on Jericho Turnpike that I had stayed in so many times before. After a nice hot shower with real soap and shampoo, we poured our wine, turned on the television and never got to see what was on. She must have been hurtin for certain for sure the next morning.

The next day I knew I had to get rid of her. She began talking that fool talk about hitching down to Florida with her. I was like, sorry miss, Black men might be good at other things, but we did not do hitchhiking that far. I felt kind of sorry that she had no place to go, and she didn't want to go back to New Castle and hook up with Stan again. She'd have stood a better chance going back into the program.

I was actually trying to talk her into making peace with her folks that lived nearby so we took the bus to Hempstead. She was sure she did not want to go back home and said she had a brother and some friends in Tampa. I kind of started to like her as a person by then and not just as a sex object, but hey what more could I do? I would have given her a few dollars if I had it to give. We said our farewells at the Hempstead bus station and then we went our separate ways.

I eventually got high later that evening with the most unlikely people—good ole Stan and his brother "Nipples." He got the nickname "Nipples" while he was in high school. He used to be fat, and looked as if he had real tits. I explained to Stan that what happened the previous night was not to be taken personal. The fact that he got ripped off again wasn't that important to him. He was just pissed about wanting some more of Barbara. I reckon if that was all I had to hear for beating him out of his clothes and money, it was worth it.

The feeling of death hovering in my head was how I felt shooting heroin for the very last time in my life. Thank God it wasn't very much since they were turning me on in the first place. In a way, as crazy as it may sound, it was as if I was putting myself through a test to see if I would still enjoy the feeling. I had given little regard knowing that I had been drug free for five months and that one last shot could have been fatal. More addicts overdosed after shooting up within 24 hours or sooner after their release from jail or a program because their system could not handle it.

Who knows that if I had never found the answer to the question at that time and I always wondered? Would I have been curious at a later date and time in my life? What if I had not established that fear of death in me? Yes, who does know what might have been. All I knew was that I did not enjoy it and I didn't die that night for a reason.

Since October of 1971 I never shot anything into my arm again.

The best therapy that I used for my own personal situation was in knowing that I never wanted to subject myself to the humiliation, and bullshit of going through anymore programs. I wanted no more of insincere people telling me what to do, and what was best for my own good.

No more sleeping in strange accommodations.

No more jail time.

No more tears, and pain for my family inflicted by me.

No longer would I have to stand before judges with my head hanging down ashamed.

No more longing for a relationship with someone who loved me for whom I was.

I felt I had deserved more out of this life, and I was determined to get it.

I spent that night with Stan and "Nipples" mostly out of fear that I might have died if I was alone. Stan was stupid, but at least his brother had a few more ounces of common sense, and would have called 911 if he had to.

A NEAR DEATH EXPERIENCE THAT WAS NOT MINE

The next day I had to face Mom so I wanted to be at my best. I knew she would be disappointed at the way I had left the program, yet be somewhat understanding enough to give me the benefit of the doubt.

After trying to locate my brother to see where his head was at, and if he wanted to come with me. I decided to get a ride and go to Mom's alone. She got a call from DETER about both of us the night before informing her that we had split. They did this not because they gave a shit, but for their own liability. If you got killed, your family could not sue them for neglect.

As we sat and talked, she started to unravel the events of her day.

During her lunch hour from work she had driven over to Mineola courthouse to arrange to have Stephen's bail revoked. She promised her parents that if he blew his chance this time, she would get their money back to them even if it meant sending him back to jail. She only got him out thinking he would benefit from the program like me. She did what she had to do plus she would once again know where he was.

She continued telling me how she was late driving back to work due to an accident after taking care of business. Old Country road was a six lane main thoroughfare, and during lunch time the traffic was always heavy. Not having any choice but to sit and creep along as traffic moved, she started feeling bad about why we just could not get our lives together.

When she finally got her turn to move past the accident scene, instinctively she looked over at the white sheet covering what appeared to be a person lying in the middle of the street. She said she could not help but get a cold chill running through her body that alarmed her motherly instincts to wonder if that could be one of her own sons.

Mom said she had almost stopped to ask the police if she could look under the sheet for her own peace of mind but did not. Although she gave benefit of the doubt and went on back to her office, she had a feeling that left her uneasy. I asked her what made her think it was one of us. She explained that part of the person's arm, and hand was sticking out from under the sheet, and she recognized what looked like a sweater of mine. It also was not uncommon for Stephen to take my clothes, and borrow without asking and Mom knew this too.

Wow, this story was very scary.

Obviously it was not me under that sheet, but the more I thought about the scenario, I started to wonder if Mom's instincts were not that far off base to be true.

Rather than sitting around any longer, we both decided to go to New Castle and try to find him to put both our minds at ease. Part of the reason to find him soon was Mom had to produce his ass in court in order to get her bail money back. I never was sure what happens when a person dies while out on bail since the court wouldn't have to worry about you not showing up.

Mom and I along with Lisa got into the car and went to find him like we were bounty hunters. I warned Mom that some of the places I would be pulling up to were not going to be the nicest places in the area. In fact I was down right ashamed of myself for knowing some of these places we hung out at. I stopped at several spots but to no avail.

When we got to William's place I got out and left the two of them in the car. He had a room at the top of the stairs in this rooming house. When I rang the bell for him to buzz me in, I just stepped inside, and stood in the lobby area while he stayed at the top of the landing. I asked had he seen Stephen during the day and his reply was, "Oh man, you hadn't hear what happened?"

I did not even have to wait for William to finish what he had to say to know that Mom's intuition was fact. The person lying in the road with a sheet over him had turned out to be Stephen after all.

William told me he was sorry he had to be the one to inform me, and offered his condolences. I wondered why not one person that I asked previously about him could tell me what everyone in the neighborhood seemed to have known by then. That was not the time to be pissed at some low life drug addict, as there were more important things to take care of.

The details that William shared with me were astonishing.

Stephen and Lump were at the mall in Roosevelt Field, and had stolen some woman's wallet. As they were running across the busy intersection in the middle of the lunch hour rush, a car came along, and hit him. Lump made it to the other side safe, and sound. Here's yet another example of a dope fiend's mentality, he watched from across the street until the police and ambulance arrived. He then went back to be within a few feet from where Stephen was laying to see if he was dead or alive. When an officer asked if anyone knew who he was since Stephen carried no identification on him, Lump never opened his mouth, and said a word. He had much to say when he came back to the Castle and told everyone what happened.

The few steps back to the car felt like I was the dead man walking to the executioner. How in God's name would I be able to tell my mother, and sister that Stephen's dead? I did not need to answer that question because by the time I did get back to the car, Mom just looked at my face and she already knew. That same motherly instinct that had brought us to that point to begin with allowed her to know in heart that she was correct.

"It was him wasn't it?" was all she said.

I lost it in the car in front of them. All I kept saying was, "If I had not left the program he would not have left either, and he would be alive right now. Lisa was in the back seat crying, and the only one that seemed composed was Mom.

After I had calmed down she asked if I knew where they would have taken his body. Since the closest hospital to the accident was Winthrop hospital in Mineola, I figured that he would be in the morgue there. But before we drove all the way over there to find out he wasn't there, we called information, and was told he wasn't there. That's all that we were told.

The only other option was the Medical Center in East Meadow next to the jail. We looked at each other and knew it was up to us to go over to the county morgue and identify his remains. We couldn't go get Dad as he was still in Jamaica at work. We had no choice. Part of us was anxious to get there and know for sure and the other part was in no rush. The ride was only 10 minutes but we took our sweet time. I did not think anyone is in a hurry to hear bad news especially if it pertains to a family member.

"Shit! Which building should we go to?" I thought to myself.

Emergency was for sick people not dead people; can't go there.

The front entrance was for folks visiting the sick, and we aint there to visit; can't go there either.

I remembered from my taxi driving days where the entrance to the building that housed the morgue was. I used to have a regular passenger, who was a nut case who worked there at night that I ended up having to pick him up every night. The first time I got the call to pick up a passenger at the medical examiner's building I sat at the top of the ramp, and kept blowing the horn to let the person know I was there. I was not going any further.

I called in to the office stating that no one was coming out, and that I was leaving. The dispatcher had yelled back that the guy just called, and could hear me blowing the horn. I then asked why the hell didn't he come up the ramp? If he could hear me surely he could have seen me. I was told he is paying to be picked up at the morgue entrance, and not up the hill where I was. What a jerk.

I practically coasted down the hill with the cab in neutral. I was scared to have gone any closer. After a couple of weeks of dealing with his stinking ass smelling of formaldehyde, and listening to weird stories pertaining to his livelihood that he felt compelled to share with me, I could not take it any longer. I told the dispatcher, Arty, if I had to deal with him one more night I was going to quit.

Before I suggested the medical examiner thing to Mom, we decided to go to the emergency entrance first. At least someone there could guide us as to what to do at a time like that. We held on to each other as we walked in. To my surprise the first person I saw at the nurses station was a high school classmate named, Lorraine. At least she was someone I had known, and I was confident that at least we would get some answers. Just as I was about to utter the words that I had up to now dreaded as to how would a person go about claiming a loved one's body, she spoke first.

As she spoke she had a smile on her face. I knew that nurses in the emergency are used to death, but I had wondered why the hell she was smiling. What had been so Goddamn funny?

We were in store for yet another surprise.

I thought one more surprise today, and Mom and I would be the one's in the morgue.

Lorraine said, "I take it you are here about Stephen huh? Well you can calm down he's O.K. He's right in there," as she pointed to a closed curtain to one of the cubicles. It was a good thing we were getting all this wonderful news while standing in the emergency room so that when one of us keeled over with a heart attack at least we would have stood a fighting chance.

Could we be hearing correctly?

I asked Lorraine one more time if she was sure she had known whom Stephen was, and that it wasn't someone else. She laughed, and reminded me that she grew up one block over from us, and we all went to the same schools together. I felt dumb for second-guessing her, and not that I wanted to hear that it wasn't him, but I could not have withstood another shock.

With that, we almost knocked one another over racing to the cubicle. I could have imagined how those contestants on that game show years ago, "Let's Make

Deal," felt being anxious to learn what was behind door number one, number two, or number three.

I cannot describe in words the joy, and feeling of a miracle unfolding before your very eyes like I had felt that evening. Mom pulled back the curtain, and there he was sitting up in a wheelchair as he drank a cup of hot chocolate, and was eating a piece of coffee cake that Lorraine had bought for him from one of the vending machines.

When he saw us, and it was obvious that anxiety was etched all over our faces, he nonchalantly asked, "What's the matter with yall?"

You had to have known him to understand his reaction to seeing us. We were just standing there in awe and we started to cry and hug him, yet wanting to beat the shit out of him at the same time. We asked him what happened, and he angrily replied, "I got hit by a car!" Other than being sore, and his knee badly bruised, he was fine. Physically that is!

He thought it to be funny when we started to tell him how the word on the street was that he got killed getting hit by a car. He felt bad when Mom told him how she passed him lying in the street with the sheet over his head. He thought that his main man Lump would have at least tried to contact a family member of ours so we did not have to go through all that hassle. He understood why Lump did not want to get involved since he figured if he was dead, he could not get in trouble for being with him when they stole the wallet.

The question remained as to why if he was alive did the police put a sheet over him, but it was never answered. He did say that he did not remember anything after he went up in the air, and hit his head on the ground, so he had probably been knocked unconscious. We let the doctor finish examining him, and decided to wait awhile before leaving just to make sure everything was fine.

Mom called Marcia and asked her to come to the hospital, and pick up Lisa, and watch her until we were through. We did not want to leave him by himself for fear if they told him he was OK, the doctor would have to discharge him.

No, Mom was planning on staying close by so she could have made sure he was not going anywhere. She even begged the attending physician to allow him to stay overnight. They must have felt compassion for us, and they let him sleep on a gurney until the next morning. Once she knew he would be stationary we felt it was time to leave since it was damn near midnight by then.

As we were driving back to her place she started to cry. She felt so awful that she was going to send him back to jail after what he had been through. That next morning we knew would be very difficult.

The next day, we returned to pick up her "collateral" and no sooner than we walked in the door to the emergency room, we could hear Stephen's mouth. He was yelling, and arguing with the discharge nurse at he top of his lungs. He had been allowed to use their crutches to get around during the night, but was told he could not take them with him.

His argument was that since he had no money, nor benefits, that he should be entitled to a set for free. He felt since he was in a County hospital, the taxpayers should have paid for his needs. After he had calmed down, and the doctor gave his release papers, we left with Stephen—crutches and all.

When we turned onto Old Country Road, and did not head in the direction of Mom's apartment in Woodbury, he asked where we were going. The time for judgment had arrived.

Mom was calm as she told him that she had no choice but to have his bail revoked so she could repay Granny, and Granddad their money. Stephen might have had his ways, but, when the truth was known, and something made sense to him, he could be very rational. This fortunately was one of those times.

The ride over was very solemn. You would have thought we were actually going to his funeral except that he was in the front seat sitting up instead of lying down in the back of a hearse. He knew that Mom was doing what she had to but he said very little going over to the courthouse.

OH THE LAUGHTER, THE MEMORIES, THE TEARS

When we got to court to take care of the remaining paperwork Mom's best friend Consuelo met us there. This allowed just Stephen and I to sit in the all too familiar courtroom to wait his turn to go before the judge. He looked so pitiful, yet all the while I was thinking, "better his ass than mine!" We been through hell and high water together, however, I was glad he was on his way to jail and not me.

Stephen asked if I would let him have my sneakers so he could at least play ball once his knee got better. He knew it would be awhile before he was coming home this time since he had several charges including the most recent to answer to. So right there inside the courtroom we exchanged my sneakers for his shoes. That was the least I could have done.

At that moment I could not help but feeling that the realization of the two of us not getting high or into any more trouble was finally at an end. It was a long, hard, and challenging three-year run. I was sad that we were not going in the same direction, and wished that at least he would use this time in jail wisely.

I wanted so badly for us to have a relationship as brothers without the negativity being the glue that bound us together. I knew it was wishful thinking, but I was glad that I would, and could be more of a positive influence by serving as a good role model.

Even though he started his drug abuse before I did, it had never crossed my mind that I could get in, and out in one piece, and leave him behind. The time we had spent during the three years of drug addiction was the most time we had spent together as brothers since we were kids growing up.

We just sat there, and I felt so alone, and helpless that there was nothing I could do to help him out of the situation. I had honestly believed that he was lucky enough to have lived for a reason, and I just prayed it was a positive one.

To kill some of the time, and break the silence after we tied our footwear, we began to reminisce about the fun times, and stuff we had gotten ourselves into.

There was the time we had conned a judge into letting him out in his own custody because we told him our Mom was in the hospital, and was about to have surgery for cancer. It was a simple thyroid procedure so we didn't think of the lie as putting the bad mouth on her. We just did our usual; we exaggerated the truth.

Stephen had gotten busted that day before, doing the pocketbook thing, and I went to arraignment as if I was his attorney. After the judge listened to our story, he surprised the entire courtroom by recessing, and calling us into his chamber. Once behind closed doors, the district attorney, and a member of the probation department argued vehemently that with his record he should not be allowed out in his own recognizance.

I would have bet my last two dollars that what happened next would NEVER come to pass. The judge listened to them, agreed, and then he rendered his decision that would allow Stephen out into my custody. The judge told everyone present that he just felt that we needed to be near our Mom, and that the charges were only a misdemeanor.

We came out of the chamber smiling, and talking with the judge while everyone else looked pissed off. I will never forget the look of astonishment on the faces of the officer who arrested him or the lady who was the victim. It must have been a total insult to everyone's integrity but ours, the little that we had.

We gave a look of, "Ha, ha we got over didn't we?" as we walked past everyone making our way to the exit door. We had gotten over, but there was little time to pat ourselves on the back. We had work to do. It was time to try and steal something so we could get high *before* we went to see Mom in Syosset hospital by 6 PM.

We laughed about the time we could not reach this lady's pocketbook through one of those small sliding glass windows in an office lobby. We knew the window was for the receptionists, and they were hardly ever locked. The door to the office was locked but not the window.

When I quietly slid the window open, alas!

There right on the top of the desk was a pocketbook. There was no way I was going to reach it, so I went outside and found a long stick that I thought would be long enough to reach the desk from the lobby. We discovered it wasn't so Stephen had held my legs as I climbed half way through the window, and hooked the strap on the pocketbook, and reeled in our catch. He almost let me slip twice but he tightened his grip around my ankles for one more victory.

If there is one thing I will always remember about my brother, and our unusual relationship, it had to be the time he had stolen $100 out of my savings account. This had taken place during the time I had been in Phoenix. I had left my passbook at home in a coat pocket for safety reasons. I did get suspicious when he called long distance to Marcia's with some "cock-a-may-me" story about how he had worn my coat up to the youth center, and someone stole my passbook.

The first thing that struck me as odd was that if he had known it was in the coat, why hadn't he removed it before he wore it? I told him I would deal with it when I got back as I had enough on my plate trying to get home in one piece. I had continued to give him the benefit of the doubt, and also ample time to fess up if he had been guilty. Of course he swore on a stack of Bibles that he had been innocent.

The next day after I had come home, the best scene in the scenario was when Stephen had gone with me to the bank still insisting he had no knowledge of who stole my money. Upon arriving I asked for the manager, and immediately ripped him a new asshole. I demanded to know how a stranger could have come into the bank, and take money out of my account other than my mother or me?

I mean it had been all right for me to have stolen from others, but I would have been damned if I was going to let someone rip me off. I had worked damn near all day for the opportunity to steal the money that was in his bank. He was polite though, and just stood there, and took my insults like a man. Once I stopped acting like a lunatic he apologized, and promised the matter would be handled quickly, and properly.

I had made no attempts to hide my feelings out loud.

I think one of the tellers that had heard what was going on called the manager over. She must have recognized Stephen, since the incident took place less than 72 hours earlier.

The manager then returned to where we had been sitting, and I thought he decided to compensate me for my loss. Instead he asked if Stephen would mind signing his name on a piece of paper. Still maintaining his goody two shoes role, he boldly, I might add, grabbed the pen, and signed his full name. Without saying a word the manager handed me the withdrawal slip used in the transaction, and slid the paper with the signature Stephen just wrote then just sat back, and did not say a word.

I could not believe it. Could Stephen have been that stupid?

I just looked at my brother, and shook my head. He had that shit ass-eating grin on his face as if to say, "Hey I tried!"

When the branch manager asked if I wanted to file charges for grand theft I had a good mind to have said, "Where are the forms to fill out?" just for him being so dumb. In fact he was lucky the bank did not want to file charges for theft by deceit.

As we walked out the bank, only after I had to humble myself to the manager, and the teller who I yelled at also, I had nothing more to say. My feeling had been that they still should have matched the signatures but that was beside the point. I had already made a big enough ass of myself.

When we got about two blocks away I asked Stephen why he did not just tell me the truth rather than going through all the hassle. This incident was worse than the time he had broken into my room that I was staying in at someone's house, and stole my drugs, and my money. All he said at the time was, "Sorry Dude"(a name he used to call me).

Once we had finished going down memory lane, I was curious to find out what had happened the day before.

He explained that when the car had hit him, and he went up in he air, and fell to the ground, his head hit the concrete. He was kind of semi conscience, yet was alert enough to hear the police ask some lady, "Is that the person who stole your wallet?" and her reply was, "Yeah that's one of them." He said the police laughed, and said there was no need to look any further since Stephen wouldn't be going anywhere.

"But the sheet! The sheet!" I kept asking.

I had been dying to find out why they had covered him up like he was dead. He told me he still did not know other than they were trying to keep his ass warm until the ambulance arrived. He was arrested at Winthrop Hospital; however, they were kind enough to just give him a summons to show up the next day. He was then moved to the medical center because he had no insurance, and Winthrop was not a County hospital. So that was how he ended up there.

I tried to offer some pearls of wisdom, and encouragement before he went before the bench. It had appeared for a moment as though what I had been saying was sinking in.

Wrong!

No sooner had the judge asked him if he had anything to say before rendering his judgment did Stephen reach far down into his bag of tricks; I mean really low down. He swung for the fences that time. He tried to convince the judge that since Mom had been under so much pressure lately, that she was not acting rational, and not responsible to know what she was doing. Boy did I feel for Mom. He had not meant what he had said, just trying to save his ass. I told Mom not to take what he was saying too personal, but she was hurt just the same.

That time his attempt at freedom at the expense of a sympathetic judge was counterfeit. I am sure the judge had heard his fair share of stories, but you could tell by his expression that he thought what Stephen was trying to do was despicable. His bail was revoked, and the charges from the precious day were bound over for another date. There really were not any losers that day. Even though emotions were kind of high it was a win win situation for all. At least Stephen could recuperate at the expense of the State, and Mom would have peace of mind knowing where he would be for at least until next year.

He then hobbled off into the hands of the guards for the ride that he was by that time quite familiar. Consuelo went on to work, and Mom and I went back to her place. I would never have had the heart to tell her that there but for the grace of God could have been me. I could have ended up in the hospital or morgue had I overdosed my second day home rather than Stephen getting struck by a car.

What I had never thought of before was, all you needed was only one time to blow it, and your life was history. Death was not prejudice, and all too final. Up until that point, I never gave it that much thought.

For the first time since elementary school had I thought about the reality of dying, and that was enough to make me want to get out of the risk business.

THE RIGHT PLACE, THE RIGHT TIME

I knew the only way to not relapse again was to go back out to east Long Island to Deer Park, and live with Mrs. Ruth, and her family on Tell Ave. I had called her up, and although I ran away from the very program that she felt strongly about, I asked if I could stay there for a while.

Her oldest son, Toby, had been in the program for a few months for doing pills and smoking weed. Her younger son, Richard, we used to call "Brainiac" due to his intellectual abilities. Mrs. Ruth's daughter, Dana, was only nine-years-old, and a real bitch if she didn't like you. Mrs. Ruth's house was like the saying; "There's always room for one more." I had ended up bunking with Richard since he had the cleanest room out of all of them. At least you could find his beds!

I checked in to the Tell avenue hotel that Sunday to live amongst five cats, a dying dog, Dana's monkey, a bird, and eight other ex-druggies. I felt like a veterinarian. The house was already almost full to capacity so I was glad I had gotten a bed. It seemed as though no sooner than I arrived at the house there had been a mad exodus of DETER residents that showed up on Mrs. Ruth's doorstep.

Her nephew had left with the promise that he would become an assistant director in a program in Amityville that was just getting off the ground. I felt like the luckiest person on earth. I mean what better position to be in to protect myself than to be surrounded by ex-addicts that seemed to have their shit together? It was almost too good to be true.

Mrs. Ruth told me that I had a place to stay for as long as I needed. She liked me the most, and was very fond of Uncle Bobby not only as her boss but someone she respected, yet had not always agreed with. I never thought she was so kind to me just for the sake of her job security, although she knew it did not hurt her chances for long term employment.

Right away I set out looking for a job in Suffolk County. I had not wanted to set foot in Nassau County again if I could avoid it. The first gig I accepted, just to have something going for myself, lasted until lunchtime of the first day! The only reason I did not walk out when the first break whistle blew at 9:45 that morning, was because I promised myself I would give it a chance.

The record for me working the shortest amount of time on a job was twenty-five minutes. That had been back in the summer of '67. That was when Donnie and I had jumped off the back of a loading dock, and ran like we stole something. It would have been safe to say that manual labor, and I never made for a good combination.

The new job had me working in a factory punching out parts all day at a machine that made so much racket you could hardly hear yourself think. The noise was enough for me to not return after lunch. My W-2 withholding form that I received that December showed a federal withholding tax of one penny. I hope Uncle Sam spent it well.

It would have been easy to get down on myself that first day for feeling like I failed again; but I didn't. Instead I walked over eight miles to the new program to talk to Louis and Bertha. Bertha had left DETER also to take a position with the new program. From the first time I had met her, even though she made me cut off my Afro to get into DETER, I had the utmost respect for her. She had a compassionate heart about her that was genuine, unlike 98% of the rest of her coworkers.

She told me not get down on myself, and was only the first job, and I had been home only six days. She told me not to rush things, and I should take my time until the right job came along. However, I knew that idle time was what used to get me into all kinds of trouble to begin with.

Before the next job interview that I went on I learned to ask more questions relating to the type of work I would actually be doing. During my next interview, when I was told I would be a "gold refiner," I thought I wasn't hearing correctly. The only image in my mind of gold refiners was back in the old Yukon days when miners sat at a stream all day sifting out gold ore from rocks.

Rather than to question anything, I looked at it as just something new I had never done before to add to my portfolio. The starting pay was $3.20 an hour plus they had a union just like the Post Office had. I viewed this, as an extra security blanket for me in the event I ever screwed up, then I knew someone would have my back. They asked when I could start, and the next day I was on the job that wound up lasting three years.

I was so happy that I called Mom, and told her the good news. At that time Dad was still kind of leery of my sudden about face in life. He had seen my efforts in times past only to see me screw up each, and every time. I respected his privacy at first, and knew that for him to accept me, the proof of the pudding would be in the eating. That was cool with me and looked forward to the challenge of proving myself worthy. Uncle Bobby and Aunt Helen were also happy that I was gainfully employed for the first time in two years.

Uncle Felix, and the relatives in Jamaica were thrilled, to say the least. You would have thought that I did something spectacular other than just getting a job, and holding on to it. He wanted to show his appreciation for my newfound happiness so I was invited to hang with him down on Delancy Street to shop for some new clothes. I had not even proven myself for very long, and there he would be trusting his instincts that his favorite nephew would be O.K.

I was so excited.

Our time together brought back to mind the good times we had taking the elevated subway downtown to shop back when I was in high school. It was Uncle Felix that taught me how to shop inexpensively. Since my image used to be one of a flashy dresser in school, no one ever knew my secret for styling in the latest fashions during my high school days.

He knew I had virtually nothing in my inventory in the form of decent clothing, so he bought me three pairs of pants, some drawers, and four shirts. Uncle Felix used to dress his ass off during his 40-year career with the New York Life Insurance Company. In the past he used to give me some of his old shirts, ties, and sports jackets if he just got tired of wearing them. I never had to worry that his stuff would be out of fashion.

My sex life was starting to bloom from the first night I spent at the Tell hotel.

All of those females that hung out there were addicts trying their hand at recovery, so it wasn't that I had to be a Don Juan to get over. None of them would have won any beauty contests. One white girl had so many stretch marks all over her body from trying to loose weight, and using steroids, that she looked like a zebra—and she was still fat! I don't think she could have given herself for free to soldiers on a troop train, but it mattered not to me at that time.

There had been this one 15-year-old named, Devona, who had the hots for me. I had enough respect not to get too involved even though she had a body that wouldn't wait. She was very fast for her age. We used to kiss, and did the heavy petting thing, but nothing more. The fact that she was white, and a minor to boot, I knew her folks would have had me under the jail. That was a good enough reason to leave her alone, but boy was she tempting.

Cathy was another white woman, who had been sleeping with Daryl, who was a former DETER resident now working with Louis and Bertha. Cathy was homely as a lemon, and wore those ugly, cat eye, plastic glasses. She was a 23-year-old widow with a 7-year-old son, and supposedly she had been raped in her

Los Angeles apartment at knifepoint. That incident happened in 1969, and her assailant had been black.

Her husband had died a year after the attack of some mysterious disease, so her story went. The thought of his wife being raped by a black man probably was what actually killed him. I don't know if that myth, "once you go black you never go back" was true or not, but she only involved herself with brothers after she moved to Long Island.

Although Louis, Daryl, and I were close since we all lived under the same roof, we were trifling, and we knew it. Cathy once slept with Louis in a motel claiming she was drunk, and knew not what she was doing. In a way that was believable. All she needed was some rum, and cola and she would get hotter than Dick's hatband.

One Sunday evening after Cathy and I had taken "Brainiac" with us to the movies, we dropped him home, and then we went to the local bar right around the corner on Deer Park Avenue for a drink. We had only stayed there for a little over an hour. When it was time to leave she was going to let me drive the three blocks home, but before I had gotten to the first stop sign, she started rubbing my inner thigh. I knew my turn would come to find out what was so good about her stuff.

She did not want to go back to her place, which I had suggested. Her reasoning was Daryl might have stopped by, seen her car, and would have wanted to come in. We detoured to an office complex about a mile from the house. God forbid I had to pay for a motel room.

Since it was a Sunday night no one was there. We started out doing the foreplay, and just as I was about to proceed further, a light came shining through the window on the passenger side. I knew it was a flashlight because it reminded me of being in jail. But, now the question was, "who was shining it?"

A security guard was on patrol in the complex, and he came up on us, and I never heard his car. I remembered thinking that I must be slipping, which was a good sign that I was starting to not always think negatively, and act paranoid.

Although we were not actually engaged in intercourse, it was still humiliating to know someone caught you with you pants down. I was glad it wasn't the police and just a security officer. At least he would be more understanding. I am also glad that Cathy didn't say I was trying to force her against her will since she was caught with her panties around her ankles. He just told us to leave the premises, and he got back into his car, and drove off. I was like, "Need you say any mo sir, you aint gots to tell me twice." I believe had the officer been white, he would have called the police.

The new program that had just gotten off the ground was called the AlbaNeck Halfway House. At first I spent a lot of time over there in the evenings after I got off work just to have something to do and remain focused. I also found myself in a position where I became aware that I was starting to substitute alcohol, and marijuana for the lack of hard drugs.

It seemed like the right thing to do since everyone else that stayed at Mrs. Ruth's house, including her son Toby had been smoking, and drinking. Louis, Daryl, and I would work all week, and then got high all weekend drinking beer, scotch, and smoking weed. I thought all was fine, and I never missed a Monday going to work because of being hung over.

It felt good opening a bank account again. I had always been good at saving for a rainy day. My goal was to bank no less than 80% of my paycheck every week. I would work as much overtime that I was allowed to work under the labor laws. I was hungry, and on a mission to be successful, once I found out what being successful meant.

I had made a few friends on the job. It was the typical factory setting where all the blacks, and Hispanics were in the back, and every office worker, and supervisor was white. We would play bid whist every lunch hour, and other than Sims taking each game so serious to the point of arguing all the time, it was something to do. I wasn't there to make a political statement using the race issue, but to just do my job, get paid, and save my money.

Since I did not have a car, I used to have to hustle a ride to work. My coworkers Caesar or Sam would always give me a lift to the Wyandanch center so I could ride home with Mrs. Ruth. Each day that I reached Tell Avenue I felt that much more secure within myself. What a great feeling that was. The only time I would go anywhere would be with someone from AlbaNeck or with "Brainiac," even though he was only 14.

I was still horny all the time and anytime a new female came around either to stay at the house for a while or just to visit, I would check them out. It became a joke to guess just how long it would take to end up screwing one of them. The average time was usually the same night we met. My track record was unbeatable. Even Louis, and Daryl were amazed at how much sex I was having. They considered themselves the kings of dipping from the "pussy well" so to speak.

MEETING WITH DESTINY

Around the first week of November, Richard started telling me about this nice looking girl that would come over around 7:30 each weekday morning. The nice looking girl would be dropped off at the house in order to catch the school bus to go to school with Toby. I didn't mean to raise my voice at him for not telling me about her sooner as she had been coming to the house every morning after I had left for work.

This girl's mother used to drive the 15 minutes from Wyandanch to Deer Park everyday. The reason was so Mrs. Ruth's address could be used for her daughter to go to school in that school district. I had not been aware that Wyandanch High School was voted one of the most dangerous high schools in America.

Richard told me the only reason he didn't fill me in about her was because he knew she was only 16, and had some sophistication about her—unlike the females I was accustomed to.

What did he say that for?

He was nice enough to at least tell me her name was Janice.

He was speaking the truth, but I was always up for a challenge. If I was to change my ways, I might as well begin by finding a decent young lady to be with. How would I ever progress any further along my road to recovery by continuing to hang with women that were no better than I was at the time?

Yes, it made sense to me. I just had to take the chance for getting rejected by Janice. It would be worth the price to pay.

I was not sure whether I needed to prove to myself that I could become a better person and live up to a woman's higher expectation or I had wanted to just feed my ego. There hadn't been a female that darkened the door of the Tell Avenue hotel that I hadn't screwed, and I had my reputation at stake. Regardless of the true reason, my curiosity had been aroused, and I was determined to meet this young lady named Janice the next day.

Well I got my wish, but I didn't have to wait until the next day. So far my luck was still holding out. Part of me was starting to get nervous as to how long it would last though.

When I came home after work that very same day that I had learned about Janice, I walked in the front door as usual to take off my boots before going any further. But this was not to be a usual evening for me as I was about to finally meet the mystery girl. I looked up into the kitchen, and there was Mrs. Ruth, and this very attractive young sister in the kitchen cleaning of all things—fish.

"Great," I said to myself. "What a way to meet such a beautiful person."

There I was all greasy, wearing a green uniform, and these ugly black rubber boots with the steel toe painted bright yellow; there she was cleaning those nasty, smelly, fish. Talk about love at first fright?

I put my image of a Don Juan, and ego on the side burner. All of a sudden none of that stuff meant anything to me. Something just told me that I could not allow anything to stand in my way of meeting her. The worst that could have happened was I would get my feelings hurt if she turned her nose up at me. I was more than willing to get my feelings hurt if it had come to that. It would not have been the first time my feelings were stepped on, and it certainly would not have been the last.

As I walked up the stairs towards the kitchen to introduce myself to her, as I got closer she looked me squarely in the eyes. I got the feeling she was about to let me know that there was no way she would ever give me the time of day. Instead she said in a clam and polite manner, "Hi I know who you are. You used to go with Linda Conroy from Westbury didn't you?" I almost fell backwards down the stairs. I'm thinking how could it be possible for anyone in this small one horse town to have known anything about me, especially when I dated Linda almost five years earlier.

When I replied that I did have a thing with Linda, she further started to recall shit that happened in the park during the summer of '67 that involved myself and other people that I knew, including Linda. I'm thinking that Janice was a psychic or something. Did I do anything to her like steal from her or hurt her feelings in some way?

For the life of me I did not know who the hell she was before that day. It was not like me to have forgotten anything since I have the memory like an elephant; especially forgetting a face.

Despite not remembering whom this girl was it dawned on me that I was suddenly remembered for once in a positive way. For so many years of my young adolescent life, I was constantly being told of all the negative stuff I'd done, I began to wonder if there was any good left in Bruce at all.

I went down to my room to shower, change, and then try to figure this person out. It was something about her mystique that got my attention. She also was the most beautiful girl I had met up to that point except for Linda. She was definitely a girl I could and would love to take home to meet Momma. I had been sharing myself with several bow-wows, and I never had the nerve to introduce any of them to my family, which should have told me something.

That evening everyone had gone out of the house. Those that were living there were at the regular Wednesday night encountering group at AlbaNeck. Louis and Daryl made everyone, and that included Toby, attend except for me. Mrs. Ruth went to Dana's dance rehearsal where the child was learning to act more like a little girl than a tomboy. Brainiac went to his friend's house to study. Janice's mother was at their house waiting for her son to come back with the car so she could come pick her up. My desires were to take the opportunity we had alone to get to know her.

My mind was still always between the sheets and my average bed down time for new female acquaintances was less than 24 hours, I didn't see why tonight with her would be any different. I'm assuming that since every other female that entered the house was "that type of girl" why should she be any different.

Well, to my surprise she was different—much different.

After I got cleaned up and smelling good I joined her downstairs in the family room. She was just sitting quietly on the broken down sofa watching TV and petting the dog on the floor next to her feet. I sat next to her and we started to talk. She explained how and when she met Linda and the Conroy family. In May of 1967, her older sister Beryl had married Linda's brother Phillip, the wimpiest brother out of the four of them.

Janice told me that not one of Linda's family members came to the wedding because they did not care too much for his choice of bride. That did not surprise me since they hardly cared for anybody anyway. Since they never got the opportunity to meet her family and vice versa, during that summer Beryl suggested that her baby sister spend one or two weekends out in New Castle since she was close to the same ages and get to know each other better. So it was during these visits that she knew me from the times I would be holding one of my comedy hour routines on the bench near the hand ball court.

After a half hour went by and I thought we had talked enough, I started to ease closer to her. I figured we were friends by now and no need to keep talking when I wasn't sure when her Mom would show up to pick her up. She stopped me right in my tracks and one 'mo time looked me straight in the eyes and said, "If you think for one minute that I'm like the rest of those dogs you've been sleeping with around here, you've thought wrong so keep your hands to yourself."

Low and behold and glory to God, for that was the beginning of a relationship that has lasted for thirty-three years.

Janice came into my life at a time when I was very vulnerable to find someone to love and in return love me. Despite all of the negative hang-ups that I still had not gotten over, she believed in me. I could not have made it through those times I was making the transition from bad to good, without Janice by my side every step of the way. What a blessing she was from God at just the right time.

I still wasn't ready to settle down with that one special person yet did not want to risk losing the feelings I had for Janice. I did not have any feelings or emotions for the other two women I was seeing so if I had to, breaking up would not have been hard to do. I was trying to have my cake and eat it too.

How pleasant to have met someone at a time when I wanted to forget a lot of my past wrongs and replace those times with positive ones. It was so different for me to meet someone that I wanted to share my life with. I became so defensive and cold towards people. For that reason the only people that I felt comfortable around were people that I felt were just like me. Part of my problem was that I wasn't sure who Bruce really was anymore but boy was I anxious to find out.

When I would be with Janice I heard more positive reinforcement for the good that was inside of me. As we both started to feel more comfortable with each other and sharing our life history, the more we found we had so much in common. Turned out that her older brother had a drug problem also. She asked if I remembered back to that very first night we met when she had to wait for her ride to come pick her up. She told me that it was because her brother used to take the family car and go off sometimes and came back when he wanted.

Her older brother Morris had also been in the program I just left. I did not get a chance to meet him as he split before I got there. I wondered why so many people would tell me I looked just like this brother that just left two days before I arrived. I did not know I had a twin at the time until we finally met and saw the striking resemblance. He also had a hell of a sense of humor just like me.

Janice expressed how strained her home life was with all the pressure and tension of living with someone who was addicted to heroin. As she spoke, I could relate to how Lisa must have felt when Stephen, and I were putting our folks through all that shit while she was so young. I had never realized how much other people suffer because of a person's addicted behaviors, especially within a family household.

We talked further as to how neither of us ever wanted to be around that kind of turmoil, sadness and uncertainty in our lives. Both of us shared how much of an influence our Grandmothers were in our formative years and how close we were to them. We shared a common goal together without even realizing it.

I knew Janice was too nice a person to have to put up with my ways and me. I actually tried to sabotage the relationship BEFORE we got too serious. After talking more and more with Janice, I felt I could never provide her with the things in life that she would be so deserving of. As often as Janice told me that she cared about me and material things did not matter that much, being the skeptic that I was, I did not buy it at all. In my heart and mind I thought who could ever settle for a person like me and I believed it and I meant it.

In the meantime, I continued to sleep around. I had enough respect for Janice to understand that at 16 she was still young and needed to wait for Mr. Right to come along. I could not have pressured her into doing anything she wasn't going to do anyway, so I never tried. I wasn't that good and even if I was; I knew that my intentions were becoming more in line with doing what was right by people.

So whenever I wanted to be with someone in a physical way, I had those that were at my disposal for that purpose only. Not to sound cocky or brash or anything like that, but it wasn't like these women expected anything more from me than I was giving anyway.

It was strange taking Janice out since I had to answer to her parents just like when I was in school. I had to adhere to the curfew, and being a gentleman at all times around them. Truth be known, I actually enjoyed that part of the relationship. Having missed out on doing nice things like that in a mannerly fashion during my latter school years bought back memories of the times when I did.

During those years of calling on a girl and dating were times when I was a much happier person. Having the chance to relive those years over made me feel as though I was that much closer to becoming a human being again.

Janice had introduced me to a restaurant in Commack name Adie's. She must have known that my passion for Italian food was the way to win my heart. Not only was the food excellent, but also the ambiance was so romantic. Whenever I think of those early days together, I just get so melancholy just knowing that I would never had thought that we would still be together thirty-three years later.

SAYING GOODBYE TO GRANNY CAME SUDDENLY

By the middle of November I was still kind of unsure whether this thing called rehabilitation was what I really wanted to do. I know I'd say it over and over that it was, but was I really sure or just scared that I would fail again? I knew that I was starting to drink in excess. I was unhappy in my job situation not knowing how long I'd be doing factory labor and smelling toxic chemicals for a living. I was grateful and proud of myself for not missing days from work and being on time everyday. I just kept having those, "I know I can do better than this" moments. It would pass with time.

My record for working without ever taking a day off came to an end on the 2nd day of December of '71. It was the saddest day of my life the day Mrs. Ruth told me that my beloved Grandmother had passed away that morning. I had left work that day early after I had splashed some acid solution in my eye. She came to pick me up and take me to the MLK clinic across the street from the Wyandanch center. It was free since they all knew Uncle Bob Washington.

After the doctor saw me, and she gave me this ugly black eye patch like the one Captain Hook wore, we left. When we got back in the car I mentioned that wearing this patch for 48 hrs. was the worse news I've heard all day. Without even starting the engine, she just looked a me and said, "Unfortunately I have some more bad news for you. Your grandmother passed this morning."

At first I was shocked, then I got angry and next I just sat and cried like a natural baby. Why did this have to happen now? Why did I have to hear from someone outside the family? I got myself together and went back to the center and called Mom. Uncle Bobby had already gone home when he got the news.

I felt so helpless and alone. Hearing the sound of Mom's voice was music to the ear. I told her I'd be on the next train to Jamaica to be with her. I was not even sure if Uncle Bobby and Aunt Helen were on their way to be with Granddad but I didn't want to ride with them anyway. I wanted to be alone. Mrs. Ruth, bless her heart, meant well to offer me a ride, but after almost biting off her head out of emotion, she understood.

She gave me a ride to the house so I could "unstink" myself and change into some decent clothes. When she dropped me off at the train station, I couldn't wait for her to leave me alone so I could go to the liquor store and buy a half pint of scotch. I didn't even skimp this time and bought top shelf. This was not the time to cheapen Granny's death by buying that $6.95 a quart shit that my factory buddies used to drink every Friday when we got paid. So with my half-pint and 6 oz cup, I boarded the train once again for a journey that was not of a pleasant nature. It was the most thought provoking 1-hour ride that I ever took.

What a joy of relief though to know that before she passed away, she knew I was OK. She was going in the hospital at the end of November for open-heart surgery at the age of 71. She was a strong deeply religious woman and no one could have talked her out of her decision to go under the knife; not even Uncle Will. She believed in letting go and letting God take care of everything.

Both she and my Grandfather suffered from heart disease ever since I could remember. Between the two of them they must have had at least a half dozen heart attacks within the past 15 years. Granny always did fine during her times of recuperation but Granddad was a different story. He was more demanding of her for every little thing, even to get him a glass of water just a few feet away.

She had got so tired of him once and told him, "You'll never put me in my grave trying to keep you out of yours!" Granny was sick and tired of all the different medicines she had to take and still wasn't up to par. She felt the surgery to repair a valve was a do or die situation. If she made it fine and if she didn't she was comfortable with that outcome too. Either way in her mind there would be no more suffering. I could understand where she was coming from. I could relate to coming to a crossroads in your life where it is either shit or get off the pot.

Two weeks prior to her death I made the decision to not go with Louis to the Bronx to visit his folks. On this Saturday in particular I did not feel like hanging out in the Bronx while the sun was shining. It did not seem to ever shine in the Bronx, which made the days seem so depressing. I knew my family was going into Jamaica to spend the day with Granny before she was to go into the hospital and something told me to take my ass into Jamaica too.

What a blessing that was. Lisa and I took the bus up to Jamaica Ave. where all the stores were, to buy her a pair of slippers for her hospital stay. Mom, both Aunt Helen and Beatrice, and Uncle Bobby were there as well as her sister in law Buddie and her dear neighbors Ralph and Frankie. In a way it was like a farewell party although no one said it. Everyone including myself that knew her well felt she would come out of the surgery in one piece.

Perhaps that day with her helped to comfort me through all the hurt I felt losing her. I couldn't even go into the viewing room to look at her since I wanted to remember her the way I saw her last. I'm glad I made that choice. I missed out on being present for their 50th wedding anniversary that September because I was away and felt like shit about that. I was told that Granny was laid to rest in her blue satin anniversary dress and she looked beautiful. I still have a copy of a photo of the two of them together at their anniversary party at Uncle Bobby and Aunt Helen's house.

As a rule of thumb during times of death in families, there seems to be a lot of unnecessary bullshit to deal with that has absolutely nothing to do with what should be important. Since this was my first experience with a family death, I saw what I had heard from other people about how some family members can be real assholes. Our family would be no different but we got through it.

I was comforted not only by the love and affection of my parents and other relatives, but Janice and Mrs. Ruth were right there with me through the entire ordeal. Even though they got lost driving and missed the funeral, they came by the apartment to help out when we returned from the cemetery.

The help was needed as folks came and ate your food, drank the liquor and asked dumb ass questions about the dearly departed. If they remembered, then their condolences would be offered. The nosiest people are the worse since they knew not when to take their tired asses and go home. They offered little help in cleaning up and then you never saw those people again until the next funeral God forbid.

Needless to say that Christmas of '71 was not very joyous in our family. Uncle Bobby tried to pick up our spirits by having everyone over to their house but it just wasn't the same. Then when his sister, Aunt Beatrice, and his sorry excuse for a son in law started arguing, like they were in a bar, over what began as a friendly family poker game, it killed the fun. Why is it that some people regardless of the situation never change?

For me I found it odd that for my first Christmas that I could actually feel good about in years was marred by Granny's death. It was as if she was sending a message to me. She hung around long enough to see me get my life back on track, knew I would be with her and the family to hug and kiss for the last time and then feel at peace to go home to glory fulfilled. Maybe this was her plan and maybe it wasn't, but it was a good enough theory for me to move on and honor her with doing the right thing and make her proud. Janice calls her my guardian angel.

OVERCOMING A FEW ROAD BLOCKS ALONG THE WAY

Right after Christmas I started to drink more often than just the standard Friday afternoons. That was when a group of us from work would go out to cash our paychecks, grab a sandwich form the deli next to the liquor store and then buy a quart of scotch. The ride back to the job took only 15 minutes so we had to drink fast. I took mine with ginger ale but Sam and Caesar had to be macho and drink theirs straight.

You would have thought after I accidentally got nitric acid in my eye earlier in December I would have enough sense to not work while half drunk. The department Caesar and I worked in was highly toxic and dangerous. I always figured that the only people stupid enough to breath acid fumes all day would be a brother, although the pay was good.

Our drinking got so bad there for awhile that when it was time to go home for the day, the five of us would actually be leaning against the wall while waiting to clock out because we could hardly stand up. Adding insult to injury, Caesar or Sam was my ride home and I was grateful that we never got into an accident or arrested for D.U.I.

Before long Sam and me started to drink on a daily basis. Caesar went on the night shift to get away from his nagging wife and the other two brothers got fired, so Sam and I became good friends as well as drinking buddies. I knew this had to stop. Why kick one habit only to start on another was the question I needed to answer. Knowing that addiction is addiction regardless if you're drinking soft drinks or over indulging in watching dirty videos.

As if this new part of my life was not enough, I won the affection of yet another female. It's not as if I was on the prowl looking either. My levels of comfort for female companionship were satisfactory as far as I was concerned. Mercedes was overweight and had these big ass bulging eyeballs the size of silver dollars. She looked like death standing on a corner sucking on a lifesaver! She was lonely as best I could figure and as my personality was one of a clown, I made her laugh a lot.

She started bringing me lunch to work on a daily basis. Barbara and Gladys used to play cards with us at lunch and they started to tease me to watch out. I didn't know her daddy was a preacher man and her brother Theodore worked in another department until they told me. Hell if that was all I had to worry about I was fine. Her brother was married yet he was screwing a married woman that worked with him and I knew what preacher men were all about. Yeah it was safe to say that my concerns were minimal.

I never had any intentions to have a romantic relationship with her. I had heard from Nelson, one of the other two drinking buddies that he tried to get next to her poontang and she acted like she was being raped. He warned me that she was a weird person. So why did I accept her advances? The thrill of another challenge was the answer. Since Nelson was only 5 foot 2 inches and couldn't have weighed more than 130 pounds, Mercedes might have been afraid she might crush him if the going got too good to her.

The day came when I could no longer refuse to accept her offers to make dinner for me. I had no more good lies left in me to use as excuses; another sign that I was changing. She planned on making a romantic dinner one Friday evening and emphasized that her folks were out of town for the weekend with their church. I thought that if her dinner was as good as the lunches, then it would be worth the risk and worry about the repercussions at a later date.

After a candlelight dinner of Lasagna with all the fixings and a bottle of wine, we went downstairs to the basement to listen to some music and talk. I was going to just bide my time until she offered desert and then leave. If my will power and curiosity was at the same level as my common sense, I'd been fine. She was another one that liked to drink rum, and after a few she got in the mood. As for me, 30 years later I'd still be trying to drink enough to get in the mood.

It had to be the worse experience of my active sex life.

She was so fat it took me about 10 minutes to undo her brassiere. The back had about six hooks to unsnap, that's how wide the support strap was. I had never seen anything like that before. That was challenge number one. After I was done with that ordeal, trying to get her girdle off was even worse. I would have had an easier time trying to shoe a horse. That was challenge number two. Challenge number three was trying to get in the mood after all that hard work.

In a flash it was over: thank goodness.

By the time she put all her "equipment" back on, I had sobered up some. She didn't smoke weed so I had to depend totally on the alcohol. When I realized again what she looked like and how much I had just struggled to get to her love nest, I said to myself, "Bruce, you should be shot and stewed for shit!"

Trying to avoid her at work, after our half hour wrestling match and the one-minute quickie, was not all that easy. Finally she got the hint and stopped bringing me lunch. I was kind of sad that things turned out the way it did because them sandwiches girlfriend made were awesome but not worth the hassle.

A year later she got pregnant. You should have heard the ladies then. I was teased that her daddy would be after me with the shotgun. I told them that unless she was a real elephant and not just looking like one, mathematically it was impossible for her to have become pregnant after our one and only encounter at doing "the nasty."

I bought my second car the week after Christmas in '71. How ironic that it was another '65 Oldsmobile, but this time it was a small Cutlass model. The car had a manual transmission so the gearshift was on the steering column. My Mom's best friend's husband in the Bronx had a friend who would sell it to me for only $150 to help me get mobile.

So with another stroke of good fortune that came my way, I got a ride up to the Bronx with John, the resident mechanic at the Tell hotel. The car needed some minor transmission work and I did not want to chance crossing the Throggs Neck Bridge and have the car break down. It was fun reaping some of the good fortunes that came from doing the right thing.

The car did very little for my image and ego however as I still hadn't relinquished my title of "ladies man." Having to drive a car like that, reminded me of what my Dad told me when I was ashamed to drive Mom's '62 Comet to my senior prom. He said, "Four wheels beat two heels!" I had to live with that plus he was right.

I think there was no better example of feeling in my mind that the world was coming to an end, than when Dad said I could not drive his '65 Pontiac Lemans to my prom. My girlfriend at the time was not the reason I felt so bad. She had no business looking down on anyone's situation considering the home life she was living in. Just having a car in her family period would have made her a happy camper.

My main concern was the image thing again. I knew I could not show up to the elegant Huntington Town House for the prom and afterwards go into the city in Mom's car and party all night. I made up my mind if it came down to stealing a car for the evening I would have done so.

As fate turned out again in my favor the brakes on the Comet went out 24 hours before prom night. I am sure Dad thought I had paid someone to sabotage the car but this time I had nothing to do with the situation. He gave in and allowed me to use the car. I had Mr. Rogers on stand by to rent a car in his name for me if it came to that. He was our driver's education teacher and taught me to drive so he must have felt confident I wouldn't wreck the car or kill myself with his name of the rental agreement.

Attending the prom also meant money for the me. I had to hustle enough money for the tuxedo, prom tickets, corsage and the after prom festivities at the Hawaii Kai restaurant in Manhattan. I couldn't stand the idea of spending my hard earned money on something as foolish as a senior prom, so I had to make my money back somehow. No sooner than I arrived at the prom, I headed to the men's room to start taking customers for some pot and some blow. I didn't sell enough to break even, but I did come close.

As it turned out the prom sucked. A popular singer name Lenny Welch who's claim to fame was his only hit song, *"Since I Fell For You,"* never showed up. Once we got past the ice crystals on the cold green peas and our arms got sore from trying to cut into the horse meat disguised as beef, we weren't about to hang around for desert. Of course I could find humor in any situation. I even got dirty looks from people at Mr. Frazier's funeral service for making folks sitting next to me laugh in the church.

The prom night would not have been without its share of laughter for me. I could not believe my eyes when I saw Marty James walk into the Huntington Town House all duded up in his tux arm and arm with his own sister Nina. I had heard rumors that nobody had asked her to the prom. That came as no surprise since she looked like death dipped in misery. The surprise was being so desperate to go to her senior dance that she would ask her brother who was a sophomore to be her date.

They even had the nerve to take one of those professional photos and she was smiling so wide she could have gotten lipstick on both her ears. It would not have been my nature to cut him some slack so I had to tease him by asking if he was going to take her to a motel afterwards, which was customary.

For Mrs. Ruth and the residents, owning this Oldsmobile was a God sent. It started to get a little embarrassing driving to the supermarket in a beat up old school bus that she had converted into a drug center mobile. Even more humiliating was having that big bus that was painted brown, sitting in the driveway next to Mrs. Ruth's late husbands boat with the big hole in the side and sitting on cinder blocks. When you were trying to impress a girl, this was not the picture one would want to paint as living in a normal environment.

I only held on to the Cutlass for two months. After meeting Janice and four months of steady employment, it was enough to convince Mom that it was a safe bet to cosign for a loan for me to buy my third car. I had saved enough for a down payment of $500. I was going to donate the Cutlass to the house as my token of appreciation. I calculated that for the two months it averaged out to only $75 a month and it would have cost me more than that renting a car so I felt I had gotten my money's worth. Just two months after the car was turned over to the house it died on the side of the road. They ran that poor old car to its death.

Although I felt some doors starting to open for me in the real world of being a responsible adult, I was caught on the blind side. I let my guard down by forgetting that there were other people out there other than just dope addicts who were not honest. This was illustrated by the son of a bitch who sold me a used '68 Pontiac GTO that I just had to have. He didn't tell me the car had damn near been totaled in an accident. I was more excited than cautious so it was just as much my fault that I got burnt as his for being a lying ass salesman.

This guy was so good at his con that he pretended to have a hearing loss in his left ear. When Mom and I went to the dealership and he introduced himself, he immediately asked if we could speak up some because he was partially deaf in one ear from the Vietnam War. It sounded believable to us and who would doubt something like that anyway. The test drive was all I needed to tell Mom that this was the car for me. My image would be restored and I always wanted a car with a stick shift on the floor.

Cousin Howie and I took the car out on the road and drove to Washington, DC to visit Aunt Marilyn and Uncle Andrew. I had met a young lady when I went down there for the Thanksgiving weekend and I wanted to see her again, plus it was an opportunity to see what the car could do once we put our foot in the gas tank.

I never shook so much in my life.

The car vibrated so much you could hardly see anything clear out the rear view mirrors. I didn't even want to drive back so I let Howie drive the 4-½ hour trip and I sat in the passenger seat. I couldn't wait to get back so I could take it back to the dealership and make them fix whatever the problem was.

The next day Howie went with me to take the car back, but we decided to stop at Mickey Dee's first. We were sitting in the car eating and up to the car came this degenerate looking white dude. He looked to be no more than 30-years-old. He started walking around the front on the car and was staring closely at the hood. We thought he might have been on a furlough or wandered away from the VA hospital that was not too far away. When he put his hands on the hood and began motioning like he was wiping something off the fake hood ornaments, we got out to see what his problem was.

He must have noticed that we were not smiling when we asked him what his problem was, because he offered an apology right away. He said that he didn't mean any harm but just had to find out if that was the same car he almost bought himself. When I asked him if it was, his response was yes. His confirmation was noticing the same two scratches on the hood ornaments that were there when he was about to buy the car.

He was smarter than I was and took it to his mechanic to have them check the car over first. The mechanic told him the entire front end was shot to pieces and that it had been in a wreck and possibly written off as totaled out by the insurance company. I asked if he was sure and he said he would bet his life on it. I thanked him and felt that yet another person was put in my path of recovery to open my eyes to things I needed to know.

My pride would not allow me to fess up and let anyone most of all my Mom know that I got beat out of $1800. Welcome Bruce to it's time to get paid back for all you did to folks over the years that caused them heartache and a sense of loss. I kind of just accepted that sooner or later I would have to atone for the sins of my past and that was cool by me. I know $1800 was nothing to sneeze at, but all I could do at that point was to go and get the repairs done. I never did go back to face the salesperson.

Due to my excitement on my car purchase I recommended Boonky Boy, who was home from the program, to go to the same salesperson so I could get my $twenty-five referral fee. After he bought his used car from the dealership, then I went back with the reason that I came for my referral check. I wasn't even going to say anything to the "deaf" salesperson and chalk the whole situation up as an expensive lesson learned, but I just had to see him one more time.

Even if I had wanted to go off on his ass I couldn't have. When I asked for him, the sales manager told me that he no longer worked for him. He told me that he was terminated for unethical business practices. First thing I thought was, "Shit! Why couldn't he have been fired before I came in the first time?"

The business manager did not help me feel any better when he asked, "He didn't pull that old hard of hearing act on you did he? He was famous for using that for sympathy selling." He could simply look at the expression on my face and see that, yup, he had gotten another sucker.

Boy it was fun to be in the real world again, and I may even get used to it!

Slowly but surely it did not take me long to cut the alcohol loose. It was good I nipped it in the bud while I was still in the healing process rather than to have waited until I got to the point I was with hard drugs. The most important lesson

I learned that time was I was getting better at reacting sooner than being sorry later.

My friend Sam had practically taken me in as part of his family with his wife Sarah and three small daughters. It was a cautious type of relationship on my part as he was now drinking that cheap ninety-eight cent wine everyday at work. His supervisors knew but since he was just another Black man loyal to the company, and a damn good smelter, they turned their heads and accepted it. They also knew that they would be hard pressed to find someone in their right mind who would stand over 300 degree heat for eight hours making gold bars.

All was going along well until my Grandfather passed away on the 4th of April of '72. He died while on vacation in St.Croix. The medical conditions down there are not too cool. We had heard stories of an ambulance running out of gas, and carpet in the emergency room, so one could have imagined the kind of care he received. Mom felt bad that he had to check out there but it probably was best. Once his body was shipped back to New York and the funeral was over with I felt so proud of myself to have been there for Mom both times within four months.

I know it must have been tough losing both her parents so close together. Poor Stephen missed both funerals since he was upstate in Sing Sing Prison doing 18 months. Yes, the days of getting slapped on the wrist for him were over. He had made the big time and I was so thankful that I was not there to share those months with him. He tried to see if he could have come down state for the funerals, but they have to escort you in handcuffs and leg shackles, which would have been too embarrassing.

Janice and I had decided that we were in no hurry to go back out to Deer Park after the funeral. We elected to catch the subway into Manhattan and go down to Times Square and see a movie. I reminisced with her about the time I had busted Granddad dealing from the bottom of the deck during one of our nightly pinochle games.

We played at least three nights a week during the month that I stayed with them while working up on Queens Blvd. I had suspected him of cheating before when he always seemed to get more aces than Granny or me. But hell, half the time I was stoned when we played so I couldn't actually put my finger on how he was getting over.

Then one night I peeped his hole card as to what he had been doing all along and I decided to say something. Forgetting for the moment that he was my 70-year-old Grandfather and not some low down trifling dope fiend off the streets, I grabbed his hand, as he was about to pull a card from the bottom of the deck. It was the principle of it all, and the moment was all mine.

That took a hell of a lot of nerve even if I was stoned because once when I was only 11 years old, he grabbed me and scared the shit out of me for running around their apartment. Ever since that incident I had always been afraid of him and for almost a year I made all kinds of excuses not to have to go visit.

Dear ole Granny was a hoot. In her quiet reserved manner she looked at him and said, "Bobby, how could you? You know better than that. He's your grandson for goodness sake!" It was like she was scolding a kid or something.

Granddad gave that innocent look like a child that just got caught with white powdered sugar around his mouth and swearing that he didn't steal the jelly donut. God bless Granny. She knew her grandchild was a drug addict, but by Godfrey she wasn't about to let even her husband of 48 years cheat me. No sir, she'd have none of that on her watch.

I'm sorry that Janice and Granny never got a chance to meet. She had met Granddad at Granny's funeral, but Granny and her would have hit it off so well. I was also sorry that I never got to meet Janice's grandmother. From what Janice shared with me about her, she sounded a lot like Granny. Her grandmother had passed away the summer of '71. They were very close. We felt so fortunate to both believe that we had our Grandmothers as guardian angels protecting us from harm.

I went on to finish telling Janice that when I told the family after he died about the cheating incident they laughed. They told me that they knew he cheated for as long as any of them could remember. The difference was no one called him on to the carpet over it and just accepted it and never made an issue over it; it was their family secret. I felt worse after that revelation and wished that they had never told me. I really think I hurt his feelings bless his heart.

As we rode the subway and the more we talked, the more I started to get the feeling I could not live without this 17-year-old woman in my life; not if I wanted to be successful.

FINDING A PLACE TO CALL MY OWN

By June I was ready to boogie from the Tell hotel. It was getting so overcrowded that at least once a week the toilets would clog up and the house smelt worse than it did already. Mrs. Ruth's own children were starting to be treated as if they were boarders instead of us. The front door never stayed locked and it was like a revolving door with people constantly going in and out all hours of the night.

I'd wake up on any given morning only to discover a new face coming out of the bathroom. I was not scared that we'd be robbed because no one would have been able to find anything to steal if they could get past the stench. What used to scare me the most were not the conditions of the house, but the next-door neighbor's son.

Her neighbor had a son whose front porch light had gone out two years earlier after he survived a horrible motorcycle accident. He ended up in the hospital in a coma and was not expected to make it through the night. You could say it was nothing short of a miracle that he came out of it. I say a miracle because that is what he believed it was. In fact he believed so strongly about it that he became a religious fanatic.

He used to keep his head shaved so that you could see his ugly looking scar from where the doctors put a metal plate. Of course that was his business, however, when he used to come in the house whenever he felt like it yelling and screaming that he just got a vision from the Lord, then it became MY business. I had wondered if I was strong enough mentally to move on to the next phase of my life, but sometimes you just need that extra nudge to step out on faith.

Having money in the bank made it easier to part on good terms. The problem was I had not been on the job long enough to apply for an apartment on my own. It was not beneath me to go back to renting a room in someone's house. Thanks to Bertha I was introduced to some white lady name Anne who had a room to rent. Her house was in Wyandanch so that was cool. At least I'd be closer to work, my relatives, and Sam and his family. The house was nice but why did I always seem to run into the weirdest people?

Anne was on welfare because her black ex-husband fucked up all her assets, and other than her home she didn't have a Godamn thing to call her own. The only time she would dress out of her bedclothes was when she had to go down to the welfare office or to the doctor. She slept in a queen size bed with two Saint Bernard dogs for so long they started to all look alike. I didn't feel sorry for her for being that ignorant to get ripped off but I was grateful for the opportunity to move into my very own room. I would finally have some privacy.

I settled in to my new living quarters the day after the fourth of July and borrowed an old black and white 12-inch television from Uncle Bobby. Although he never said it to me, he seemed happier than me that I moved out of dear Mrs. Ruth's house. He had been to her crib on a few occasions so he knew the deal.

Maryanne had been living with Anne for almost a year since she kicked her habit and was employed at AlbaNeck also. She lived upstairs by herself. I had met her previously over at the halfway house and she seemed like a nice person. What struck me as fascinating with her was that she had the filthiest mouth I'd heard from a female, yet the kindest, and most honest person I had met other than Bertha.

Maryanne would cuss you out in a heartbeat if your hand called for it. She used to cuss out everyone at the halfway house and that included the director himself. When she was right you couldn't argue her down.

I felt sorry for Maryanne as she had a heart of gold but could not find a decent man to love her for whom she was. She had a boyfriend who was insanely jealous and had every reason to be. He wasn't ugly nor was he pretty. Guess you could say he was in between; he was pretty ugly!

I knew she liked me so we spent some evenings together up in her room. She used to get the best pot in Wyandanch and one evening we got bold and got it on before "Superman" came to visit after he got off work. He didn't have a key so when we heard a car door slam around midnight, I gathered my belongings and made it down to my room before he rang the doorbell. The next day she laughed as she told me he never noticed a pair of men's high top Pro Ked sneakers at the foot of her bed that weren't his.

My other heart's desire was to have a bathroom that had ALL the fixtures working at one time. While I was in Deer Park the toilets hardly worked, now I move to Anne's and it used to take an hour to run hot water in the tub to take a bath. I wasn't asking for much. Even in jail you got to toilet yourself and shower with hot water without any hassles.

After only a month living with Anne I began to start my apartment search whether I qualified or not. I could not get used to turning on hot water to bathe, go to the Mount Ave. Park to play a game or two of hoops with cousin Howie, go home and the tub would only be 1/2 full. In all my years of living on the edge, I vowed from then on if nothing else I would stay clean.

Though dating Janice made me feel like I was back in high school again, this time around I could enjoy myself when we went to a movie or out to eat. This time around I did not have to be the center of attention wherever I went. I could relax and feel it was OK to have another person have center stage. I stopped feeling so intimidated by others and felt if I spoke up for something I did not agree with, I didn't have to answer to anyone for it.

You could say that at 22-years-old, I was just starting out fresh and anew or as some folks call it being born again. I wanted so badly to take my time this go around and not be so hasty to taste the forbidden fruits of life, especially anything negative.

Caesar lived out in a town called Central Islip about 20 minutes from Wyandanch. I had been to his place only once to visit but was impressed at how quiet and peaceful it was. The only other time I had heard of Central Islip was in '68 when Stephen spent a couple of months there for his addiction before he was transferred to Woodbourne. When we would go out there to visit from Westbury it seemed like it was in another state.

Since I was in the market big time for an apartment all of a sudden it didn't appear to be that far off the beaten path. In fact I considered it more as a security blanket because it was so far removed from my old environment. Most apartment complexes would offer a referral fee so Caesar was excited about the prospect of earning $100 if I applied and was approved.

REUNION WITH BITTER SWEET MEMORIES

Although I had experienced quite a bit in my short life span, I never experienced what I considered all out blatant racism. I felt some in high school but it was more that I was a stone cold fuck up than anything else. The short-lived riot of '68 was started because I got into a fight with an Italian dude in the hallway at school. He accused me of stealing his wallet from a gas station the night before while he was working there. He remembered me coming in with Markey boy and Tommy and asking to use the restroom.

He was right about what I had done, but the fight escalated when one of his friends jumped in and then it became two against one. I still could have lived with that, except as I was on the floor getting my ass whipped again, I happened to look up and there stood Mr. Southern watching, and not making any attempt to break the shit up.

That was the beginning of my week suspension from school and the white folks getting all riled up over us "niggers" disrupting their school system. There were one or two aftershock incidents during my week long hiatus, which fueled the Long Island Newsday's racist's comments in the paper. During this week also, Martin Luther King was assassinated and then the black folks went into mass hysteria and looting and burning became commonplace.

Throughout all of this time of turmoil, I still did not feel as though there was a problem with racism. Prior to drugs altering the character of many of us black kids in the late '60's we all got along quite well from third grade on. In spite of all of our boldness as the years went on into high school, we were not crazy enough to fuck with the Italians up on the hill. They would shoot your ass, and think nothing of it with little repercussion for their actions.

One week before graduation the administration held a little get together for all the seniors. I attended and it was amazing that just two months prior to graduation the school was in such chaos and here we were laughing and socializing as if nothing happened. Patrick and I shook hands and gave a love hug and agreed that our little skirmish should not have resulted in a mini riot.

I was very reluctant to attend my 20-year high school graduation in November 1988. If not for the encouragement from one of my dearest friends, Sandy, Janice, and Mom, I would not have gone. I knew that I had nothing to be ashamed of in regards to my current life and owed no explanations to anyone. My apprehension was based solely on fear that I would be remembered for only the bad person that I was in my final two years of high school. My argument was why should I have spent over $300 to go back to where I felt I would not be welcome.

After checking out the updated mailing list of who RSVP'd, and making sure that Janice would be back from a business trip in order to attend, I made my travel arrangements to attend. Janice was to fly to New York the day after. I flew up to Baltimore where Kelvin was living at the time. Kelvin picked me up from the airport, and the two of us drove up to New York. He had promised to let me drive his Jaguar part of the way, but never did.

Not that getting to drive a Jag was the only reason I took the longer route, but I wanted to spend some time just talking with him. We had just gotten back in touch after many years, and at the time he was the only successful brother from our neighborhood. I was fascinated that he made it out of New Castle in one piece, and went on to become a doctor.

His Dad, God rest his soul, used to be one of the funniest parents I knew growing up in New Castle. I got to know him well because of his entrepreneur spirit. I always admired that quality. He also used to hang out and loved the hustle also, which made him well known in the community. His real estate and taxicab businesses made us youngsters feel that we could be successful businessmen also.

So to know that one of his five sons made his way on through the tough times, and financial burdens of medical school, to become successful, had to give him bragging rights. He was always talking about his son the doctor, and rightfully so.

I am blessed to have Kelvin as one of my best friends. In fact he is like a brother to me. All too often when those from whence they came from become successful, they act like they are too good to even say hello to those that they used to eat their lunch out of a brown paper bag with.

To my surprise, with over 300 classmates, spouses and faculty members as chaperones, only one asshole had to bring up the race incident. He had always been a creep in school anyway so I overlooked his stupidity and enjoyed the evening. They organized the affair really nice and the committee would send out monthly updated lists of who responded. I had no idea that so many people after 20 years would show much of an interest.

The committee felt that if they kept updating us on who was coming, and then someone just might have seen a name that would entice you to attend. If for no other reason than to see that one person after 20 years would have been a valid reason. Their strategy worked on me. I was surprised when I saw so many names of classmates that I just had to go.

Janice just had to go also, even though she had only met a handful of my friends and a few classmates six years into our marriage. I wanted to show her off to everyone that was there. After all she was the main reason for me being where I was in my life and if she couldn't have made it then I wasn't going to go.

I didn't see Janet Clifford's name on the monthly updates, so when she walked up to me at the reunion, I was speechless for a moment. We hugged so hard and she told me the only reason she was there was she saw my name on the list. Since she still lived in Westbury it was not a problem for her to come at the last minute. She looked fantastic and still had her red hair and freckles. She was honest when she told me that she just knew I was dead. Janet was one of the few white chicks in school that was down with us.

She used to smoke more pot than us and although there was never any sexual part to our relationship, we were always good friends. She even bought a photocopy of the page in her yearbook where I wrote one of my famous morbid farewells that if I died she'd have to come to the funeral.

I was also glad to see my English teacher Ms. Seebert. She was kind of controversial at the time when I had been one of her students in 10th grade because she was young, gorgeous and loved Black men. She once had them print a poem that I had written for her class in the school paper. She was so glad that I attended and when I introduced her to Janice she turned to her and said with emotion, "I just knew he'd turn out O.K. and I never doubted he'd overcome his troubles."

That was just one more warm and fuzzy feeling I could add to the bank along with all the others. I was saddened to learn however that she was battling ovarian cancer and to this day I never made the attempt to find out if she is dead or alive. I didn't want to know.

MOMENTS OF TRUTHS TO BE DEALTH WITH

Meanwhile, back out in Central Islip while going to several apartment complexes and being made to feel as though I wasn't welcome because I was Black was very demoralizing. Here I was investing all of my time and efforts to do the right things and be a productive person in society only to feel unwanted. That sucked big time. I was just about to go back into my militant bag after the last incident took place in another one horse town called Hauppauge, when luck struck again.

Caesar not only was trying to get the referral fee, but he was trying to hit on the rental agent and she was receptive. He came to work one day and told me that there would be two vacant apartments in October and to go out and see his "friend" and she would hook me up. Even though I was trying real hard to do things on the up and up, reality still was, "it's not what you know but who you know." Worked for me. I filled out all he paperwork, turned over my pay stubs, bank records and the waiting began.

I decided to ask Dad much to my reluctance if I could move back in with him for the waiting period, which was hopefully only six weeks if all went well. He knew from the times I would stop by and visit that this was by far the longest attempt made to try and turn my life around. I ran my idea past Mom first. We both agreed that it would be a good idea and this way I could save my money for when the day came to move.

Of course Mom had always been more open-minded than Dad but out of respect we still had to honor his privacy. He'd been alone now for two years, and anything out of his normal routine could be a distraction for him.

Together Mom and I went over to Rushmore Street to present our idea. I knew it wasn't going to be easy to convince him to stick his neck out again for me, but I felt it important to try for two reasons. Reason number one was to prove I was sincere more than ever. Reason number two was to show him that I would not let him down again.

Well, we got the response we expected. Dad was never one for a definitive yes or no but was famous for his bringing up past shit regardless of his final decision.

Hell, it was his house and we all left him, he didn't leave us, so I had to be humble and "eat a little cheese" and sit back and let him have his say.

Mom started to get noticeably pissed since she was tired of always hearing excuses, and as for me, I felt like I was back in the middle of their relationship and I didn't want that to happen. Just as I was about to say to forget the whole thing, Dad agreed to give me another chance. I knew that it was his opportunity to vent his frustrations for having to live alone for two years because of all the shit that happened in the past, especially when he kicked me out the house on my graduation night.

The main purpose for the arrangements was to save some money. I would need two months deposit at $210 a month. I used to vision on a daily basis how the apartment would look with furniture, and my own added touch. When the agent showed me the two choices, I selected the one bedroom on the second floor with the balcony facing the open front courtyard and the street. In my mind it was the most beautiful place in the world.

I had already told Janice about what I had done, and she was happy for me. She may have not known it at the time but this apartment was for us. I didn't want to live alone anymore. I had too many lonely nights by myself already, and since I kept wishing for someone just like her to come into my life, why would I not want to spend my time with her?

Anne was sad to see me have to move out. Not that she really gave a shit about me, but she'd be losing out on my $100 a month rent. As for me, I had put my stuff together as fast as humanly possible for the move back to Rushmore Street before Dad had a change of heart.

It would have been my first time back under his roof in two years and I could hardly wait. What a feeling of joy that the occasion was on pleasant terms. I swore I would never do anything to bring hurt, and pain to him ever again. I owed him at least that much.

The kid here had become so frugal, and past the point of cheap, that I would even take my lunch to work. This was a far cry from the Bruce that used to be so ashamed of having to take his lunch to school in Jr. High school because Dad couldn't get off of 35 cents for lunch money, that I would throw my brown bag away before I got to the bus stop.

I wouldn't take Janice or my other two companions anywhere that cost money. If it wasn't free we weren't doing it, and that included going to a motel to get laid. I would call that strong resolve for someone like me but all I was focused on was to save every dime for the apartment that I hadn't even gotten yet.

It felt so good eating dinners with Dad during the week and spending time with him when he came home from work around 7:30 in the evening. From time to time I would even cook something for us so he wouldn't have to do anything when he got home but sit down and eat. I was convinced in my heart that he had started to see for himself the changes in me. I used to feel kind of sad that Stephen wasn't here to share the new found bonding that was felt in the house we grew up in.

The last thing I wanted to do was have Stephen feel that I had gotten so big headed that I had forgotten about him. I could never have done that. During my brief stay with Dad, I had taken Janice with Mom and I to visit Stephen. Janice would tell me years later that it was the most uncomfortable feeling she's had in her life. She had refused to even go see her own brother in a county jail so I never imagined the impact on her to visit Sing Sing. She knew how much it meant to me at the time so she did not say anything.

As I made my way slowly into the cafeteria at work at 10:15 AM that 7th day of October 1972, to call the rental office to find out the status of my application, I had to admit I was not too optimistic. Even with the help of Caesar's lady friend, my hopes were kind of dim. I had felt that the apartment was asking God for just a little too much too soon after He had just delivered me from drug addiction.

I had never tried to accomplish anything of this magnitude before so I was prepared for the big letdown if it was to happen. I was so nervous the sweat on the tips of my fingers almost made it difficult to press the buttons to dial the phone. I remembered hanging up twice before anyone answered so I could gather my courage to hear what the verdict was going to be.

This was so different from going to court and being nervous as to your fate because now so much depended on my stability, credit, and work history as well as my background check. These were things that I had never owned before, and I was not sure just how well society would view them.

On the third attempt, the lady answered the phone. By this time I had grabbed a chair from one of the tables, and was sitting down. "Well Mr. Codrington," she said, "Everything looks O.K. and the apartment will be ready for you to move in on the 15th of the month. We need a week to paint and clean it up."

She went on to advise that the rent would be prorated, and I would only be charged from the 15th through the end of October. She asked me if that would be satisfactory. I just sat there in total shock. I never had anyone ask me a question like that before. I did not even know what the word prorated meant, but all I heard was everything was O.K., so I could care less about anything else.

The second time she asked if that would be fine, I just said sure. It was already the 7th of October so eight more days was not gonna kill me, so I gave her the impression that I wasn't worried about anything.

I thanked her, and when I hung up the phone I could not help but yell out loud, "Yes I did it, I did it!" Those employees that were on their break in the room must have thought I just won a million dollars or I was just crazy. At that moment I did not care about what anyone thought of me. I knew what I thought of me and it felt damn good so that was all that mattered.

My first call was to Jamaica to tell Dad, and the folks the good news. Mom was next on the agenda, and then of course Janice. What a happy day that was for not only me but for all those that had faith in me during those 12 months. All the sacrificing and efforts was paying off.

I didn't cry until I went into one of the stalls in the men's room and flushed the toilet several times so no one would hear me; a trick I learned in jail. The john at work was not the best spot for my emotional bubble to burst but it made do for the time being.

Sam had already promised me he would help me move since he had a pick up truck and Caesar was not only happy he would receive $100 but was glad to have me as a neighbor.

Everyone was so happy for me that I began to feel insecure all over again like all this good fortune was too good to be true, especially for me. I still hadn't felt that I paid enough dues on the good side of my life to merit all this happiness at one time. Nothing to it but to just enjoy it for as long as it lasts.

PRECIOUS MOMENTS WITH DAD

That Sunday afternoon Dad and I were sitting around reading the paper and watching some of the baseball playoffs on TV. He handed me an advertisement for Seaman's furniture store and asked if I liked the picture of a bedroom suite. I didn't want to say yes right away since I had planned to take the pullout sofa bed from the basement with me to sleep on.

I saw that he was serious, and I felt if I turned down his gift offering then I might have hurt his feelings. The advertisement listed the sale price as $299. The suite consisted of a double bed, mattress and box spring, a night table, a men's chest and a woman's dresser with a mirror. It seemed like a good buy to me but then of course I wouldn't have known the difference in pricing anyway. When would I have had time to buy anything nice using heroin?

Dad asked if I wanted to go over to Hempstead and take a look at it. I was getting a little nervous about his new attitude until I realized that he was my dad and that he loved me, and this was his way of showing it. He never was good at expressing his emotions other than when he got pissed off, so it had been awhile since I saw his temperament outside of me getting scolded for fucking up. We got in the car and drove over to Seaman's with me thinking all the while that we were just going to look.

The furniture was beautiful, and I pictured how it would look in my brand new master bedroom. Boy the word "master" really made me feel important. I would have my very own "top drawer" in my own chest just like Dad. The top drawer was his office. Growing up, I had always wondered what all was in there. It was such a secret place that was off limits to everyone, and that included Mom.

Without realizing it, growing up and observing Dad's routine about life was a learning experience that I would later incorporate into my adulthood. I felt as though the top drawer was like my right of passage into manhood. I often wondered if Dad knew the real significance of his gift.

Dad loved to talk to strangers so the salesman and him were having a good old time talking baseball. They both asked how I liked it as I was bouncing on the mattress like a little kid for the first time. The mattress had little to no comfort but it was no big deal in the grand scope of things to come.

I told him that I liked what I saw and felt. I could see the salesman's mouth watering in anticipation of a sale. I was laughing to myself as I thought he might as well wipe that grin off his face because I knew Dad; he NEVER bought anything the first time out.

When we first moved to Rushmore Street in 1959, I remembered that a Kirby vacuum salesman came to the house, and stayed for almost three hours! He was talking faster than he was thinking. When the time came for the conclusion of his marathon demonstration, Dad simply thanked him and got up to shake his hand. The poor guy looked like he had just heard that one of his family members had died. He assumed the sale, and Dad assumed he wasn't buying shit without sleeping on it first.

When I thought we'd be on our way home after checking things out, Dad came out of his bag with another shocker. He asked the salesman could the merchandise be delivered within two weeks. The salesman immediately went over to his desk to check the delivery schedule for Central Islip. I just stood quietly. I didn't want to act too surprised, and show any disrespect by not thinking in my heart he had it in him to do something that nice.

The man came back after checking the schedule and assured Dad that it could be delivered by the 22nd of October, one week after I move in. After the sale was written up I believed that not only did he buy me a gift, I felt I had given him one also. My gift could not be seen but only felt in the heart. That moment we shared would last for my lifetime. As we walked back to the car for the drive home, I felt as though my life truly had a new beginning to what I had only thought to be a tragic ending.

I called Janice that Monday to tell her the good news that we would have bedroom furniture, and not have to sleep on the sofa bed. The sofa bed had sentimental value because it had belonged to my Grandparents, but in all honesty it was a bitch to sleep on. After I said the word "we" to Janice I collected my thoughts and wondered why I just came out with that word. All along my intent was to have Janice share my apartment with me but only for a short time while her Mom and twin sister could find a place to stay.

If lying to one's self was a crime, I'd been guiltier than hell.

During the time of all of my good fortunes, Janice had to move up to the Bronx to stay with her older stepbrother, and his family. The living environment at her home was not too cool. Her Mom was being treated for a heart ailment, and the stress of her husband and son Morris not acting right, forced her to leave and take Janice and her twin sister with her.

I was not at all familiar with domestic violence at 22-yrs-old. The only time I had heard of abuse in the home was when Ralph's mother shot her husband to death right on the step at their front door. The man was a hard working mason but he was tipping around on his wife and that was taboo. This happened Memorial Day weekend of '71 and no one believed Marge when she used to come up to the bar, and tell folks that she was gonna kill that nigga. Otherwise I never grew up around physical abuse nor saw it displayed by anyone related to us.

I knew Janice needed and deserved a chance for a better life. She had already sacrificed a lot at such a young age by having to drop out of high school to work to financially help her Mom. For the past year we had been together sharing just about everything, I knew she was such a smart person, and had so much to offer society. Her home situation was not her burden to bear but she took the responsibility of helping her family without thinking only of herself.

I had never seen such a display of unselfishness in a positive way before. Yes I knew she was a special person. I also saw my offer to her as a way of giving back something of myself for all the good fortune that had come my way with her right there every step of the way. I felt as though God placed her in my life for a reason.

IT'S MOVING DAY!

When Saturday the 15th rolled around, Bruce was ready for Freddie! I had my utilities and phone hooked up, in *MY* name. I went out to the apartment that Thursday to make sure things met *MY* standards, and picked up *MY* keys. To think that I had a mailbox that belonged to me was astounding.

Sam knew what time to be at Dad's with his pickup truck. Janice's older sister Beryl arranged to bring Janice and Janice's stuff over to Dad's. I was confident that I had left no stones unturned. The only thing that I did not have control over was the weather. It was raining cats and dogs, and windy too. A small inconvenience for such a grand occasion was how I saw it. If that was the only rain on my parade then I was thankful.

When Sam arrived at the house and we started to take some of the furniture from the basement out to the truck, Dad excused himself and said he's be right back. I felt that he was getting a little sad that I was leaving after we had such a good time together and did not want to be around to watch me move. Where he was going in all that bad weather was between he and himself. We tried to keep the stuff covered with a big heavy-duty piece of plastic but the wind was very strong and kept blowing it off the furniture.

We kept on plugging away for about an hour and still no sign of Dad' return. Janice arrived and I was so glad that they made it in the bad weather. I was so glad to see her because now I felt the whole process was complete.

Beryl gave me a hug, and then she helped Janice unload the back seat, and put her stuff in my car. Just when I thought they had gotten everything into my car, Beryl popped open her trunk and it was packed with more stuff. It appeared that Janice had her whole life's belongings with her for just a "temporary" arrangement.

When Dad returned just as we were about to pack the last load into the truck, he looked like Santa Claus. He had gone down to the local appliance store and bought for us a toaster, blender, electric can opener, and a clock radio. He also had ordered some dinnerware to be delivered at a later date. I was so touched and I tried to hide the tears that were welling up in my eyes. He finally believed in me.

Although I was giving him $twenty-five a week he had saved it and used it to help me further get my feet on the ground. He was very fond of Janice so it wasn't like he was spending his money, and I was going to share my things with someone he did not care for or didn't even know. After a hearty hug from us to him, and vice versa, we piled into the Pontiac GTO and followed Sam for the 45-minute drive to our new home.

After we unloaded and dried off, Sam knew enough not to hang around. This indeed was a very special moment for Janice and I. Sam was a sensitive guy even though he was an alcoholic, and so he gave me a long bear hug before he left. I had to remember for a minute that he had watched my growth over the past year also, and was just as happy to see that I made it just as everyone else had.

When I closed the door behind him, I just looked back at Janice and had to pinch myself to make sure this was all real and not a dream. We just sat on the sofa bed and looked around our new home and hardly said a word.

Praise God and glory to His name, we have not been apart since.

WHAT A FEELING IT WAS
TO BE LOVED

When we got up the strength to unpack I sensed our relationship was there to stay when I saw all the things she bought new. She had "his" and "her" items for the bathroom and two coffee mugs that said the same. I wondered why she was getting so comfortable with me yet I knew in my heart that I was so glad she felt the same way I did.

I admit it was all very flattering to know that 17-year-old Janice would actually want to spend the rest of her life with me. Was this love or infatuation? Her attitude was almost like she was convinced I would be OK and never relapse; now all I had to do was convince myself.

I never did ask her parents for her hand in marriage. We tried to set the stage to tell her Mom by inviting her out to the apartment for dinner. Janice was to cook her favorite meal of chicken and red beans and rice. From the moment we picked her up from the train station and drove home, we had planned what and how to tell her that in 10 days we were going to become husband and wife. I knew that her Mom liked me a lot and felt I would be good enough for her daughter, but I wasn't sure if her feelings were like Janice's in terms of the abstaining from drugs.

The meal was delicious and the visit was enjoyable until the time came to take her back to the train for the ride back to her place. We never did get around to telling her our plans. We found out after we were married that she knew what the deal was when she came to visit. She knew we were living together, that Janice's story about visiting that day was a lie and that we would get married soon. Moms seem to know stuff like that.

When I told my friends at work I wouldn't be in to work Tuesday the 30th of October because I was getting married, not one person other than Sam believed me. To them it was just another joke. It was customary to pass the envelope around the factory so take up a collection from your fellow union members if someone died, had a baby or got married. As much as I had given over the past

12 months now that it is my turn to be on the receiving end, I wanted as much as they could give.

The wedding plans came together so suddenly, and 15 days from the time we moved in together, we were saying, "I do's." Leave it to Janice to get things done quickly yet efficiently. I had to borrow a tie and sport jacket from Uncle Bobby the day before since I did not own any. We got up early on the big day so we would be on time, and when we got to the town of Babylon, we could not locate the county building where the judge's office was. My manly pride and stubbornness did not stand in the way of me calling for directions, plus Janice would have killed me if we were late.

By 10 o'clock on October 30th 1972 we were in front of the Honorable Judge Marquette Floyd who was a friend and Kiwanis brother of Uncle Bobby and agreed to do the ceremony for free. Mom's best friend Consuelo stood up for Janice and Uncle Bobby stood up for me. Mom and my new mother-in-law Raymonde were the only other people present.

Dad had to work, and I didn't make a big deal that he wasn't going to be there so that was fine with us. The ceremony was short and went on without anyone objecting when he said, "speak now or forever hold your peace."

Right after the ceremony, we took a few pictures, which we since have lost over the years, bid farewells to all except for Raymonde. We promised to drive her to her doctor visit at Columbia Presbyterian Hospital in Manhattan not far from the George Washington Bridge. The ride took over an hour but it was the only way she could have made the wedding and not miss her important appointment.

Her visits usually lasted about two to three hours so we left, and drove back into Jamaica to kill some time. We had very little money so shopping was not an option. We just strolled along the avenue holding hands, and looking in the store windows. When we got hungry we opted for a sit down meal instead of wolfing down a hot dog from one of the street vendors; after all this was our wedding day and nothing was too good for my bride.

There was a five and dime store named Grants that was advertising in the window a turkey meal with all the trimmings, desert and beverage for only $1.99. There was nothing more to think about. That was where we were going to have our first meal as a married couple. I felt so grown to be making my first decision as a husband. So with the five bucks I had in my pocket we marched right in and sat right down at the counter.

I felt like Lou Costello from that old Abbot and Costello routine when they only had enough money for one meal and Costello had to act like he wasn't hungry when the waitress asked what he wanted. Splitting our first meal was more special and romantic anyway, plus we needed the change for the toll to get back across the bridge.

The next day I went in to work and Janice took the day off. Her boss believed her when she told him she was getting married. Mine situation was different. I found out that the majority of the employees honestly did not believe I got married and so Sam did not bother to pass the hat. I wasn't too angry, just hurt that when I was serious about something so important it wasn't believable. Would you believe that I had to bring in a photocopy of the wedding vows with our names written in and a copy of the marriage certificate? One hundred and fifty dollars later I felt it was worth.

Janice had taken the day off to fix up her apartment and to make our first real dinner as man and wife. The fried chicken was perfect and her boxed macaroni and cheese although a bit soupy was excellent. She made corn and biscuits and it made for a meal fit for a king. I had never seen Janice that happy as she was being in her own kitchen in her own place with her own husband. My memory of our first home cooked dinner as a married couple keeps me grounded, even after all the meals we have been blessed to receive.

The transition from a hard-core dope fiend to becoming a married man within the span of 12 months was still all too new for me to comprehend. The questions that stayed in my head were; will it work or won't it? Have I finally found the peace and happiness I had been searching for since I was 15-years-old? Did I act too hastily by giving up my freedom of being single? Would Janice continue to settle for a husband who worked in a factory with no future there of ever advancing? The one answer that I came up with at the time was the only way to find out is to try it for a while and wait and see.

What a good choice!

NEW JOB AND GOOD NEWS
AT THE SAME TIME

On the road to becoming a good citizen I have to be honest and say that I did suffer a few minor setbacks. After October 30th I felt the need to earn more money without taking on a part time job. The reason was nothing more than my manly pride to provide for my wife. Starting in the spring of '73, I had a deal worked out 3 days a week with the night watchman to turn off the cooking equipment in my department and then punch my time card to reflect that I worked until nine or ten in the evening. While I was home watching the boob tube, I was paid time and a half for the hours after 4:30 PM. The only thing I had to do was throw the guy $20 a week for his services.

I wished that the dope fiend mentality would have gone away for good, however it always seemed to creep back into my life when it was necessary. My arrangement was going along quite well for three months until one night he forgot to punch me off the clock. When the supervisor came to me at the end of the week, as he noticed that one night my time card showed I never left, he asked me what time did I leave. He had his head down with pen in hand waiting to write the time manually. As soon as I told him 9 PM I kind of wanted to retract the words but it was too late. He just looked up at me and grinned, put his initials to authorize the time card and that was the end of any overtime.

I started to become very content doing my factory job and not taking on any additional pressure from the outside world. I was smart enough to know that the longer I stayed there I'd probably end up like Sam who'd been there damn near 10 years. That would be enough to make anyone drink in excess.

I had no skills other than selling so my choices were limited. Then in March the opportunity came my way to go to work for Alba Neck with Louis, Bertha and Daryl. The program was in need of a therapist and the entry level position did not require any formal education. It shouldn't have: it only paid $7000 a year.

I was just starting to work on making more rational decisions and not just act off my gut instincts, but I wasn't there yet. This was an opportunity that I had dreamed of. I truly was interested in reaching back and helping those addicted, and helping them to get their lives together. Although I despised Lester, the founder, and director of the program, I felt as long as I stayed tight with the other three, I'd do well.

When it rains it pours.

I had to give my answer by December when another blessing came our way. I took Janice to the doctor so she could take a pregnancy test. There were none of them there kits back then to do at home testing. I was so nervous that I went and stood outside Dr. Gerhardt's office, as she was finishing up her exam so I could smoke.

After three cigarettes in less than 10 minutes, she emerged from the building before she even buttoned up her coat. Janice was ALWAYS cold by nature so I just knew that she was too excited to even think about being cold.

Although we had only been together three years we read each other's mind very well. I simply reached out to her and she practically leaped into my arms and there was no need to say a word. We were to become parents the 2nd week in August. We went straight from the doctor's office to Mom's. We told her Mom and my Dad the next day.

It was only then that I realized how thankful, and lucky I was that I was so naive about sex in high school. I had always wanted when the time came for me to be a father that I would be ready, willing and able. Several of my friends became fathers in high school and several girls got knocked up too. Tommy and Tracy were both 17-years-old when their son was born.

He looked just like his daddy, was named after him, and 17 years later from the day he was born, he was in jail just like his daddy was when he was 17-years-old. Of course having a mother that was a drug addict, and a father who committed suicide gave the child a slim chance of not getting into trouble.

Linda Conroy had two sons, quit high school in the 10th grade, and never did a blessed thing in raising either of them. The daddy's parents raised the first son. They were retiring to St. Thomas and asked for custody so they could give their grandson a chance at life. Linda's second son was given up to adoptive parents at birth. If she had any more I didn't know about it.

Before Linda turned 18 she was messed up on drugs, and living with a man name Bryce who was 10 years older than she was. They lived in a broken down house, with the plywood draperies, that Dee and her family used to live in when they moved from New Jersey. The house was only three blocks from where Linda grew up. She never made it any further than that.

I saw her last in the winter of 1974, and she looked like she was dead but didn't get a chance to lie down yet. It was so sad to see such a beautiful girl that I'd known since she was thirteen end up that way.

I had heard all the awful things about her about the kind of life she was living with that sorry ass good for nothing nigger she was hooked up with. But when I actually saw this once beautiful young girl looking like the years had kicked her natural ass, I thought back to when she got her family and came to the park to kick my ass. Hell, if they were so big and bad towards me, they should have had Bryce fitted for some cement shoes.

My joy and happiness in becoming a dad was done the right way, and for that I was glad. I may have done a lot of terrible things to myself, and hurt some of my family members, but it could never have been said that Bruce had kids scattered here, and there and did not take care of them.

Janice and I made our first major decision together. We agreed that if changing jobs would make me happy, and feel like I was doing something worthwhile she would have no objections. I remember thinking I was hoping Janice would make me realize that the program's HMO would not cover the pregnancy and hospital bill since it was considered a pre existing condition. I further wanted her to make it crystal clear to me that taking a $5000 a year cut in salary was a dumb thing to do with a baby on the way.

I began my new job as an intern therapist on January 4th 1974.

My job was eliminated in September; one month after our son was born.

THE CHRISTMAS HOLIDAYS COULD ONLY GET BETTER

I thought I was good at selling so I tried selling those expensive vacuum cleaners door to door. I didn't make any money but I sure made a lot of friends. My next venture was getting involved with a multilevel marketing company pushing powder in a can to help people lose weight. Mom's dear friend, "aunt Rosie," was my first and ONLY customer.

Since the bills had to be paid, and Christmas was just around the corner I swallowed my pride, and went back to work at of all places—the Post Office as a holiday temp. UPS was on strike, and the Post Office was begging for help. I'd be damned if I was gonna forfeit all the hard work to get to this juncture in my life due to lack of job or funds. Quite a difference from working the Christmas in 1969 when I was stealing and selling everything that I could get my hands on.

As usual things were going well.

I went to work, minded my own business, and never missed a day. Why this particular supervisor felt the need to page me while I was in the bathroom, and scared me to death I didn't know. The first thing I thought was that something happened at home to Janice or the baby.

When I jumped off the commode, and raced as fast as I could to where the guy's office was to see what the page was about, he calmly just asked me who gave me permission to leave the floor. When I gave him some sarcastic answer he told me to get off the time clock and leave. I didn't believe him to be serious, so I just returned to my duties, mumbling to myself. It was not until I saw him go over to the time card rack and clock me out that I knew this idiot was serious.

My anger got the best of me and I threatened to kick his ass and went after him. I chased him as he ran to the safety of his office, and before he could close the door, I stuck my foot in the doorway and got inside. He grabbed the phone to call the police and I snatched the receiver out of his hand, and was just about to hit him so hard his ancestors would have felt it, when several of my fellow workers ran in and stopped me.

They suggested that I should leave before the police arrived since someone else had called 911. I thought that leaving to be a good idea also. Before I left though, I couldn't help but slap the guy in the face with my heavy industrial work gloves. Messing with someone's money, and job right before Christmas was like going on a Kamikaze mission. No doubt that if I had nothing to loose, I would have been back in jail for assault, and attempted murder. The whole incident was so uncalled for.

Unfortunately our second Christmas together in '72 was sadder than our first when Granny had died. Janice's father passed away in December of '72 and although their relationship was not what you would have called very close, it was still her dad. For me I suddenly was dealing with the death of my father-in-law. I had waited for the right girl to marry and gained a father-in-law, then within 45 days he was gone. This death thing I was not too comfortable with, plus it was coming too close together and I was not used to going to funerals for family members.

When our third Christmas rolled around, we were ready to make up for the previous two. I fulfilled a childhood dream of having the biggest Christmas tree I could find. Notice I did not say, "that I could afford" as money was not going to be an issue this year. By this time of the year we had traded in the GTO for a '73 Chevy Vega with a hatchback trunk. The timing was perfect because when we went shopping and bought our first tree together it was so big Janice had to sit in the back and hold the hatchback down with a rope so the tree wouldn't fall out. It was that big!

I applied and received my very first credit card, thanks to George. He was a credit manager with Nikon and would always tell me to establish some credit worthiness about myself. Dad was anti credit cards so I was scared to own one of them suckers. The other reason I was paranoid was with all the credit cards I had stolen from people during my "bad" days, my thought were what if someone got a hold of mine? Not that I believed George over my own father, but I felt comfortable to manage my debt in a wise manner so I went for it.

With credit card in hand, I bought a full-length rabbit coat for my wife. It had pieces of leather in different colors sewed into the fur with a leather belt to match. I had even paid to have it gift-wrapped and it looked so pretty under the tree that I didn't ever want Janice to open it. You couldn't have told me that there was any prettier gift received by any other woman that year. I also bought Janice a sewing machine. She was used to sewing her own clothes and was taking an advanced adult education sewing class on Wednesday evenings at Central Islip High School.

Christmas was always a special time for me growing up. There were so many vivid memories of the happier times when family were together and made the spirit of giving and love so much meaning. When my turn came around to have a family of my own I wanted to settle for nothing less than a fun filled holiday season. I felt I had missed out on four Christmas' during my absence from the main stream of society and a sense of family was all that mattered to me from 1973 until my feelings changed 23 years later.

I had enough money for Kaleem' first Christmas. That was my main concern. I was not going to let some racist postal employee ruin the moment for us. Kaleem was the first baby in the family in a long time so he was spoiled rotten. He was only 4 months old and all I wanted him to feel was love and security from his family.

I TRIED TO MAKE A
DIFFERENCE

I got a call from Louis three days after Christmas to ask if I would like to come back to work at the program. This time I would be an outreach worker and evening therapist for the outpatients. Of course I said yes even though I didn't know how long it would last this time. My intent was to take it one day at a time and continue to look for something else. After all I had all day to supposedly be "outreaching" with no one monitoring my coming and going so it was perfect for me.

During this go round at Alba Neck, Janice was put to the test in May of '75. I had such a soft heart and was very caring for those residents that lived there 24/7. When Mother's day rolled around there were four dope fiends that had no opportunity to visit their Mom's. Lester and the staff agreed to allow everyone to go home to spend the day with their families with adult supervision. I could not bare to see those four poor souls having to stay at the halfway house with a staff member on duty with three other addicts that I didn't care too much for, plus one of them had syphilis.

I called Janice to ask if she would mind if I brought them to the house for dinner and she agreed. Since I was doing the cooking anyway and all we were having was spaghetti and meatballs, salad and some garlic bread how much effort was it to cook a little more. When it was time to eat, the three guys ate like they hadn't seen food in 10 years. It was unbelievable. It must have been conditioning from their being in jail a lot. I misjudged my rations and Janice and I ended up getting as the saying goes, "the crumbs off the table."

While the guys were on desert, the only female in the bunch was making googily eyes at Janice. I should have told Janice that Veronica was confused regarding her sexuality, so she would have been more prepared when given the once over look.

Before I quit in July, I could have written a book and titled it, "The Program." My observation of 90% of the staff members was that they had some serious sexual and personal hang ups. The shit they used to sit around and talk about in our staff meetings was very bizarre. They tried to convince you into believing that certain issues they would bring up were in the residents best interest and make them better counselors. I always felt that their topics were about their own fucked up behaviors, and they could care less about the people they were there to help.

I'll give just a few examples of the type of people placed in positions to help drug addicts be better people. Jack was a former DETER assistant director before I went there and was kicked out for relapsing. He was then placed on the methadone maintenance program. After living with a black woman who was a recovering alcoholic and dope fiend they got married.

In one of our staff meetings he had the balls to ask for our feedback on the solution he came up with to help Rodney who was assigned to his care. I thought he was joking when he came out of his mouth to say the brother was having a problem with premature ejaculation. I know that it can be a problem in us guys, but I didn't agree on his solution to have him masturbate with a stopwatch and see how long it took for him to get his rocks off.

His theory was the better he got at it, the longer he could have sex without having an orgasm. I couldn't bring myself to even go along with some of the other sicko's by giving any dignity to such an absurd thing to talk abut in a drug program.

Another time a therapist name Peggy started to talk about how she liked to play with herself in the presence of her lover so he could see the objects of her desires. She brought this up because she was Alegra's therapist and Alegra also happened to be Rodney's girlfriend and she was frustrated of course because Rodney came too soon while they were screwing. Not that I am a prude or anything but this started to get disgusting to me.

Dennis was a part time therapist and also held a Ph.D. in clinical psychology. He chimed in when Peggy was finished talking to share how much a woman playing with herself drove him up the wall so he felt it was a good idea for both Rodney and Alegra. I thought the man and Peggy were going to lie down on the floor and go at it the way they were reacting to each other.

I used to spend more of my time talking and hanging with the residents than the staff because they were more normal. They used to like me a lot and thought I was the nicest and most sincere staff member they had. I was glad I was tight with them because they would tell me when the director would ask them to prepare lunch for his staff meetings. The cheap son of a bitch could not even go in pocket to send out for some real food. Of course his answer to having them make our lunch was that it was a learning experience.

As I would watch the others eat after saying I wasn't hungry, I would laugh inside at what they were really eating! Whatever the residents could find to throw into the mix, that is what they served. I was told afterwards that a lasagna they once made had everything in it from cigarette ashes, semen, armpit odor and I won't even say any more on that subject. The staff often forgot that pay back was a bitch when you treated them badly and that they were still dope fiends; but had feelings to.

HOW DO I LOVE THEE, LET ME COUNT THE WAYS.

If I am not mistaken those words were taken from a love story. But just what exactly is a love story? Is it a story about before or after you've fallen in love? If you have never been in love, then how do you know when you've found love? If you find love, then how do you know when it began?

These questions had been on my mind so many times, ever since I found the love of my life in October of 1971. I did not want to mess up this opportunity to try my hand at something I knew nothing about but was willing to learn. When you've never had a person that even remotely resembled a soul mate, it is kind of hard to vision what it would feel like to be in love.

After being attached at the hip for the past thirty-three years to my best friend, lover, wife, "shrink" and mother of our two lovely sons, I would like to take a stab at sharing what I believe this thing called love is all about.

There but for the grace of God go I in terms of divorce, widowership or being in an unhappy relationship and not knowing how to fix it. While growing up, my idea of what two people in love represented was simply observing how family members acted around their spouses. If a relative seemed happy and stayed together then I assumed they were in love. If a relative argued all the time and split up, then love was not a part of their relationship. But what happens to adolescents when that "happy" picture is clouded. Some relations stayed together but were not truly in love.

Despite being the product of a home that was divided when Mom took my little sister and moved out and left Dad, my view of marriage still had high expectations. I was determined to learn from the mistakes and observations learned from some of my closest family members. My goal was to find someone to love and marry before I turned 30. In my mind if I could not accomplish that goal then my chances of ever finding my soul mate were slim to none.

It was not until I realized later in life that none of the choices I made were mine but God's, did I understand that the stage was being set for many years of marital bliss and I had nothing to do with it. I took what I always used to call "luck" or "good fortune" and replaced those words with the word, "blessings."

Accepting the role that God has given to Janice was the hardest part of my releasing that macho manly image that refuses to allow some men and women to move on to a more loving and long lasting relationship. If my role were to be the primary breadwinner and corporate executive instead of Janice's, then that is exactly where I would be.

I am not and have NEVER bought into the American corporate dream of work hard and you'll get ahead. Based on how I grew up and what I experienced from the time I was 15 years old prevented me from ever letting my guard down.

Do I regret the street life education I earned a doctorate in?

I have to say unequivocally no. My education taught me that being humble was part of life and the sooner I learned that, the quicker I could adapt to whatever situation I was in at the time.

Don't try and change the person you are involved with. It never works.

Janice quit smoking on her own when her cigarette lighter fell out of her pocket at the altar one Sunday eight years ago in church. She also gave up watching those idiotic soap operas on her own. She moved up the corporate ladder without once kissing anyone's ass. Accept the role God gave you regardless of what you may think your role should be. It doesn't matter. I have learned to appreciate the things I have that are not all of a materialistic nature.

My goal when I first got married was to never have Janice to want for anything again in her lifetime. When you have sacrificed like she did for he sake of your parents as well as your siblings at the age of 15, you've missed out on so many wonderful things to make memories of. Can you ever get those things back? The answer is no. However you can begin to build new memories that can last forever.

Having her chance to do this with someone that she had grown to love very deeply made it all the more sweeter to savor. I never wanted more for myself than I did for Janice. I wasn't sure if that was the right attitude to take going into marriage, but it was good enough for me.

Stumbling blocks along the path to building a happy marriage are such an important ingredient to the mix. The more you have the stronger your marriage can become. I did not say that it would automatically become stronger, but the odds are in your favor if you learn how to use these stumbling blocks to your advantage.

Reminiscent of the days gone by when we first started our married life with hardly any material things yet a lot of love. We didn't have our first television set until six months after we were married. I say our first because the one I had borrowed from Uncle Bobby only got three channels and none were prime time networks. Janice covered our first dining set, which consisted of a folding card table and two chairs with contact paper to make it look nice.

Talk about color schemes!

Our living room consisted of red shag carpet, I painted the walls blue, and our sofa was blue, a French provincial green armchair, a wooden bench and a plastic lamp with an orange lampshade.

I always wanted a fish tank so I bought a 10-gallon tank and at one time had as many as six fish. We used to think that several of the fish were suicidal because when we would come home from work sometimes there would be a fish lying on the floor. Either they jumped to their death or the black Molly I had was kicking their ass so bad that they took their chances at liberty or death.

Is the grass greener on the other side of the fence? Perhaps it may be. Will you still have to cultivate it and keep it manicured so it will always look nice? Sure you will if you have any pride at all. Is the effort to start a new lawn harder than trying to maintain the one you already have?

Should differences in a relationship be satisfied and terminated at the irreconcilable stage? Are the excuses for terminating marriages always justifiable? Should society work on more excuses to work on saving marriages as they do excuses to end them?

Questions are fascinating. They always have been for me. Seeking answers are even more fascinating. It does so much for the human spirit.

KEEPING A SIMPLE APPROACH TO MARRIAGE

The journey along the path to peace and happiness when falling in love is a journey that should be shared. It should be shared because there is always an area of our lives that can benefit someone else. Relating to other people's circumstances has been so successful when used in therapy. The "walking in your shoes" philosophy is so real when you can verbally and visually connect to another human being. You actually can feel their joy, sorrow, pain, loss or victory.

I have been free of heroin, cocaine and other drugs now since October of 1971.

I won't lie and say I gave up smoking pot at the same time I stopped using heroin and cocaine. My thinking at the time was to take the most critical stuff and eliminate that from my lifestyle and whatever comes next, well so be it. Smoking weed kind of reminded me of the good old days before I began my downward spiral into hard-core drugs.

My love for life was larger than my love life or for drugs. Plain but not so simple. If you don't know what there is to love, then you will never overcome any of the obstacles preventing you from living a life of love. Sounds redundant I know, but when shit is made too difficult folks tend to shy away from trying the unknown or what they perceive to be difficult.

Janice and I were often asked what is the secret to our success at marriage when the divorce rate is over 50%. We used to feel as though we were in the minority considering marriage was such an important aspect of life. There were times that we would feel guilty that we were happy and in love when surrounded by friends and family members that were not at the same level in their relationships.

I was talking to a close friend of ours, whom recently got married, about how Janice and I met and he was so fascinated. I told him that when we were asked how did our relationship survive during the baby boomer generation I had a hard time answering. He said to me, "Bruce, it is not what you knew when you started out but what you didn't know that made it successful."

I have tried to put a pulse on the key ingredient to a lasting relationship and have decided to stop looking. It was easier to simply accept that there is no single contributing factor, just different personalities and levels of acceptance by both parties. My advice to the lovelorn or those that are seeking their soul mate is to know when you have found the right person.

I don't mean when you think that you've found the love of your life, I mean when you know you've found the right person. One can search over and over and never know when the love of their life appears because it may be disguised in the form of fear, caution, and lack of humility. If there was ever a stronger quality in a relationship that would definitely bind it closer, I would have to say that being humble earns my vote.

Either one or the other person in a relationship has to have a strong sense of humility. If both possess that characteristic then more power to them, but one is sufficient. It matters not which one so long as humility is recognized and built upon.

I know that the years of my addiction and having gone through several bullshit therapeutic communities for self-help made me a very humble man. If I had allowed my stubborn pride, image, and egotistical personality to dictate over my life during the period of recovery, then I would have never made it. I had to learn humility as much as I may not have liked it in order to save myself from a lifetime of destructive behaviors.

Humility kept me from not giving up on Janice when I first met her and not try and take advantage of such a fragile yet strong-willed young lady. I knew that the long-term benefits of not losing her to someone that could have made her life much more fulfilling was worth me being humble.

I knew who I was at the time when we met and did not try to be someone that I wasn't. It was a more of an understanding of the minds than anything else because we both knew that in order to achieve what we wanted to achieve, I would have to change more of my ways than hers.

I accepted and could live with that. Janice was not trying to be the dominant one in our relationship, she was just being honest and I knew she was right. I humbled myself to not feel as though I had to give up more of who I was than Janice had to give up more of who she was. Who cared!

The first several years together I would often search to find a simple analogy of my past and my present. Whatever the circumstances might have been, I'd ask myself how I would handle things if I was still addicted and then turn the answer into a positive solution. When I needed money and felt my back was up against the wall after I had lost my job at the halfway house, I hustled and found a temporary means to make an honest living rather than feeling sorry for myself. I just knew there was money to be made somehow and my instincts steered me in the right direction.

The criminal mind is a terrible thing to waste when used in a positive way.

Each area of a relationship is different. I knew that I could no longer be as selfish and spoiled as I had been and make our marriage work. I knew that I had to work at whatever job I could get to provide for my family and not worry about how the job made me look or feel. I had to change my whorish nature and not feel as though sex was so important that I had to conquer them all in order to prove my manhood. I had to learn to respect the feelings and rights of my spouse because she was entitled to have her own regardless of how big or little they were.

I had to ask myself, "Is missing out on the benefits outweighing the need to feed my stubbornness, ego and lack of humility?" If the answer was yes then there is very little chance that the relationship would survive the tests of time. If my answer was no and the benefits are that meaningful then the willingness to put my feelings on the shelf or someplace else would carry me through.

Whatever the benefits are is just as important as the desire to savor them in your relationship bank. The more deposits you make into your relationship bank, the more fun you will have in your relationship.

Let me explain.

We are taught to open a bank account to either write checks save money or both are we not? When we deposit our money in the bank we would like to know that we have some level of comfort that it is protected or insured. For the most part, the money that we deposit is earned through hard work. Because we work hard for our money we tend to not want to waste any of it or as they say, "Get the most bang for our buck."

If we are lucky enough to leave our money in an account long enough we just may earn a little interest on it. As customers we also expect a certain level of professional customer service from the banking institution we are dealing with. Most important, we expect that when we want to make a withdrawal that our funds will be available. That pretty much sums up a lesson in simple banking protocol.

Take a look at yourself and visualize for a moment that you have your own personal bank. Let's call it the "Relationship Bank and Trust Company." Your account can either be savings for a rainy day or checking to withdraw your resources when you need to. For your deposits we are going to substitute memory for money. Because you work hard to earn memories you want to be just as careful not to waste any so you can also get the same "more bang for the buck."

If you leave your memories there long enough you will earn additional memories in the form of interest that can also be compounded daily or reinvested. Of course you would expect the most professional customer service in order for the bank to maintain your business. In short you expect to be treated as though you were someone special.

Saving up memories in a bank should be a priority in a relationship. Just like when you need money for a rainy day, an emergency, your future or just for some fun, you can use memories in the same way. There is no better need to withdraw a memory from the bank than when your relationship needs some fun.

THE GIFT THAT TRULY
KEEPS ON GIVING

In 1995, after my worse experience with trying to have and love our pet dog, Prince, I vowed never to have a dog again. I just had to go to the "Relationship Bank" when it came time to do something special for Janice for our twenty-third anniversary. I knew she did not feel the same way that I did towards dogs, so I relented and decided to surprise her with a new puppy.

I was still very reluctant until I drove 30 miles north of Atlanta to pick out her anniversary gift—a little Peek-A-Poo puppy. I felt better once the breeder explained to me that she was not without pedigree. Hell all I wanted to know if the little animal would tear up the house like Prince had done. Once assured that with proper love, her temperament would prevent her from ever going nuts I went inside to look at the litter.

Talk about another love at first sight. There laid the cutest little thing that I had ever seen. From day one I did not look at her as an animal, but part of our family. I could not believe that I even had thoughts like that, or had it in me to be so emotional over a dog. There were only two left to choose from since the others were accounted for already. One was black and the other was white. I picked the black one of course.

The hardest part of the process was to know that I had to wait approximately a month in order for her to be ready to be separated from the mother. It was even harder trying to keep the secret from Janice. I told the boys, but that was all.

When the day came to pick her up, it was raining so hard that I had to pull over to the side of the highway and wait. I was so anxious to hold her and take her home. I had Kynon to plan to call his mother to pick him up from skating that Friday evening so that she would not be home when I arrived with her surprise.

I remember placing this little ball of black fur in a box and talked to her all the way home. She began to whimper, and I had to tune out to not feel sorry for her that she no doubt misses her mommy. Still raining, I took my time and we were not in the house 10 minutes before I heard the garage door open and Janice would be coming into the kitchen.

Not prepared for such an early arrival, I quickly grabbed a red bow from the closet, placed her on the floor by the hall leading to the kitchen and had the camera ready. Talk about catching a moment to remember. Man it was awesome. We named her Shultzi, and she has been a blessing to us from day one.

LAUGHING AT YOURSELVES IS HEALTHY

I have one memory of when Janice and I were driving back from Atlantic City to Long Island in '76 and not having any money to pay for a toll in Staten Island. We had so much fun playing the nickel and dime arcades. This was before the casinos were built so you could only lose but so much.

I remember we got tickets for five dollars apiece to see Harold Kelvin and the Bluenotes when Teddy Pendergrass was still with the group. For an added opening attraction there was an act that featured a diving horse. I think I wanted to see the horse dive into the tank more than I wanted to see the group perform.

After we checked out of the fleabag motel where we slept with the light on, we ate breakfast played some more games and then got suckered into one of those boardwalk auctions where the guy talked so fast you hardly knew what he was saying. We walked away broke with a kerosene lamp that we must have ended up paying for three times over; but we had the time of our lives.

We were doing fine coming back on the Garden State Parkway since the tolls were no more than a dime and one or two might have been a quarter. However, when we reached Staten Island heading to the Verazanno Bridge, we did not realize that the Gothal's Bridge from New Jersey to Staten Island required a $1.twenty-five toll. The reason was simple. Going over it was free so our thinking was it was free. Made sense to us. The return trip was when they collected the toll. When we saw the sign and the cars stopping ahead of us, we didn't know what to do. I mean we literally had no money at all.

As I stated before, the worst part of being an ex-addict was that you would always have the knowledge and ability to resort back to your old trifling ways if the situation called for it to save your ass. I could not have thought of a better opportunity to dig back into my bag and come up with some way out of this embarrassing moment.

When we reached to the booth, I was honest when I told the collector we had never been across this bridge before and did not know that we had to pay on the return trip. I am sure as a New Yorker he was used to the same old story so he told us to pull over to the side by the building that housed the toll authority and fill out our name and address and phone number for them to mail us a bill and we could send in the buck twenty five.

We never stopped looking behind us the entire 15-minute ride to the Verazzano Bridge scared that the police was chasing us for just driving off. Once we crossed the bridge into Brooklyn we stopped worrying but couldn't stop laughing.

There are many other memories, some good some not so good, that I have accumulated over 30 years. Just like photographs in an album, memories can be used to bring a smile to your face, warmth to your heart, laughter at a time when you are feeling down and most of all a quick reminder of why you love the one you're with and want to be with the one you love for better or worse until death do you apart.

When I would be asked from time to time for some marital advice I would offer a simple slogan from the heart that says, "stick around for the memories." You made them now hang around so the two of you can stroll down memory lane together. There is no sense in not sharing that which both of you have made and why would you want to give those precious moments to anyone else except until death do you part?

Janice tells me that I have a memory like an elephant. I say, "Good for me at least it's free!"

WE ALL HAVE GIFTS WE JUST NEED TO KNOW WHAT THEY ARE

I found that using my negative past experiences helped me to become a better husband and father. Breaking the law for me was a life long lesson in knowing how it felt to lose my freedom. I could have chose that it felt good or that it felt bad enough that I would never steal again. By using hard drugs at an early age I knew how it felt to be high on heroin and cocaine. I could have chose that it felt good and continued to use or chose to never want to stick a needle in my arm or any white powder up my nostrils again.

I learned from trying and screwing any female that would stay still long enough was not the best way to find my soul mate. I could have chose to place getting as much sex as I wanted over finding my true soul mate or chose not to put so much emphasis on it and expressing true love in the right ways with the right person.

Janice was invited by a female co-worker to give a talk back in the summer of '91 at the woman's church. When Janice asked why she was chosen to speak before her congregation, the woman told her because of the way she carried herself and that at the time she was happily married for nineteen years. Janice asked what suggestions the woman had for a subject, and Janice was told to just speak about her life and why she was so happy and confident within herself. Janice felt honored yet humbled by the mere thought that her inner peace and self-confidence was taken notice by another person, especially in the work place.

Her message to the congregation and visitors comprised mostly of woman was a simple one. Her talk was titled, *"Choices."* She shared about the choices she had made in her life to get her to where she was to that day. It was very emotional for many in the pews especially myself. It was the first time I had ever heard Janice put into words how she felt about the choices in her life.

When she shared how there was not one family member of ours that thought our marriage was a good idea because we were too young, it touched me deeply.

The fact that our family did not deter us from knowing that our love was real and we were at least willing to give it a try spoke volumes for our commitment to our vows. When she finished speaking, many of the women in the audience lined up to shake her hand and thank her for sharing her testimony. I had no doubt that some had marriages that were standing on shaky ground.

About two weeks after this wonderful talk on marriage, we were asked to participate in a panel discussion on relationships. We had joined a black newcomers group when we moved to Atlanta to fellowship with other blacks that relocated from different parts of the country. Leigh, the founder was a single female whose biological clock was ticking down faster than she wanted it to but had a heart and smile so big, you just had to love her.

She was good at coming up with things to do and having fun doing them, but mainly she was interested in many of the singles in the group finding someone to have a relationship with. Since the group boasted having damn near 85% single members, that left the rest of us as being married. The single females outnumbered the males three to one, so the competition was fierce.

Leigh came up with the idea to do a talk show type forum with a panel and discuss relationships. Janice and I were nominated to be the married couple on a panel of two divorcees, one single women and man looking to get married, and one single woman and man that did not trust marriage.

We rehearsed in someone's home for several weekends, and then the event was to be held at a downtown restaurant where Leigh arranged to have dinner afterwards and those on the panel ate as guests of the audience. She arranged to have as advisors a psychologist who had a radio talk show and a councilman who later went on to become the mayor of Atlanta in '97.

Part of loving and respecting your other half is accepting their faults. Janice has very few of them (smile) but one that tests my nerves is her punctuality. She always seems to be operating behind schedule. She'll argue, "Whose schedule; yours or mine?" We were supposed to be downtown by two o'clock, forty-five minutes before the audience arrived, so we could make sure everything was ready to go. Janice had to get her nails done so when I was dressed and waiting, after I had gotten off work early, and she came in around one, I got a case of the ass.

She proceeded to get ready and since we were approximately a half hour from downtown without traffic, we did not leave until almost 1:50 PM. She knew I was pissed but tried to make conversation just the same. My way of showing I was annoyed was to drive 50 miles per hour on purpose and not talk just to piss her off.

So here you had the loving all American Black couple on their way to discuss the joys of marriage in front of Lord knows how many people and we aint speaking to each other. At one point Janice suggested we not go and her second suggestion was when we got downtown she would take the train and go back home. Both of these ideas did not seem too good.

When we got to the restaurant, she asked that I let her out while I went to find a parking place. At first I didn't want to stop and let her out fearing she might just leave like she threatened to and I would be stuck having to explain why she was not with me. After she got out, I kind of watched her in the rear view mirror and she did go inside the restaurant. I parked and ran back to meet her in the lobby area.

When I would get angry one of the dumb things that I used to do to get back at Janice was threaten to buy a pack of cigarettes. I had quit but I knew she would be pissed if I smoked just to spite her. My dear wife always has an answer for me that would make me feel like, "why did you even open your mouth Bruce?" I could never doubt her logic because it was so different than mine and thank goodness for that. She would tell me that since I was the one who had asthma and that if smoking was going to hurt anyone it would be me not her.

As we headed up the stairs to the banquet room where everyone was waiting, I stopped at the cigarette machine and was about to put my seventy-five cents in for a pack of Salem, when I looked and saw that my brand was sold out. I just stood there trying not to laugh since after all we were not speaking to each other.

When I turned away from the machine and caught her trying not to laugh as well, we both just burst out laughing. She nicknamed me "pinhead" and when I would screw up and knew I was at fault, I would earn a "pinhead" award. I think we stopped counting them after 31 years.

We hugged and ran up the stairs, me thinking we would be walking in late. Janice knew better. She knew that black folks had a tradition of never being on time, and of course she was right. There was not a soul present during our little talk show forum that ever knew that just a little over an hour ago, we both had big time attitudes and almost didn't show up.

It is no secret that in a loving relationship that there will always be "spiritual debates." The word argument or disagreement sound so negative. A true relationship would not be possible without continuously learning from one another and more often than not may not see eye to eye on certain topics. I have learned more from Janice than I believe she has learned from me. My deep love for her allowed me to accept that there are no scorecards in marriage when it comes to learning and accepting. The key is to keep the playing field even and if nothing else this is what couples should work hardest at. You can save the win lose mentality for your bowling league, golf game, lottery, gambling, etc. as there is no place for who is a winner or loser in marriage.

ACCEPTING THAT IT WAS TIME FOR MORE INTERVENTION

The inspiration to write my journey to love evolved in 1993.

Brenda was a therapeutic counselor that I was assigned to when I was having a hard time coping with why I changed jobs so often as well as learning about anger management. I hadn't been in therapy since 1971 so I had to get used to talking and sharing of myself all over again. When sharing your inner most thoughts and fears with a total stranger it may take some time to establish a confidence level before you truly open up.

I liked Brenda because she seemed to care about me and not just use up our sixty minutes together just for the sake of her getting paid. After we got through some of the reasons why I felt I was unable to receive any gratification from any of the jobs I had, we got down to who I was as a person. This happened on our fourth session.

The anger in me stemmed from my feelings of always feeling that whatever happened to me that was negative; I was being punished for my past wrong doings. I would get pissed off at shit and take things out on my family and those I cared about because I felt comfortable with them. It was also easier than risking any repercussions from the secular world. The bottom line I was playing it safe; or so I thought.

I had always felt such guilt about not being with Janice when her water broke and she was starting to go into labor with Kaleem.

After moving to Atlanta in 1983, my intent was to do something spectacular with a business of my own. With the cost of living much cheaper than New York and the most money we'd seen in our lifetime from the sale of our first home in the bank, I felt the situation was perfect. Of course each setback at first was due to lack of knowledge in what the hell I was looking for, then after that I chalked up every disappointment to the "oh whoa is me" syndrome.

But why was I so angry all the time was a question that Janice forced me to seek answers to. Janice flat out refused to put up with living in an environment of yelling, slamming things, not speaking for more than twenty-four hours and most of all having her children exposed to any of those behaviors. My heart did not want to be that way because one of the things that we shared prior to our marriage was that our children would never be exposed to a unhappy home life not as long as we could help it. Janice in her own subtle ways could move mountains. In the summer of 1990, she gave me two choices. Those choices were seeking help or seeking help, end of discussion.

I always felt that I was above learning anything positive from therapy, yet I was never averse to going to therapy. Those feelings were a result from never getting anything positive out of therapy due to the individuals that were in control of the sessions. My attitude towards counseling at the time was very resistant and close-minded. Then I met Brenda.

One of the questions that she asked me was if I was honest with myself and was I afraid to be honest with her. I knew I was not honest with her but thought I was doing a half ass job being honest with Bruce. She got me to open up about my past and as hard as it was to share with someone not from the world of the addicted, she made me feel so comfortable I told her about my drug history and some other things.

Brenda asked me why I felt so guilty about the circumstances surrounding the birth of our first child. I explained that not only was I working without benefits and unsure of my future, I allowed my negative attitude to put a damper on what should have been my chance to rise to the occasion. I shared that I was feeling unworthy of earning anything that was good as if I hadn't done anything to deserve it.

Brenda got me to write down on a piece of paper certain accomplishments in my life up to the present and she asked me to hand it in to her the following week. I had to struggle to find instances that I thought to be valid.

During our next session she asked me to read out loud what I had written. When I read how I overcame drug addiction, and a life of crime, she told me to stop and read that portion again. Then she asked me why I wrote that particular accomplishment down, to which I answered that to me it was a big deal. But, I felt at the same time it was not that significant in my struggle with low self-esteem, and kicking myself in the ass whenever things didn't go my way.

She wanted to know how I kicked the habit and stayed clean for nineteen years. When I started to give her how I accomplished such a feat, she asked why I was not as proud of that as I was in staying married for just as long. I had always took for granted that one had nothing to do with the other, however she pointed out that the same determination and goal setting that went into recovery was just as important.

Perhaps my train of thought was about not making a big issue over rehab and more recognition of surviving marriage for nineteen years. By doing this I could avoid my negative past. She explained that is exactly why I should give recognition to overcoming a drug habit so that I would not have to feel ashamed to talk about it. It is a part of who I am and the story and experiences will never go away so I needed to learn how to incorporate my old self with my new self and welcome the results.

BLESSED TO BE A REAL FATHER AT LAST

Dad had been in Barbados on vacation so we were staying at his house to be nearer to the hospital in Plainview. I had gotten one of my famous attitudes the night before over something stupid and so the next day I went to Belmont racetrack to play the horses. I knew Janice hated for me to gamble and we had many "heated debates" on the subject since we got married. The due date was a week away so I wasn't worried that I'd miss out on the main event and saw no harm in going.

My heart wasn't into it, but I didn't want to back down and show that egotistical sign of weakness that plague men so often. Janice went with Mom and Consuelo to an open-air flea market to do what she loves to do—SHOP. When I came back home, after losing of course, and called over to Moms, she gave me a tongue-lashing. She said, "Where the hell have you been? Janice's water broke and we had to take her to the hospital and you should have been there."

I felt like two cents. Mom was right; I should have been the one that took her to the hospital instead of watching some four-legged nags running around a racetrack while losing money we did not have.

I drove the fifteen-minute ride to Central General Hospital in Plainview doing seventy miles per hour on the Expressway. When I got there I knew that I needed to first apologize for leaving the house that morning with an attitude and secondly for not being with her for the trip to the hospital.

When the baby doctor told me I might as well go home, as her contractions were not close enough for anything to happen, I didn't want to leave her side. However, Janice convinced me to go back to the house, wait and then when the time was near I'd be notified. I would then be able to return in time to be in the waiting room for the good news. In 1974 being a part of the delivery was not popular so the best a father could opt for was to be close by for the first hand news of whether it was a boy or girl.

I made peace with Mom and then went on over to Dad's to wait by the phone. By then it was around 6 PM. I was outside in the front of the house talking to our neighbor Mrs. Williamson when I heard the phone ringing. I bolted towards the door and raced for the phone to pick it up. Janice had given birth to a healthy 5lb 15-ounce boy. My emotions were happy, overjoyed, scared but part of me was angry. Damn, didn't the doctor have enough experience to know that by the time I left and drove home that in less than two hours she would be ready? He screwed me out of being there to get the news in person was what I was thinking.

So glad that twice in the same day I did not let my anger prevent me from enjoying the blessing. I ran outside and hugged the neighbor and then ran back inside to call Mom and my mother-in-law. I was confused as to what to do first. I only knew that I wanted to be there with my wife and son and nothing else mattered.

Unfortunately before I could get out of the house my dear sweet mother-in-law called right back to say she'd be ready and waiting down in the front of her apartment building when I got there to pick her up. Pick her up? She expected me to drive the opposite direction to Hempstead, pick her up and then drive back in the other direction to the hospital. The things you do for those you love. At least she was waiting downstairs so we had time to hug and kiss before she got in the car.

By time we arrived we were just about the only local family that hadn't seen our new bundle of joy. I had to get over my feeling stupid that Mom, Consuelo, Myrna and Lisa met us in the lobby to tell me what a beautiful son I had. How could I have been present for the beginning of this, go through nine months of supporting Janice and then when the big day arrived, be at the end of the list for seeing our creation?

Raymonde and I got the two passes from Myrna and Lisa and we went up to the fourth floor. I got off the elevator and when I saw the sign that read "maternity wing," I almost froze and didn't want to go inside. What a miracle that was seeing him and seeing my last name on the nameplate that read "Boy Codrington." I remember feeling sorry for him that he had a big nose just like me, but as long as he was healthy that was all that mattered.

Janice was in recovery and we had to wait thirty minutes to see her. She was given something for the pain and a local to put her into twilight land and would be awake by then. She looked good for what she had been through and the first thing we said after I gave her a big kiss was we needed to name the baby. For nine months we knew we had to come up with something, and here we were without a name to call our first love child. How pitiful was that!

By now you probably know that I had always been a spontaneous person, and there would be no reason to do something not spontaneous at that time. I was listening to the radio in the car while driving back from the hospital earlier that day and heard the name Kaleem. To this day I never could remember what went with the story the voice on the radio station was talking about but all I knew was I liked the sound of the name.

When I suggested to Janice to name our son Kaleem, she wanted to know where I had came up with a name like that. After I explained that I had heard the name on the radio, she laughed and asked, "How do we know that the person on the radio was not giving a news report about a murderer or a child molester?" I had to agree with her since I had not heard the entire information before I had heard the name Kaleem. We went for it anyway.

Next all we had to do was pick a middle name from a book of African warriors. We chose Onajae, which meant "Mighty Warrior." We felt we did Kaleem proud.

Now a far as our second son, Kynon, the events surrounding his birth were a whole lot different.

"I don't know my dear." I said, "I have done a lot of things in my life, but watching a natural childbirth?"

Oh well, just another chapter in my book of life where a first became a welcomed challenge. After all, we were not talking about just any childbirth; we were talking about our second child. We had waited seven years for that moment so the least I could do was be there in the delivery room with Janice. I did agree to go through with the natural childbirth classes with one stipulation. That stipulation was that cousin Kelli had to take the classes also, just in case I chickened out. As I mentioned previously, witnessing blood, pain, and suffering was not part of my make-up. However, once that agreement between Janice and Kelli was approved, we signed up for the nine-week class at Mercy Hospital.

On June twenty-five, 1981, I had just arrives at my new job as a manager trainee with Red Lobster. I parked my car as usual in the rear of the restaurant parking lot. I got out and was heading towards the kitchen door; George Cabrera was standing there having a smoke. He stopped inhaling long enough to tell me turn right back around and head home. He said Janice had just called and felt she was going in to labor. Awe shit. Even with the nine-week course behind me, and that horrible, disgusting, video of a real birth, I was nervous as hell.

I did not remember much in the way of how I made it home. I was shocked to have rushed through the front door to my house, only to discover Janice, Kelli, and her companion Tom, sitting on the living room sofa. Janice was, and still is, the calmest person I had ever met. She knew the time was near, yet it was not the time to go into the labor room. Her suggestion to a hypochondriac like me to relax fell on deaf ears.

Janice talked Tom, and I, into carrying an old refrigerator down into the basement. I thought that if she weren't ready to go to the hospital after we were finished doing this, then either Tom of I would be on our way instead. Tom's heart was not in the best of health at the time; I had asthma and hypertension. Thank God that the dynamic duo handled the task with ease.

Mercy hospital was only a ten-minute drive from our home. We felt that this experience would be without any issues whatsoever. Prior to my leaving Friendly Ice Cream, Corp., Janice and me became very close to a waitress name, Karen. Karen was also a nursing student at Mercy hospital. She agreed to look out for Janice when it came to that little extra tender loving care. Janice was still not ready when she checked in. At least this time I was the one that signed the mother of my child into the hospital-not Mom or Consuelo.

We knew that after waiting seven years to conceive, there would be no way that we should not have a name picked out. If the baby was a boy—Kynon. If the baby was to be a girl—Kara. I wanted a Daddy's little girl so much, but Kara? It was not one of my favorites but could have learned to live with it.

Kaleem was only seven and was in awe of all that was going on around him. He knew that he would soon have a little brother or sister, and was so excited. He was looking forward to having someone to boss around. Mom and Dad were there also waiting patiently for their new grandson or granddaughter. As time went by, Kelli said she had to leave for an appointment. There went my back up so I knew I could not have copped out even if I wanted. If the truth were known, I wouldn't have missed being with Janice at that time for anything in the world

With my family growing, my pride of accomplishments in life just kept getting stronger. When Kaleem was born, I had no job or money to pay the hospital bill before I brought him home. I had joked with the clerk in the hospital business office that they would have to hold my wife and baby as ransom until I could pay the bill. In a sense that is how it appeared to me at the time. They allowed Janice to get dressed, they placed Kaleem in her arms after she got settled in the wheelchair, and then they waited for me to come back with her exit papers. Mom paid the television and phone bill for us. Although I joked about it, I felt like shit for not being better prepared for our first child.

Because he shared so much of the harder times that we went through, Kaleem was always special. He bought joy, peace and laughter into our lives at a time when we needed it the most. He is so much like his father that it is scary. He still is truly unique.

Kynon, on the other hand, came into the world of his crazy family with a little more stability. At least we could say that he was paid for at the time of checkout. We gave him the middle name—Monroe, Uncle Felix's middle name. We felt it an honor since Uncle Felix was never blessed to have a son of his own. My brother and I were the closest he would get to having sons, although we were just his nephews.

The experience of watching, live and in living color, the birth of a baby was breathtaking. My strong, loving, determined, wife never even asked for an aspirin throughout the five-hour labor period. Janice did not even take anything for the pain and discomfort during the delivery either.

My reactions to crisis were not the same as Janice.

I almost had to be carried out of the delivery room when Janice let out a gut-wrenching scream during one of her contractions. I panicked; she started laughing. "Oh great!" I thought. "Janice done finally lost her mind and is freaking out." What did I know? How could I have not trusted Janice to know that there wasn't anything to panic about; it was just a cramp in her left leg.

I did well for my first real drama in a long time. When it was all over, I'm sure I was more relieved than Janice. My timing was still a little off in the area of sensitivity, or a fancy way of saying, "I did not know when to keep my mouth closed." While the doctor was giving her an episionamy repair, as her legs were still in the stirrups, I leaned over and said, "That was cool. When can we do this again?" I won't even repeat what Janice's answer was. I will only say that she did not curse once up until then.

When I left the delivery room to go share the exciting news with the folks, they were already half way down the hall walking towards me. They cold tell by the look on my face that everything went well. How could things not a have gone well? Janice was in control, and all was well with the world. I took Kaleem and hugged him and led him by the hand towards the elevator.

We were allowed to ride up to the third floor with Kynon where he would be processed into the "real" world. They placed him in the "baby room" and turned him towards that large window to make his first grand appearance to the world. I watched with great emotion as Kaleem just stared at his new, little, baby brother without making a sound.

Janice looked so beautiful after just giving birth. I was so proud of her for not acting like three of our fellow classmates. I felt sorry for these women's husbands. During the classes, we became sort of friendly with several of the couples.

Three couples from the class were in the hospital with Janice, and the women were not very nice to their spouses. In fact they were acting like raving lunatics. I had heard how pain could cause people to become like *"Dr. Jekyl and Mr. Hyde,"* but to witness this type of transformation was amazing.

Janice has never asked for much for herself, so for this blessed occasion all she asked for was some baked ziti from Sal's Pizzeria. I returned that evening to the hospital with a dish of baked Ziti. I just sat and watched her savor each mouthful, and realized how many more blessings were in store for me in the years to come.

TWENTY-FIVE YEARS AND WE AINT KILLED EACH OTHER

I, Bruce take thee Janice to be my lawful wedded wife, to have and to hold, to love and to cherish, through sickness and in health, through better or worse, for richer or poorer 'til death do us part.

While Janice was orchestrating yet another big moment in our life, I was making sure I had my funds together for my special anniversary/wedding gift to her. Jokingly when this whole idea was born, I used to say, "I just want to show up at the church. PERIOD!"

However, for a special event like this, I couldn't come half stepping.

Janice elected me to be handle all the finances. Bless her heart; Janice was not the type of person that you'd want to manage the household expenses. Her idea of balancing a checkbook was rounding up amounts in her ledger of the checks that she wrote. When the statement came in the mail it appeared to her way of thinking that there was always money left over. Now this works fine if you don't care if your checkbook balances or not. But if you do, like I was trained up to do, this wasn't too cool.

Solution?

Let Janice have her own checking account separate and not equal to the household account. Seemed like a fair and logical solution to me. I would pay her first and foremost every payday her "allowance." This way for example, when she wrote a check for $19.78, she could write in her ledger; $20.00. The most logical illogical rationale for her accounting system was she never worried about bouncing a check. So simple.

I decided twenty-four months prior to the twenty-fifth anniversary that I was going to systematically, save $200 a month. Had not a clue as to what I would spend it on, but whatever it was to be, every dime was going to that purpose and nothing else. This had to be my biggest challenge thus far. I was not making a whole hell of a lot of money, but I knew from past experiences how to "make it work."

Every two weeks when I got paid, I went to Fidelity National Bank, where I had opened a savings account. I would deposit $100. When I reached $500, I would then buy a six-month Certificate of Deposit. Hell, the interest wasn't much, but I knew I couldn't get my mitts on it that easily. When the six months were up, I'd go over to the jeweler and add to the layaway. Miraculously when the 30th of October rolled around, it was payday and I had the final installment in my pocket. Talk about walking tall. I felt so proud of myself.

I refused to have had my bride this time around, united in Holy matrimony, with a ring that I had to borrow from my mother! Not that there is anything wrong with that, but after twenty-five years I'd expect some progress in the financial area of my life. If not that would be pretty pathetic.

The diamond ring that Janice wore from 1980until 1997 came eight long years after we were married. Consuelo had a friend who knew a jeweler downtown in the diamond district of Manhattan. He designed the most beautiful diamond ring I had ever seen up until then. I applied for my first MasterCard from European American Bank, and I had just enough on the credit line to make the purchase—$1500, and not a penny more.

I was so excited.

The plan was to give Janice her very own diamond ring that Christmas of 1980. I would have settled for that and I think she would have too, but Mom talked me into getting the band of gold that was designed to fit the "engagement ring." I must admit that Mother knows best. The combination of the two made Janice extra happy.

I wanted to do something even more special for the twenty-fifth year of marital bliss, but I was unsure of what I could do. I am not one for creativity or planning. I am so self-conscious about things getting screwed up, that I tend to make my surprises far and few between.

Whenever I was in doubt, it was time to go to the bank—the "memory bank."

I dipped into our "memories" savings account and low and behold, I found an idea. In the August 1986 issue of a popular black women's magazine, my lovely wife was featured along with two other women in the fashion section. The article was about real, everyday, working women that have to juggle their family schedules as well as dress for success.

A close friend of the family, Barbara Bryson, had been the fashion writer during that time. She knew that the feature required a mother, wife, and a career woman—all wrapped up in one. When she called Janice to tell her to submit her photo and biography, Janice thought Barbara was crazy. Janice is one for being adventurous (wonder where she got that quality from?) so she forwarded the information.

Well, was Janice surprised when she got a letter and follow up phone call stating that she had been selected for the issue. At first she thought it was Barbara playing a joke, however, it was no joke.

Janice would be flying off to the "Big Apple" in June to be professionally photographed, and interviewed by Barbara for the article. I remembered Janice bitching about how hot it would be while doing a photo shoot, but hey, what the hell? It was free and an experience of a lifetime. I remembered the anxiety and anticipation as everyone in our family, and her co-workers waited for the issue to hit the newsstand.

Praise the Lord, as He ceased to amaze me.

I had only imagined how beautiful the photos would have turned out; however, the interview that Barbara conducted was extraordinary. When I purchased the magazine that I had long awaited for, I was truly moved to tears when I read Janice's responses to the questions asked of her.

She also looked exquisite in the clothes that she was outfitted in. I feel as though I earned the right to brag, plus it is my story, so I will. Janice, in my opinion, is the most beautiful woman inside and out that I have ever known. Janice shared how juggling family, trying to get off to the office on time, and dressing for success, was accomplished. But, it was the end statement she made in the interview that moved me to emotion.

"Bruce is very supportive. I wouldn't trade him for anything in the world."

Now this may not sound like such a big deal to someone else, but we are taught to express our feelings for each other, right? How can anyone deny the love, respect, and consideration a man has for his wife, than for her to shout it out for the whole world to hear? It is one thing for a man to feel as though he is appreciated; it is another to know it in his heart when he hears it first hand from the love of his life.

FROM THE LOVER IN ME I SHARE ALL OF MY HEART

Knowing that I loved to write gave me the idea to compose a short love story of my love for Janice. Then I thought, "I do that often without any special occasion needed so that is not anything new." Think Bruce! This is the silver anniversary. You've had the love of your life tolerate your ass for twenty-five big ones, so come up with something to knock her hat into the creek! Something she will never in a million years expect.

My thinking took me to a place where I knew I was comfortable. The though process kept coming back to writing. However, this time not only would I write something special, but I wanted EVERYONE in Atlanta to read how I felt about my beautiful bride.

I remembered I would always make it a point to read the wedding announcements in the Dixie Reader section every Sunday. Engagements and weddings were published weekly and some folks even sent in photos of themselves. I thought that to be so cool. But, my favorite reading were the anniversary announcements. It was important to share that couples can stay married for a long time and continue to celebrate their love.

Ah ha! I finally had the perfect surprise.

I called The Atlanta Constitution, our local newspaper, and asked for an editor for the "Dixie Living section." I spoke to a nice lady name Judy and told her of my idea. Well you would have thought she new us personally the way she reacted. I thought she was going to start crying on the phone. I know stereotyping is not nice, but I could tell by her voice and conversation that she was a "sista girl!" The fact that she went on to praise and glorify His name for hearing that a young couple stayed married for twenty-five years, made me sense she just had to be black.

So I couldn't help but to make it crystal clear that yes; we were a beautiful black couple that wanted to shout out to the world our love for one another. Call it what you want, but the most important aspect of my idea was to be a positive role model for all God's people. We just happened to be a young black couple that made it that far. She was so excited to be able to be of assistance in this wonderful occasion.

Geez Louise! I forgot to tell what my idea was so you can understand why Judy reacted the way she did!

I was going to write an announcement in letterform and include a photo of the two of us. Nothing fancy, just a few lines to highlight the moment. But, Judy would have none of that! As I mentioned, she acted more excited than I was about all of this. Judy came up with the idea to go one step further. Something I had never dreamed of.

A poem!

She suggested I write a love poem to Janice and she would make sure it was published November 2nd in the Sunday paper. Our "marriage" was going to take place that Saturday, November 1st. I asked if it could be the week earlier since the paper would come out after the wedding.

Judy had an answer and solution for that obstacle. She said if it came out the week prior, it would not be as much of a surprise to Janice. Chances are some of her friends and coworkers would read it and be on the phone that afternoon talking about; "Girl. Did you see what Bruce wrote about you?" Janice never reads the paper so the odds of her knowing before anyone else were not too high.

"But," I said, "I want her to have the poem on her wedding day, not after."

"Don't worry Bruce," she said. "I have a solution for that as well."

Her solution was to mail "copy sheets" to my job. The Dixie Living section of the paper would go to print that Tuesday evening. She said since there is no news to report in that section it went to press five days earlier. The layout would be composed on Tuesday morning of that week and she would even overnight the rough draft prior to printing.

"But will they get to my job in time?" I asked.

She assured me that not only would she send them special delivery with a signature required, she would send at least ten copies. That set in to motion the challenge for me to sit down in quietness and create a poem. I had two weeks to do it.

The last time I wrote a poem was in the tenth grade when I was stoned to the bone on some good pot. While listening to some Latin music in the basement on Rushmore Street with a mellow high off of the pot, I wrote a poem for Ms. Seebert's English class. To my surprise she was so impressed with my literary skills that she recommended that it be published in the school newspaper.

I was kind of embarrassed. What would my friends think of me doing such a sissy thing like writing poetry? I also did not think it was that good. Hell in my mind anyone after smoking some good weed could write a heavy poem reflecting on the times they lived in.

It stuck in my head and remembered it like it was written yesterday and not in 1967. It went as follows:

> "The world is what you make it. They give and we just take it.
> And don't be psyched into believing that you are not a human being.
> Countless years of our free labor is gone, but still give us their standards to live
> on. What gives them the right I could never understand, when yet they are not
> much more of a man!"

This time there was no pot smoking to stimulate my talent and creativity. However, I did not find it all that difficult once I realized I was speaking about the love of my life. Then the creative juices just started to flow like I was put here on earth for this soul purpose.

Two days later and after much editing, my poem was complete. I was ready to express it to Judy, but first I had to find a photo of the two of us. A recent one at that!

I could not believe we reached our pinnacle of twenty-five years together, and the only portrait photo of us was one from my twenty-year high school reunion in 1988.

It did kind of look stupid to have a nine-year-old photo from when I was only thirty-eight years old. One need not be an Einstein to calculate that Janice and I would have had to be eight and thirteen years old respectively in order to have been married twenty-five years and still look so young. Oh well, who's going to know the difference. Our secret was kept amongst the relatives and to everyone else; who cared?

Judy said she immediately called me at work when she opened the mail and read the poem; Once again she was almost in tears describing over and over how sweet it was for me to do this. She said it was the nicest poem she had read in a long long time and the only one she ever received in her department after working there for eight years. I just sucked it up and figured she was just an emotional basket case.

The fact she shared with me she'd never been married and can't seem to find a good man out there, lead me to believe she was sincerely happy for us. I felt compelled to invite her to the ceremony. What the heck. One more guest can't hurt and who knows, maybe she would have wrote something about the ceremony at a later date; if she had shown up!

As promised, I received the rough draft that Wednesday. I had to go in to the men's room at work when I saw my poem in print. Writing it was emotional enough, but actually seeing it and knowing all of Atlanta would read our love story, was too much for me. I cried like a natural baby.

They were tears of joy and a sense of accomplishment that I never dreamed of. Just 30 years earlier, I was a drug addict not caring whether I lived or died. The mere thought of anyone wanting to love me for who I was seemed an impossibility. All the hurt and pain that I had inflicted on myself, family and those that I stole from felt like it had all been lifted off my shoulders at that very moment.

So the poem went like this:

"Dear Janice,

To say I loved you then would mean I loved you when, I was so young, unsure and very immature. Throughout all my doubts worries hurts and fears somehow I knew you'd always make them disappear. I love the feeling of being loved by you and the blessing from God is that I still do. Those warm and tender moments we share back then and now will always be dear. And in my heart mind body and soul, together with you I cherish to grow old. For as long as we have each other to laugh to hold to share and to cry it will be true love and happiness 'til the day that I die. Thank you my love for twenty-five years of just being who you are and for our loving sons Kaleem and Kynon."

I just stood, looked in the mirror, and wondered who that person was that lived the kind of lifestyle that I did. Was it really me? Could I have been so trifling? How did I overcome the odds of earning the label of a "recovering addict" and never spend one day after October 1971 in any type of drug therapy?

Yes Bruce, you are that person and you'd better be damned proud of it!

You now have the words to break the chains of feeling undeserving as a person. In thinking that your recovery was no big thing took away from the glory and self-fulfillment that warranted recognition. Society has always been too quick to criticize and so slow to praise. We are bombarded day in and day out with all the negativity of the world and the people in it, yet when a human-interest story merits consideration, no one is interested.

After I had gotten my composure, with rough copy safely in hand, I returned to my desk to call Judy to thank her for a wonderful layout. I've read hundreds of announcements in the Atlanta newspaper from 1984 until 1997, and if I do say so myself, mine was by far the most creative and romantic. Always knew you had it in you Brucie boy.

I received the ten copy sheets that Friday before the wedding, said my good-bye's at work and headed home to everyone that had arrived that afternoon. The sorry ass supervisor could not even let me go home an hour earlier than five o'clock to get home to family, friends and loved ones who had traveled as far as California to be part of the love celebration. We also had to be to the church for rehearsal by 7:30 PM.

Of course, I had to get stuck in the horrendous Atlanta traffic and the frustrations prior to he biggest weekend of my life began to take its toll. "It is gonna be all right Bruce," I said out loud to myself, "Just relax and look forward to the fireworks."

When I pulled up to the front our home, my heart was beating a mile a minute. I was so excited to visualize so many family members under one roof: and it was for a happy occasion for a change.

I heard a familiar, "hey bro" as I got out the car in the driveway. I turned to look behind me and there in the cul-de-sac across the street was my sister Lisa and my six-year-old nephew Kenton. I almost forgot it was Halloween night and they were out Trick-o-Treating. Kenton was dressed in his costume and it dawned on me that this was their first time visiting the new house.

I went on inside through the garage, and when I opened the door to the kitchen; I was overwhelmed to say the least. The first faces I saw sitting at the table were Dad, Uncle Felix, Aunt Neat and Mom. I hugged everyone, especially Uncle Felix and Aunt Neat, who got an extra dose. They were the ones that I wanted to come the most since they both were terrified of flying it was like a miracle unfolded before my eyes.

I turned to see Aunt Faye, cousin Larry, Uncle Peter, Janice's half brother Fred, Morris and Deirdre, cousin Marcia, Uncle Bobby, Aunt Helen, Consuelo, and the list goes on and on. I had very little time to laugh, cry or do anything since I had to haul ass to the church.

Of course my prodigal son Kaleem was not there yet and I was panicking. I always do when it comes to tardiness. I got that trait from Dad. I got to meet cousin Kellie's husband Jay for the first time when they arrived with the wedding coordinator and friend Connie.

As we drove to the church with the wedding party, I had to listen to Mom complain about how much further we had to go to get there. Aunt Helen was not in the wedding, however, she had to go with Uncle Bobby. It was just a Helen and Bobby thing amongst them. The rehearsal went well, and then I had to hear Mom complain during the 20-minute drive home that she was hungry. It was just a Mom thing.

Kelvin was there by the time I had returned home. I missed him earlier as he was out buying food and spirits for everyone. He was so happy for us and he brought his daughter, Noelle, and his son, Shane with him for the weekend festivities. Having the family and friends together under one roof was the most well organized feat that Janice had accomplished.

The idea for a silver anniversary celebration started out as planning a vacation to a romantic island—just Janice and I. Then we thought to ourselves, "How selfish to not share the moment with friends and loved ones." Our goal from day one was to make our marriage special. Because we felt after twenty-five years that our goal had been met, why not allow the love to flow for an entire weekend? Hell, why not let friends and relatives experience the love with us. So that was how our silver anniversary plans began to take shape for the event of our lifetime. The plans began March of '97.

WAS NOT EASY, BUT WAS SURE WORTH IT

Janice does well planning things. Of course I being the financial guru in the family, my job was to keep "the wedding" plans on budget. I did not know the first thing about planning a wedding. However, since I love to write and create artistically, I wrote and designed the wedding invitations. Nothing fancy, just a few words to express how much that person's presence would mean to us. I had been working as a travel agent at the time; so I was able to help organize the "New York" entourage make their plans for the same flights.

Uncle Felix and Aunt Neat were deathly afraid to fly. We knew this, however, if they could not have made it there would have been no wedding. That is how much they meant to us. Both of them was such a positive role models in our lives, that part of who Janice and I had become was a direct result of their influence. I made up my mind that if I had to drive to New York and pick them up, they were going to attend—period.

Since there is always a family member that don't take any shit or prisoners, we were blessed to have that "one" person. Bring on Aunt Faye. When she got her invitation she called the folks and told them she will pick up there tickets when she goes to get hers and her son Larry's.

Aunt Faye lived ten-minutes away from them, so they were thick as thieves as well as being family. When she heard Uncle Felix start to stutter and making excuses for not going, she damn near cussed him out. Of course she had to respect their fears the same as we did, but she felt that there was no way they could miss out on this special occasion.

Even though Uncle Felix was Dad's brother, Dad could not try and talk him into going. Their love and respect for each other taught Dad to back off when he felt the discussion would lead to and argument. I even wrote them a letter that was placed inside their invitation expressing how much it meant having them there with us. I knew however that I would respect their decision one-way or the other.

Aunt Faye would not hear of it. They were going to be on Delta flight 617 at noon on October 31, 1997, with everyone else and that was all there was to say. She made their reservations on the phone first. The day she was on her way to Kennedy Airport to the Delta terminal to purchase four tickets, she simply called to say she would stop by for a check from Aunt Neat. Then she hung up! She took the ten-minute bus ride, walked the four blocks to the house, and left twenty-minutes later with a check for their tickets.

I did not know at the time how making their decision came about. However, I won't forget the day I got a letter from Aunt Neat saying they would be there; I cried tears of joy for two days. From that point on, nothing mattered to me. I knew that this was going to be the most memorable event of my lifetime.

Janice secured the site for the reception. Dear friends of ours reserved the clubhouse in their half million-dollar home subdivision for only $100. The tuxedos for Uncle Bobby, Uncle Peter, Kaleem, Kynon, and me were ordered one month in advance. Janice arranged the music through a co-worker that was a DJ. The church and Pastor Rogers were set. Although I was a travel agent, we just went to a local agency to make out plans for Ocho Rios. I did not want to screw things up.

This would be our first time hiring a Caterer, so because this was the most expensive part of this whole idea, we wanted to make sure we found the right one. We was referred to the Ultimate Occasion. Not to sound prejudice or anything, but we tried to patronize black owned business' for all our needs. Because I was still somewhat skeptical trusting that black folk could take care of business, this decision was the most difficult.

When we met the brother who owned the Ultimate Occasions, I was impressed. He was in partnership with his mother and another family member. They had a banquet hall that was available for rent and I toured the kitchen facilities. He permitted us to attend a setup prior to a wedding they were catering several weeks before we had to make our final decision.

Of course I was still nervous as I handed over my American Express card for them to process $2300 for the contract. I remember telling Janice when we were selecting the menu that all I cared about was having Swedish meatballs. I was easy to please.

We made arrangements through a salesperson that I knew at a local hotel. It was only five miles from our home and eight miles to the church so it was convenient. The only arrangement left to make was transportation from the airport. We chose another Black owned business to provide two vans. There were

10 family members arriving at the same time so it worked out well. Janice had the day off so she met everyone at the hotel when the vans arrived.

The day came for the final payment for Janice's diamond ring. I had calculated the last payment to fall on that Thursday, October 30, which was a payday. It was no surprise that the day was the official anniversary of our twenty-five years as a married couple. That made the moment so much sweeter. I was so nervous going over to the mall to pick up the ring. I had been looking at it for ten months.

Although I started my savings plan a year earlier, the decision to spend the money on a ring was not made until January of '97. Janice had picked out the stone and the setting. The owners and employees became like our family. They were so excited for us. I guess when you are in a business like theirs, it is heartwarming to meet and see a couple so much in love after twenty-five years.

Kaleem had to come out to the mall from his house to pick up his tuxedo, so I asked him to meet me at the mall. The truth was I was so paranoid about walking out to my car with this little tiny box with the most prized possession I ever owned in my pocket. Of course if anyone tried to rip me off, the weekend would have turned into a funeral festivity because I would die first trying to defend myself. All went so smoothly though and I hugged Kaleem when I got in my car to go home to Janice with her reward for putting up with me all those years.

My sister-in-law, Morgan was there when I arrived home. She flew up that afternoon to help her twin sister with the last minute details before Saturday. Morgan was to sing at the wedding so having her there two days in advance made us feel more comfortable. I decided why wait until Saturday to give Janice the ring. It is our anniversary so why not tonight?

I called Janice into the room, and asked her to sit on the edge of the bed. Morgan was present also. I got down on one knee like I always saw in the movies, and asked her to marry me again. Now Janice aint no fool. She knew what was in the box. Morgan cried as she though it to be the most romantic thing she had ever witnessed.

Janice kept starring at the "rock" the rest of the night. She must have thought, "And it's all mine, free and clear and it only costs me twenty-five years of patience with Bruce."

Saturday morning rolled around. Everyone had arrived from near and far to the hotel. We made welcome letters for everyone with instructions and a itinerary for the three days. Kelvin and I went to take care of the wine and champagne order. It felt so special just the two of us having some time together before all the fanfare. We have such a special relationship.

Although he and I grew up in New Castle and went to school together, he did not get caught up in the lifestyle that I did, yet he never looked down on me. When we met again after graduation, it was seven years later in 1975. We were at a wedding for Aleah Frazier and he had just graduated from medical school. He often reminds me of how I was walking around the reception stopping people and saying, "Hi, this is Kelvin and he's a doctor." He was embarrassed but let me have my moment to share my pride that he made it that far.

His sense of humor was like mine and we laughed about the fun we used to have when we were in the same classes in school. I once told him that I was glad he did not have to use too much bedside manners as a doctor, because he'd have the patients laughing all the time and that they probably would never get well.

George spent the night at our best friends' home. Raymond and Betty are like family since we met in 1990. Poor George had some health problems after he lost his job with Nikon. I always felt that he never got over the way they just let him go after twenty-one years with the company. It was the only job he ever held since college and he was such a creature of habit that he did not know how to deal with that.

He began to drink more heavily and went back to smoking cigarettes after quitting for almost fourteen years. Although he was on kidney dialysis, my closest friend through thick and thin flew down with everyone else on flight 617. He would not have missed it and for that I will always admire him for his strength and courage.

OK, OK, so much for the mushy stuff about George.

The truth told, George would not have missed out on a party with free booze, and food. He was always one to be the life of the party and we just accepted him for that. If he had to come in an oxygen tent, he would have.

Raymond's responsibility was to lead the caravan from the hotel to the church. Everyone knew to be in the lobby at 1:30 PM. The ceremony was to begin at three o'clock sharp. Connie and her sidekick Jennie were like Generals in an Army. If anyone were late, they would not disturb the ceremony once it began.

Now Raymond's driving left a lot to be desired. We used to tease him because he drove so slow that he should have gotten a job driving a hearse. This one time though it worked to our benefit. We did not have to concern ourselves with him losing anyone that was following behind him to the church.

WILL I BE ABLE TO SURVIVE THE MOMENT?

Our limousine arrived at the house around 1:45 PM.

I was so nervous, yet not too nervous to take a few moments to reflect on how wonderful my life was. I went off into the bathroom of all places to be alone for a few moments with my thoughts. I needed some time to pinch myself to see if all of the events up until that moment were for real.

To say that my emotional state of mind was off the charts would have been an understatement. Realizing that I was standing in the bathroom of our 4500 square foot home that was just a year old, surrounded by so many family members, friends and loved ones and having a limo sitting in the driveway waiting to take me to a church to renew our vows after twenty-five years was more than I could have ever asked for.

Each person that came from afar had a special meaning to me, especially Uncle Bobby and Aunt Helen. For them I had to use my literary skills to create a special letter that would await them on their bed in the guest room along with their flowers. I just had to let them know that I was eternally grateful to them for taking me in, trusting me, and giving me the extra motivation that it took twenty-six years earlier to get my life together.

The type of loving people that they were, they did not want to take any credit for my return from the emotional dead. Aunt Helen had told me that I had to do for myself what no one else could have done and that the support was all that I needed.

To this day, they have that letter framed and hung on the wall in their home.

Having so much to be thankful for I could not have been more proud as my sons were down the hall, helping each other with their tuxedos. My joy and pride resulted from my prayers that they would always be close as brothers. I would never want them to have had a relationship like Stephen and me, and they have lived up to that commitment.

Sadly, although Stephen was living in Atlanta with his wife and sixteen-year-old daughter, they were not part of this blessed occasion through no fault other than their own for not wanting to be part of our lives. I could not say that I was not hurt that they could not share in the moment with everyone, but knew that in my heart that I did try to be a good brother to him.

Sounds funny, but the night before and earlier that Saturday of the wedding, when everyone was gathered in the hotel lobby and our home, laughing and having a good time, then that would have been enough for me. The ceremony was just and added bonus.

I was thinking to myself a strategy to not become overly emotional during the ceremony in front of a church full of people. I decided then to resort to my sense of humor to get me through. If that did not work, all I had to do was turn around and look at George, as I knew he would make me laugh just by his facial expressions.

My thoughts and going down memory lane were abruptly interrupted when Janice yelled at me that I was holding up the process. That must have been the first and only time that she was ready ahead of me.

I dried my eyes, and grabbed my stuff and headed downstairs to the limo while Uncle Bobby was shooting one of his infamous video recordings. It was that time.

We got to the church in time to get dressed. I went into the men's room to get myself together and was so nervous, I couldn't fix the cumberbun or hook the tie to the shirt properly. I almost did something that I am still working on—cussing.

It would also have been worse if I did it in church.

Right at that moment as if God knew I was about to get into the flesh, as they say, in walks brother Chuck. He had a sense of humor about everything, yet he was the most dedicated Christian and pillar of the church that I knew. He once surprised his wife, who also was to sing at our wedding, by arranging for their vows to be renewed in church one Sunday. It was so touching, and that was only for their tenth anniversary.

After he helped me get myself together and made me laugh he left to go finish lighting the candles for the ceremony. There I was alone again. I made sure my hair was neat, no boogers in the nostrils, no toothpaste on the corners of my mouth, and no food stuck between my teeth. Yeah, I must say I was looking damn good for a 47-year-old man.

I had been working out vigorously the previous two years to look my best. I did not want to stand in front of everyone in the church with a beer belly. Most of all I did not want to be on the beach in Jamaica with one.

I put my tuxedo jacket on, inched it up onto my shoulders, went to button it and low and behold. There I stood in a jacket that was two sizes too big.

I won't lie this time. I did cuss in church, God forgive me.

"I can't believe this shit." I said. "How could I have picked up the wrong jacket?" Well I had picked up the wrong jacket and it was only forty-five minutes to show time, and there wasn't anything I could do about it. The salesperson at the tuxedo store gave me a size 44 and I needed a 42. The funny thing was I realized it that Friday evening, and went back Saturday morning and picked up a size 42. Unfortunately I forgot to exchange it with the one in the plastic bag before I took it to the church.

Not much to do at this point but suck it up and go with the show. I did try to con Uncle Peter into switching jackets with me but he was taller and the longer sleeves would have made me looked worse. It was also too late to ask Raymond to drive to the house and get the other jacket. He would have made it back in time for our 26th anniversary, so that was not an option either.

After Uncle Bobby and I received our last minute instructions from Pastor Rogers, I peeked through the glass of the door leading to the sanctuary. I was overcome with emotion as I saw the church filling up with people. Up until then I just visualized the family and friends, but many of our church family attended.

I was quite moved when I saw three of Kynon's friends and one of Kaleem's. We were like surrogate parents to many of their friends and for them to take time out, especially on a Saturday afternoon to honor us, was a blessing. Uncle Bobby kept asking if I was all right and told me not to worry about anything. It bought back vivid memories when he said the same things to me twenty-five years earlier.

SHOWTIME

It was 2:55 PM and Gina began to play "Joyful, Joyful" on the piano. That was our cue to enter the sanctuary and take our places at the altar. I tried not to look at many faces as I walked the few feet to the altar. I did not want to get emotional. We had rehearsed the night before so I knew what to expect. The accordion doors separating the back of the church were drawn close after Mom, Uncle Peter, the flower children, and Consuelo marched in and took their places.

Kaleem and Kynon stood on opposite sides of where the two doors joined. Uncle Bobby got me to laugh again as he whispered in my ear, "Yo Bruce, don't Kaleem and Kynon look like members of the Fruit of Islam?" The funny thing was that they did. They stood like soldiers looking around as if they were protecting the doors behind which their mother was being kept until her debut.

Morgan began to sing *"Betcha By Golly Wow"* to an instrumental tape that Janice bought a copy of. The song had such special meaning to us. It was our love song from when we first met. By now many of the guests were looking around and wondering what was going to happen next. I am sure many had never heard of the song and since it was not a traditional church wedding song, many looked puzzled. It did not matter since we knew what was going on and it was our time to shine.

Well just when I thought Janice had run out of surprises and shocks of a lifetime with me, she totally blew my mind that time. When Morgan got to the stanza of the song which read, "If I could I'd catch a falling star," the doors were pulled back to reveal the shock of my lifetime.

As I watched the doors open, there stood the most beautiful woman in the world. Everyone stood as customary to do at weddings, but I was wondering what several people were laughing at. Kaleem and Kynon each held out a loving arm for their mom to hold strong to, and they marched down to join us at the altar.

I do not remember much about what happened next with my reactions, but I just kept shaking my head and laughing. Janice had done it again. She made what could have been just and ordinary occasion something more than that. When they arrived at the altar, and Morgan had just completed the song, Janice just

235

kept smiling at me. Uncle Bobby asked if I felt like I was going to faint. I must have turned two shades of pale.

I found out later at the reception that the people were laughing at the looks on my face when the doors opened and I saw Janice. How could I have been so naïve to think that Janice would NOT show up in a wedding dress? I honestly did not think of it. But, aside from that, her dress was so elegant and she looked so breathtakingly beautiful in it. I think that was what overwhelmed me.

Up until that moment, I could only envision what Janice would look like in a wedding dress. Part of me went back into that pity party bag and feeling like shit for not being able to have had a real wedding in 1972. But part of me understood as I gazed in utter amazement at Janice's undying beauty that this was the way it was meant to be. I knew that I would not have appreciated a marriage ceremony such as this in the frame of mind that I was in when we got married.

Yes I knew I loved Janice twenty-five years earlier, but no I did not believe that strongly that I would have been a good husband for her to want to keep me around forever. Shows just how insecure I was, but God and Janice knew better.

Pastor Rogers has a good sense of humor also. He had known our family for twelve years. When he asked that everyone could be seated, he started saying what a blessing it was to be together on such a beautiful occasion. He said, "We are all here to celebrate the renewal of vows for Bruce and Janice." Then he paused, smiled, and said, "And she fooled you again didn't she?" Everyone in the church cracked up. We then prayed together and got busy with the ceremony. I was glad when it was over. All the candles and stress had me sweating like a pig. At least I knew if I had fainted that there was a doctor in the house.

I never told Janice until after the wedding, but I was still worried about the Caterer showing up on time and running off with our money. I know, I know I should not have been so pessimistic but all my sins I guess were not washed away at the same time. In fact someone caught me on videotape, as we were receiving people on the line after the wedding, asking our friend Cathy, "Did the Caterer show up?" She had arranged for the clubhouse and was the contact for the Caterer to get the key from to get inside and set up. She just looked at me and said, "Relax. Everything is fine. You worry too much."

Of course the introduction as Mr. And Mrs. Bruce Codrington was customary at receptions, but I was more nervous for this part of the festivities. Having to descend two flights of stairs was not the problem; seeing a crowded room full of people that were so special to us got my emotions to the brink of tears.

This would have been the second time that I would have emotionally lost it, but I kept my composure. I am sure it would have been understood by those that knew me when, that I would have had every reason to show how much that I was thankful to be there.

We could not have been more pleased with the quality of food or the service provided by the Ultimate Occasion. The song that we had our first dance as bride and groom was what else?—*"Betcha By Golly Wow."* This time the tape was played with Phyllis Hyman singing.

Janice and I chose the song because that was our favorite song when we met. As we danced, I could not keep my eyes off of her. I was holding in my arms my life, my world, my strength, my best friend and most of all my soul mate. I could hardly believe that God placed Janice in my life when He did, but most of all kept her there through it all.

What an added blessing we had to honor Uncle Bobby and Aunt Helen as they were on the eve of celebrating their 51st wedding anniversary.

After his toast to us, I grabbed the microphone and surprised them and announced their anniversary. I caught them totally off guard, but it was a fitting tribute to honor them. With the champagne flowing, dancing to the beats of the DJ, and just seeing everyone having the time of their lives made the effort so rewarding.

I made two collages of family photos. I had a photo of every family member that was in attendance. I made one poster board with just Janice, me, Kaleem and Kynon of our lives over the past twenty-five years. That culminated the lean years as well as the prosperous ones. I hung each on the wall of the clubhouse for all to see. I also hung a copy of the poem I had written in the newspaper.

TIME TO SAY OUR
GOODBYES FOR NOW

It was hard saying goodbye to everyone when Sunday arrived. We had all the family members to the house for a brunch and fellowship and then it was time to head to the airport to see everyone off, praying that their memories would last as long as ours have. The hardest part of saying goodbye was to accept that an opportunity to get together again for fun and laughter would not be anytime soon, if ever.

As Janice and I drove back from Hartsfield Airport to our home we just looked at each other with such admiration and love that it is hard to describe. We were sad it was over, yet could not wait until Tuesday to be on a plane flying first class to Jamaica for some fun in the sun.

As fate would have it, part of my inner fears of saying goodbye in Atanta that Sunday did become a reality. Since that day, we have mourned the passing of: Aunt Neat, George, Dad, Stephen, Janice's brother Morris, cousin Howie, Uncle Felix and Aunt Helen.

Life is funny isn't it? God is so wonderful and merciful, that he allowed in his time to spare each person that was part of this wonderful occasion to be present. I prayed a lot prior to October 31, 1997. I prayed that nothing would put a damper on our celebration of love, and my prayers had been answered.

Now, as life goes on, I have learned to be thankful for all that I had been through, yet I must learn to have faith for what is yet to come. I have learned from each chapter of my life from the good, the bad, and the ugly. I do not know how or why God gave me a second chance at life. I do not know why God blessed me with Janice and my two sons. What I do know, is that I have made those that loved me a reason to be proud.

For all those that had, and still do play an important part of keeping me grounded when I still have a tendency now and then to "lose it" I am eternally grateful. Although many of the people in my journey through life have gone on to glory, I consistently am blessed with so many new faces to keep the spirit alive.

The full circle of my life from sleeping on the streets as a junkie to having the second wedding of a lifetime had been quite an adventure. I know there is much more that I have to look forward to, however, I try to just take one day at a time. I place so much faith and trust in Janice as she plans the next chapters of our lives together. And just like when the anniversary plans began to unfold, she was serious when she told me that all I had to do was just show up.

I am so thankful to God that I did—thirty-three years ago.

0-595-32916-0

Lightning Source UK Ltd.
Milton Keynes UK
UKOW02f2301190915

258887UK00001B/85/P